Becoming a Responsive Mathematics Teacher

This resource presents and describes a model for teaching and learning mathematics responsively in the elementary and middle grades. Developed through the Responsive Math Teaching (RMT) project—a seven-year collaboration between teachers, teacher leaders, school and district administrators, and researchers from a network of K–8 urban schools—this book equips any mathematics educator with the tools to enhance instruction and increase equitable outcomes for students and communities historically underrepresented in mathematics. Chapters pair research-based instructional practices with real examples to show how this model has been successfully implemented in actual schools, often under challenging conditions. Each chapter includes classroom vignettes and then breaks down the topic into jobs or responsibilities for teachers, indicating their specific role in supporting their students. The authors provide tools to assist teachers in the decision-making needed to carry out these responsibilities in the classroom. Topics include the components of a responsive mathematics lesson, comprehensive lesson planning guidance, building a responsive classroom community, and supporting responsive teaching as an instructional leader. Whether you are a classroom teacher, teacher educator, or leader, this book can guide you in understanding and reframing your responsibilities, challenge existing norms around mathematics, empower your students as problem-solvers, and ultimately cultivate joy in mathematics teaching and learning.

Caroline B. Ebby is a mathematics educator and Senior Lecturer at the University of Pennsylvania Graduate School of Education, and a former middle school mathematics teacher.

Brittany Hess is a Research Specialist and mathematics instructional coach at the Consortium for Policy Research in Education (CPRE) at the University of Pennsylvania Graduate School of Education, and a former classroom and mathematics lead teacher.

Lindsay Goldsmith-Markey is a mathematics teacher educator in La Salle University's Department of Education and a former classroom teacher and mathematics specialist.

Lizzy Pecora is a Senior Research Project Manager at The Wharton School of the University of Pennsylvania.

Jennifer Valerio is a mathematics teacher educator and Associate Director of the Urban Teaching Residency Program at the University of Pennsylvania Graduate School of Education, as well as a former mathematics classroom teacher and coordinator.

Joy Anderson Davis is a Math K-8 Learning Specialist for the School District of Philadelphia, serves as an academic consultant for the Academy at Penn, and is a former teacher and instructional coach.

Also Available from Routledge Eye on Education
(www.routledge.com/go/routledge-eye-on-education)

Math Problem Solving Through Small Group Instruction: A Guide to Increasing Proficiency in Grades K-5
Dani Fry Jackson

Teaching 6–12 Math Intervention:
A Practical Framework To Engage Students Who Struggle
Juliana Tapper

There Is No One Way to Teach Math:
Actionable Ideas for Grades 6–12
Henri Picciotto and Robin Pemantle

Mathematics Teaching On Target:
A Guide to Teaching for Robust Understanding at All Grade Levels
Alan Schoenfeld, Heather Fink, Alyssa Sayavedra, Anna Weltman and Sandra Zuñiga-Ruiz

Exploring Math with Technology:
Practices for Secondary Math Teachers
Allison W. McCulloch and Jennifer N. Lovett

Introducing Nonroutine Math Problems to Secondary Learners:
60+ Engaging Examples and Strategies to Improve Higher-Order Problem-Solving Skills
Robert London

Coaching Math Workshop
Nicki Newton

Fluency Doesn't Just Happen in Multiplication and Division:
Strategies and Models for Teaching the Basic Facts
Nicki Newton, Ann Elise Record and Alison J. Mello

High-Impact Tutoring in Math and ELA:
An Evidence-Based Approach to Help All Students Succeed
Nicki Newton

Becoming a Responsive Mathematics Teacher

Centering Student Thinking in K-8 Classrooms

Caroline B. Ebby, Brittany Hess,
Lindsay Goldsmith-Markey, Lizzy Pecora,
Jennifer Valerio, and Joy Anderson Davis

Taylor & Francis Group

NEW YORK AND LONDON

Designed cover image: Getty Images

First published 2026
by Routledge
605 Third Avenue, New York, NY 10158

and by Routledge
4 Park Square, Milton Park, Abingdon, Oxon, OX14 4RN

Routledge is an imprint of the Taylor & Francis Group, an informa business

© 2026 Caroline B. Ebby, Brittany Hess, Lindsay Goldsmith-Markey, Lizzy Pecora, Jennifer Valerio, and Joy Anderson Davis

The right of Caroline B. Ebby, Brittany Hess, Lindsay Goldsmith-Markey, Lizzy Pecora, Jennifer Valerio, and Joy Anderson Davis to be identified as authors of this work has been asserted in accordance with sections 77 and 78 of the Copyright, Designs and Patents Act 1988.

All rights reserved. No part of this book may be reprinted or reproduced or utilised in any form or by any electronic, mechanical, or other means, now known or hereafter invented, including photocopying and recording, or in any information storage or retrieval system, without permission in writing from the publishers.

For Product Safety Concerns and Information please contact our EU representative GPSR@taylorandfrancis.com. Taylor & Francis Verlag GmbH, Kaufingerstraße 24, 80331 München, Germany.

Trademark notice: Product or corporate names may be trademarks or registered trademarks, and are used only for identification and explanation without intent to infringe.

ISBN: 978-1-032-88223-9 (hbk)
ISBN: 978-1-032-88222-2 (pbk)
ISBN: 978-1-003-53671-0 (ebk)

DOI: 10.4324/9781003536710

Typeset in Palatino
by KnowledgeWorks Global Ltd.

Access Support Material: www.routledge.com/9781032882222

Contents

Meet the Authors	ix
Preface	xiii
List of Tools	xv
Acknowledgments	xvii
1 What is Responsive Mathematics Teaching?	1
2 Launching a Task	23
3 Facilitating Productive Struggle	45
4 Discussing Learner Thinking	73
5 Connecting, Consolidating, and Reflecting on Evidence of Student Learning	106
6 Planning for Responsive Mathematics Teaching	140
7 Building a Responsive Mathematics Community	171
8 Supporting Responsive Mathematics Teaching	196
References	231

Meet the Authors

Caroline B. Ebby, Ph.D., is a Senior Lecturer at the University of Pennsylvania's Graduate School of Education, where she led the Responsive Math Teaching project, a multiyear research-practice partnership with the School District of Philadelphia that was funded by the U.S. National Science Foundation. A former middle school mathematics teacher with over 30 years of experience working to improve mathematics instruction, she teaches practice-based elementary mathematics methods courses for preservice teachers and graduate courses in teaching, learning, and leadership. Her work bridges research and practice, partnering with K-12 educators to design and support professional learning that centers on formative assessment and fosters responsive, inclusive mathematics instruction. A key area of her scholarship focuses on building teachers' capacity to use research on student learning and formative assessment practices to guide instruction and build equitable mathematics learning environments. She is a member of the national training team for the Ongoing Assessment Project (OGAP) and led the development of OGAP tools and routines for K-2 additive reasoning. Dr. Ebby has authored numerous research and practitioner-focused articles and is co-author of *A Focus on Addition and Subtraction*, *A Focus on Multiplication and Division*, and *A Focus on Fractions*—a series of books that translate research in mathematics education into practical, accessible resources for teachers.

Brittany Hess is a Research Specialist at the University of Pennsylvania's Graduate School of Education, where she also works as a K-8 mathematics coach and teaches in the Urban Teaching Apprenticeship Program. Prior to this role, Brittany worked as a special education teacher and instructional mathematics lead in the School District of Philadelphia. As a member of the Responsive Math Teaching Project, she led professional development, facilitated collaborative lesson planning groups, and coached teachers and leaders in Philadelphia public schools, in addition to serving as a qualitative researcher. Brittany has also worked on several research projects that studied the impact of learning-trajectory-oriented formative assessment and professional development through the Ongoing Assessment Project (OGAP) on students, teachers, and schools. Brittany holds an M.S.Ed. in Teaching, Learning, and Leadership from the University of Pennsylvania.

Lindsay Goldsmith-Markey is a mathematics teacher educator in La Salle University's Department of Education, where she teaches courses in mathematics methods, the development of mathematical thinking, and mathematics content. Prior to that, she served as the Director of Professional Development for the Responsive Math Teaching project, designing and leading professional development in responsiveness for teachers in the School District of Philadelphia, and played a lead role in the development of the responsive teaching tools featured in this book. For the first decade of her career, Lindsay taught elementary grades and middle grades mathematics in the School District of Philadelphia and the Boston Public Schools. Lindsay's work is focused on using experiential and practice-based methods to help preservice and in-service teachers develop increasingly positive mathematics identities, deepen their conceptual understanding of elementary mathematics, and grow their capacity to teach learners responsively. Lindsay holds an M.Ed. from Harvard University and is nearly finished earning her Ph.D. from the University of Pennsylvania in Teaching, Learning, and Teacher Education. She believes strongly that everyone is capable of being a creative and productive mathematical thinker when mathematics learning is centered around problem solving and sensemaking.

Lizzy Pecora is a Senior Research Project Manager at the University of Pennsylvania's Wharton School, where she supports a variety of research initiatives, faculty projects, corporate partnerships, and community-based programs. Prior to this role, she worked at the University of Pennsylvania's Graduate School of Education as a senior research coordinator with the Consortium for Policy Research in Education and the project manager for the Responsive Math Teaching Project. With a multidisciplinary background in education, she has worked with school districts, nonprofits, and industry partners to design and implement innovative, community-engaged initiatives that bridge research and practice. Across all of her work, she is driven by a commitment to strengthening educational access and fostering collaboration between K-12 and higher education, with a focus on aligning initiatives to the needs of practitioners and communities. Lizzy holds a B.A. from Allegheny College and an M.A. from Villanova University.

Jennifer Valerio, Ed.D., is currently the Associate Director of the Urban Teaching Residency Program at the University of Pennsylvania Graduate School of Education, where she also teaches elementary and secondary math methods to novice teachers. Prior to this role, Jennifer spent 16 years as a K-8 mathematics teacher and curriculum coordinator in the Garnet Valley School District in Glen Mills, PA. In 2015, Jennifer joined the Responsive Math

Teaching Project, where she worked with Philadelphia public school teachers in planning and debriefing responsive mathematics lessons. Jennifer's doctoral research and subsequent conference presentations have focused on using practice-based approaches and collaborative lesson design to support teachers in incorporating responsive math teaching practices into their daily mathematics instruction. Over the course of her two-decade career in education, Jennifer has taught at the elementary, middle school, high school, undergraduate, and graduate levels and has facilitated professional development in a variety of settings. Jennifer holds an Ed.D. in Teaching, Learning, and Teacher Education from the University of Pennsylvania.

Joy Anderson Davis, Ed.D., is a mathematics educator and instructional leader who currently serves as a Math K-8 Learning Specialist for the School District of Philadelphia. In this role, she partners with school leaders to design and implement student-centered mathematics programs that build teacher capacity and deepen student understanding. In addition, Joy serves as an academic consultant for the Academy at Penn and as an instructional coach for the Penn Learning Network. A former elementary school teacher, she has spent the past twenty years supporting schools in developing and enacting curricula that center student sensemaking and meet the needs of diverse learners. Joy served as an instructional coach for the Responsive Math Teaching Project and provides customized mathematics consulting services to schools through the RodJoy group, which she founded in 2015. She was recently recognized with the Penn GSE Alumni Educator of the Year Award honoring her leadership in addressing school challenges and advancing meaningful, equitable learning opportunities.

Preface

This book grew out of a seven-year collaboration with teachers, teacher leaders, and school and district leaders from a network of K-8 public schools in the School District of Philadelphia. A central goal of the book is to share a set of frameworks for instructional practice that resulted from this partnership, along with explanations and real examples that illustrate how these frameworks can be used by teachers, leaders, and teacher educators to enhance mathematics instruction at the elementary and middle grades.

This book is designed to support teachers in using research-based instructional practices to challenge disempowering norms around mathematics and create space for joy and justice in the classroom. We present and explicate a model for mathematics instruction that is responsive to the needs of learners and the mathematics that they need to learn. This model has been tested in schools with real teachers, often under challenging conditions, and adapted to meet their needs while staying true to the vision of the project: to increase equitable outcomes for learners and communities who have been historically underrepresented in mathematics. It includes tools to help teachers change their practice, over time, to become increasingly responsive to their students and their students' thinking. When teachers use the tools and embrace the responsive teaching approach, they learn to recognize and build on learner assets, thereby providing entry points for students who are left out by more prescriptive approaches to the teaching and learning of mathematics.

Many teachers are motivated to teach mathematics in ways that are very different from how they learned mathematics in school and how they might have been asked to teach before. We have found it helpful to support the process of learning new ways to teach through reframing what a mathematics teacher's responsibilities are and what they are not, giving them permission to let go of practices that minimize student thinking and sensemaking. Making sense of a problem, figuring out a problem-solving strategy, and following that strategy to a solution are responsibilities of the student, not the teacher. When the cognitive load of problem solving is shifted from the teacher to the student, the teacher's job becomes twofold: understanding what each student is thinking and supporting them to move forward toward the mathematical goal. This is the heart of responsive teaching.

The beginning of this book focuses on the components of a responsive mathematics lesson, while the latter half zooms out to think about broader practices, including planning for responsive teaching, building responsive classroom communities, and supporting ongoing teacher development. In each chapter, readers will find vignettes that provide examples of what the topic of that chapter looks and sounds like in action. These vignettes are based on the very real experiences of our partner teachers in their classrooms and professional learning communities. Practical tools are provided that can assist educators in learning how to make shifts in their practice through anticipating in advance and decision-making in the moment. These tools and other resources are also available as online downloads at: www.routledge.com/9781032882222

Ultimately, this book is an invitation. It invites teachers, leaders, and teacher educators to engage deeply with the complexities of teaching mathematics responsively—to listen closely to students, to reflect critically on their own instructional choices, and to reimagine what mathematics learning can look, feel, and sound like in their classrooms. The tools, examples, and frameworks shared here are not the endpoint, but rather starting points for learning, reflection, and growth.

List of Responsive Math Teaching Tools

Chapter 2 Launch Tool

- Establish Individual Understanding of the Task (Table 2.1)   31
- Establish Collective Understanding of the Task (Table 2.2)   33
- Build a Bridge to Solving (Table 2.3)   35

Chapter 3 Facilitating Productive Struggle Tool

- Build a Bridge to Solving (Table 3.1)   53
- Help the Learner Move Forward with Their Idea(s) (Table 3.2)   57

Chapter 4 Discussing Learner Thinking Tool

- Determine Which Student Ideas the Discussion Will Focus on (Table 4.1)   85
- Getting a Learner's Strategy or Idea Out in the Open (Table 4.2)   88
- Help Other Learners to Engage with the Strategy or Idea (Table 4.3)   90
- Surface Important Mathematics Behind Each Strategy (Table 4.4)   93

Chapter 5 Connecting, Consolidating, and Reflecting Tool

- Help Learners Make Connections to Explicitly Bridge Their Thinking and Strategies to the Mathematical Goals (Table 5.1)   114
- Provide Opportunities for Learners to Solidify Connections, Consolidate, and Reflect (Table 5.2)   123
- Collect Evidence of Student Understanding to Inform Subsequent Instruction (Table 5.3)   134

Chapter 7: Building a Responsive Mathematics Community Tool

- Build Listening and Sensemaking Skills (Table 7.1)   183
- Build Discussion Participation Skills (Table 7.2)   186
- Build Collaboration Skills (Table 7.3)   189

Chapter 8: Facilitation of Collaborative Learning Communities Tool

- A Template to Plan Facilitation Moves for Discussing Learner Thinking (Table 8.1)   212
- Supporting Collaborative Learning Communities (Table 8.2)   224

Acknowledgments

We are deeply grateful to the many teachers and school leaders who participated in our professional development and research, opened their classrooms, and generously shared their practice to learn with us. This work would not have been possible without our ongoing partnership with the School District of Philadelphia, the collaboration of our colleagues at the University of Pennsylvania's Graduate School of Education, and the support of the William Penn Foundation and the U.S. National Science Foundation.[1]

---

1 This material is based upon work supported by the U.S. National Science Foundation under Award No. DRK12 1813048. Any opinions, findings, and conclusions or recommendations expressed in this material are those of the author(s) and do not necessarily reflect the views of the U.S. National Science Foundation.

1

What is Responsive Mathematics Teaching?

> *I hated math as a student. It always felt like a bunch of rules and formulas that didn't make sense to me. A few years ago, I realized I was recreating that environment for my own students. My kids were staring at me and the board, desperately trying to memorize things that had little meaning to them. Learning about responsive teaching helped me change that. It gave me the tools to help my students see math as something they could make sense of on their own terms. I'm still learning, but now my students ask a lot more questions and share a lot more ideas in my class. Seeing my students engage with math in ways I never did is special. It has not only helped my students grow but also begun to heal my own relationship with math.*

Responsive mathematics teaching is a powerful instructional approach that moves beyond a one-size-fits-all model to recognize, leverage, and adapt to the diversity of student ideas, needs, and experiences found in any classroom. It involves listening attentively, making skilled real-time adjustments, and facilitating discussions that build on and extend student understanding and mathematical knowledge (Robertson et al., 2016). While learning to teach responsively takes time and effort, educators who commit to this shift often experience profound growth and transformation in their practice.

The inspiration for this book emerged from a sustained, collaborative project between the authors and hundreds of educators, each navigating their own path toward more responsive practices. No two teachers changed in the same way, but they all grew—transforming not only their instructional approaches and their students' experiences but also their perspectives on their roles as teachers, their understanding of mathematics, and their relationships with students. The reflection that begins this chapter and the others woven throughout it have been synthesized from comments we collected from teachers and teacher leaders who were committed to changing the way they taught mathematics in order to engage learners as active meaning makers and problem solvers. These experiences offer a glimpse into the many ways that educators have embraced responsiveness. They illustrate the challenges, discoveries, and rewards that come with adopting a more student-centered approach to teaching mathematics and the transformative power of teaching mathematics in a way that centers curiosity, collaboration, and making connections.

This book is an invitation for each reader to consider their own journey toward increasing their responsiveness—as a mathematics teacher, a school leader, a teacher educator, or a school partner. Whether you are just beginning this work or have been reflecting on becoming more responsive in your practice for many years, this book offers a detailed framework and practical guidance to embrace and deepen responsive teaching practices. In the pages that follow, we share a model for teaching and learning mathematics that grew out of a seven-year collaboration with teachers, teacher leaders, and school and district leaders, grounded in the idea that mathematics instruction can center both the learners and the concepts to be learned.

Throughout this book, we explore what responsive mathematics teaching is, why it matters, and how it can transform a classroom, school, or district. We also introduce practical tools, strategies, and insights to help guide incremental shifts in teacher practice. This work is not about quick fixes or perfect lessons—it is about building a classroom culture where all students feel empowered to think deeply, collaborate meaningfully, and see themselves as capable mathematicians. As you read, we invite you to reflect on your own practice, consider your role in fostering equity in mathematics education, and envision how responsive teaching can help you take the next step in your journey.

What Makes Teaching Responsive?

Traditionally, mathematics instruction in the United States has focused on delivering content through presenting step-by-step procedures and then having students complete practice problems until they can obtain correct answers (Stigler, 1999). This kind of instruction positions students as empty vessels, waiting passively to be filled up with information by their teachers (Freire, 1970). The problem with this approach is that students are not, in fact, empty at all. Each learner comes to every mathematics learning experience already knowing and understanding many ideas about mathematics, about themselves as learners, and about the world in which they live. The teacher's responsibility is thus much more dynamic than presenting mathematical content in a uniform, prescribed way. Rather, teachers need to be able to help learners connect what they already know and can do to new concepts and skills. This requires a kind of teaching that is centered not just on the mathematics being taught but on the students who are learning it as well. Responsive mathematics teaching does just that.

Fundamentally, responsive mathematics teaching unfolds *in response* to students' emerging ideas and the resources they bring. Responsive teachers work to elicit information about what their learners currently understand and think and then respond in ways that move the learners forward in relation to developmental goals. This means that the teacher is always being responsive both to learners' ideas and to the mathematics to be learned in an effort to intentionally close the gap between the two.

Responsive teaching is not a set of prescribed steps, but rather a dynamic cycle with teachers at the center of the pathway between learners' current understanding and the mathematics they need to learn, as illustrated in Figure 1.1. By continuously eliciting students' thinking, responding in real time, and guiding students toward deeper understanding, a responsive teacher brings students' ideas closer and closer to the mathematical learning goals. This ongoing refinement highlights the responsive nature of the approach, as instruction evolves to meet students where they are and continually advance their learning.

Responsive teachers begin by identifying a clear mathematical learning goal for students. They then identify tasks or activities that allow students to explore the mathematical concepts and build new relationships in relation to that learning goal. These tasks or activities can be presented in a variety of formats but always require students to think about what to do and why, rather than simply replicate a prescribed procedure. Next, they invite

Figure 1.1 Responsive mathematics teaching.

students to approach the task in ways that make sense to them, based on their existing ideas and understandings. As students work independently and collaboratively to grapple with the task, teachers pose questions to find out what students are thinking and then gradually nudge that thinking forward (Munson, 2018). Finally, they support students in actively making sense of each other's ideas, exploring the ways in which their ideas are interrelated, and consolidating their learning in order to draw connections to more formalized mathematics.

By engaging in iterative cycles of meeting students where they are and guiding them forward, responsive teachers facilitate learners' capacity to construct their own deep and meaningful understandings of the mathematics they need to learn. Collaboration between students throughout this process helps each student to weave their newfound ownership of mathematical ideas together with those of their classmates. When this happens, the learning community builds rich and collective understandings of mathematics, enhanced by the variety of unique ways of seeing and understanding things that students bring to the classroom and the more formal disciplinary knowledge and conventions that the teacher and curriculum offer.

Why is Responsive Mathematics Teaching Important?

The way that mathematics has traditionally been taught involves a teacher explaining step by step how to solve a problem while students listen passively or provide brief answers to the teacher's questions. Students are then typically asked to reproduce the steps that they watched the teacher do to solve a set of similar problems (Stigler et al., 1999). In this approach, students are positioned as receivers of knowledge rather than as active participants in constructing their own knowledge. Correct answers, quick recall, and single solution pathways are valued over creativity, productive struggle, and variety in approaches to solving. Authority for determining what is correct resides with the teacher and the textbook. Students who get confused or produce incorrect answers are seen as less capable of learning mathematics, and they tend to continue to take on that identity as they progress through school. Nicole Louie (2017) notes that this approach to teaching mathematics creates a *culture of exclusion*. When the only way to be good at mathematics is to be fast and correct, many students are denied access to mathematical sensemaking, relational understanding, and the opportunity to develop positive and powerful mathematical identities.

This culture of exclusion rests on the incorrect assumption that some people have a natural mathematical ability, while others have little or none—a myth that can have damaging consequences for learners. It is also important to acknowledge that the impacts of this exclusion are not equally distributed across schools or society at large. People who are seen and see themselves as "good at math" are often from historically privileged groups, including white, middle-class, and socioeconomically advantaged backgrounds. Moreover, the prevailing stereotypes about who has this natural ability tend to fall along racial, gender, linguistic, and economic lines (Ladson-Billings, 1997; Nasir et al., 2008). These assumptions often lead to deficit framings of the students, families, and cultures from marginalized communities.

Responsive mathematics teaching, on the other hand, shifts the definition of how mathematics is learned and reframes traditional notions about what it means to be good at mathematics. It is about cultivating the belief in students that "I can do math, because it makes sense!" When students are allowed to figure out their own ways of solving problems—ways that make sense to them—and also to explore the whys and the hows behind those ways, they develop powerful mathematical identities as doers, thinkers, and creators of mathematics. This sense of agency helps them to grow the confidence needed to take academic risks as well as the desire to continue learning and doing mathematics. It also empowers them to persevere through the natural struggles that come with solving problems. This conception of mathematics—as a sensemaking endeavor—aligns much more accurately with the way that mathematicians outside of K-12 schooling view the discipline (Boaler, 2015; Lockhart, 2009).

> *Real math, whether it's being done by professional mathematicians or elementary school students, is about figuring things out, not about following directions. It's about breaking problems down in order to understand what needs to be solved, exploring interesting and unique approaches to solutions, and engaging in discussions with others to strengthen and expand ideas. Math is fundamentally creative, collaborative, and rooted in reasoning. I was not taught this as a student, and for a long time, I didn't teach this way. But I realize now that my students can do what I didn't. They are capable of doing "real math" and I am capable of supporting them.*

At the heart of responsive mathematics teaching is the belief that everyone has the natural ability to think mathematically and, with the right opportunities and support, can make sense of challenging mathematics. Moreover, each learner has unique strengths and perspectives to bring to the table. It is the responsive teacher's job to make space for those strengths and perspectives to emerge, to celebrate them, and to help students see each other's strengths as resources; in other words, the responsive teacher recognizes and builds on the assets of each and every learner in the classroom to advance everyone's understanding of mathematics. When teachers approach mathematics instruction in this way, all students are provided with the opportunity to achieve high levels of understanding and success, and the culture of exclusion is replaced by a culture of inclusion.

Learning to Be a Responsive Teacher

> *After spending three years working to make my math teaching more responsive, my classroom looks completely different. It's active and vibrant and the energy in the room is palpable. My classroom is now full of actively thinking students. They talk with me and each other to make sense of the problems we're solving. They struggle productively to come up with their own ideas and then talk to each other, in big and small groups, about the different ways they see things and the different approaches they take to solve problems. I no longer believe that it is my job to tell students what to think. Instead, I'm focused on supporting them in developing their own thinking.*

Learning to be a responsive teacher can initially feel like a challenging endeavor because there is no script to follow. By its nature, responsive teaching requires adapting to the students in the room and the ways they engage with and think about the problems they are solving. The same task explored with two different groups on the same day might unfold in entirely different ways, depending on who the students are and what they know and think. Given this, teachers often wonder, "How will I know what to do if different students all use different strategies?" and "How can I plan my lessons if things could go so many different ways?" These are natural responses to an approach to teaching that challenges the status quo. However, just because there is no precise recipe for each lesson does not mean that responsive instruction cannot be planned, or that it needs to feel overwhelming for teachers. With time, effort, and support, teachers can learn both how to be adaptive in the moment and how to anticipate and prepare for contingent scenarios.

In the sections that follow, we introduce two supports for teachers to develop the adaptivity and anticipatory skills needed for responsive teaching. First, we present four guiding principles that drive and circumscribe responsive teachers' in-the-moment decisions. These principles help responsive teachers evaluate different teaching choices they can make at any given moment. Second, we outline a potential lesson structure designed to allow space for students to make sense of the problem(s) they are solving, come up with their own ideas, and then work collaboratively with peers and the teacher to refine those ideas and connect them to formalized mathematics.

Using a lesson format like this allows the responsive teacher to feel a sense of structure, within which they can adapt what they do to suit the needs of their students. The guiding principles can be thought of as a set of guardrails to help keep teachers on track as they make choices. The lesson structure can be thought of as a playground—an open space, with familiar boundaries, stations, and equipment, within which the teacher can not only be innovative but also stay focused on the overall learning goals.

Guiding Principles for Responsive Mathematics Teaching

Every teaching and learning situation is contextual. A teacher's decision about what to say or do in each moment depends on a range of factors: the individual learners; their prior knowledge, current ideas, and emotional states; the mathematics being explored; and the relationships among everyone involved—to name just a few. Not only do teachers need to react to all these variables, but each teacher also has their own personality, style, and way of interacting with students. Consequently, there is rarely a single correct way to respond in any given teaching moment. While variability is natural and expected, responsive teaching rests on the assumption that there are some constants that underscore the kinds of teaching decisions that are most likely to lead to positive outcomes for students.

These constants come in the form of four *guiding principles* that teachers can keep at the forefront to make the kinds of choices that promote a culture of inclusion, rather than exclusion.

Responsive teachers:

1. Prioritize mathematical sensemaking
2. Promote collaborative learning communities
3. Support the development of positive mathematical identities
4. Ensure that all students have access to mathematics.

In the following sections, we describe each principle, review the research behind it, and discuss why it is important for responsive teachers to embrace and allow it to guide their decision-making.

Guiding Principle 1: Prioritizing Mathematical Sensemaking

A primary goal of responsive teaching is to help students make their own sense of mathematics. Traditionally, mathematics has been taught in such a way that places individual sensemaking to the side and instead asks students to adopt specific lines of reasoning explained to them by their teachers or textbooks. Often, students do not follow these particular ways of thinking and consequently either memorize or accept things that make no sense to them or become discouraged and assume that they cannot understand the content. Learning mathematics becomes focused on the production of correct answers via the application of memorized steps and procedures with little understanding of any *whys* behind the *hows*. This approach to teaching mathematics also ignores something inherently beautiful about mathematics—that there are many different ways to solve almost all mathematical problems.

In contrast, responsive teachers prioritize making space for students to actively engage in making sense of the mathematics they are grappling with. This involves presenting problems without prescribing specific solution methods and intentionally slowing down the learning process so that students have time to develop their own ideas, navigate problem-solving challenges, persevere through mistakes, and engage in discussions with their peers. Making space for this kind of engagement allows students to build new relationships, gain a deeper understanding of mathematical concepts, and develop insights into multiple ways of approaching mathematics (Hiebert & Grouws, 2007).

Prioritizing sensemaking allows students to be creative, exercise perseverance and resilience, and engage in the vital mathematical practices of logical reasoning, mathematical argumentation, and critique. As students explore and construct ideas alongside their peers, they exercise and refine their understanding of mathematics. The understandings they develop are deep, meaningful, and long-lasting because they are cultivated by each student personally. When students are active sense makers, rather than passive receivers of knowledge, they build agency as mathematicians and a sense of empowerment. This motivates and encourages them to persevere as mathematicians and allows them to experience the joy of doing mathematics.

 When making a pedagogical decision, responsive teachers can honor this principle by asking themselves: *Will this decision help my students actively engage in mathematical sensemaking?*

Guiding Principle 2: Promoting Collaborative Learning Communities

Dialogue is vital to the pursuit of mathematical sensemaking. When people learn, they begin with their own ideas, but it is through conversation with others that they negotiate and refine the development of those ideas. As learners express their thoughts, listen to the thoughts of others, and try to fit different ideas together, they build increasingly sophisticated understandings of the concepts they discuss (Vygotsky & Cole, 1978). Despite this well-supported understanding of how learning occurs, mathematics learning is often treated as a solitary endeavor where individual mastery is prioritized over collective exploration, and conversation is limited to interactions between teachers and students (Hiebert et al., 1997). In typical mathematics classrooms, when students speak, it is usually to answer a question the teacher has posed, and it is almost always the teacher who confirms or denies the correctness of the idea under discussion. Students who struggle in these classes often wait passively for guidance, stumble through their struggles alone, or receive one-on-one support from their teacher. The expectation is that students will absorb an understanding of rules and procedures from the teacher, and there is usually little space made for learners to reason through thinking with peers.

Responsive teachers structure their classrooms differently by embracing the notion that learning happens in community, through the collective negotiation of ideas around a shared learning goal. Cultivating this kind of learning community requires, first and foremost, a focus on building relationships. Safe and comfortable relationships—between students and the teacher and among students—help everyone feel ready to take the risks needed to engage in productive discussions about complex ideas. Responsive teachers devote time to cultivating an environment where curiosity about each other's ideas is encouraged and collaboration is a vital part of problem solving. An important part of this work is ensuring that students develop ownership over a set of core values that govern the ways community members interact with each other around mathematics. These core values support students in having productive discussions about mathematics with others in their learning community.

This work often begins with the collective development of classroom norms. Classroom norms can be explicit (e.g., a list of rules the class creates and agrees to follow) or implicit (e.g., the patterns of social interaction that are seen as acceptable by the community). To support students in actually living the community norms, teachers need to do two things: help students build the skills and beliefs required to embrace them and ensure that students honor them. This involves using teaching moves that scaffold student dialogue, model acceptable behaviors, gently redirect inappropriate behaviors, protect students in vulnerable moments, call attention to brave and helpful contributions, uplift important but overlooked truths about mathematics learning (e.g., mistakes are useful sites for learning), and empower students to trust in their ability to learn mathematics collaboratively.

When a responsive teacher cultivates a classroom community built on strong relationships and a shared set of core values, the students in the class can engage regularly in conversations that help them collectively construct deep and meaningful understandings of mathematics (Kazemi & Hintz, 2014). The teacher can act as a facilitator, strategically leveraging the diversity of ideas in the class to help a collection of individual, "rough draft" ideas evolve into formalized, group knowledge that all students had a hand in creating (Jansen, 2020). In a collaborative learning community, students learn how to have their own mathematical ideas, share them articulately with others, make sense of and evaluate others' ideas, and draw connections between ideas. In short, they construct new knowledge that is connected to their prior knowledge but enriched and augmented by the experiences, approaches, and thoughts of others. Importantly, they also learn to believe in themselves and their peers as sources of mathematical authority, increasing their sense of competence (Cobb et al., 2009). They no longer need the teacher to tell them if something is right or wrong. Instead, they come to understand that all members of a mathematical community can figure out whether a mathematical idea holds true or needs revision. The experience of being a member of such a community helps students to feel engaged in and connected to the mathematics they are learning and prepares them to think logically and critically about new ideas, just like professional mathematicians.

 When making a pedagogical decision, responsive teachers can honor this principle by asking themselves: *Will this decision help me to further develop our collaborative learning community?*

Guiding Principle 3: Supporting the Development of Positive Mathematical Identities

When students participate in a productive, collaborative mathematics community, they are more likely to develop positive mathematical identities and see themselves as capable of learning and belonging in mathematical spaces (Martin, 2000). The development of positive mathematical identities has not always been a priority in mathematics classrooms, however. Instead, it has traditionally been socially acceptable for students to see themselves as "not good at math" or "not a math person." The cultural norming of this idea—that there are "math people" and "not math people" has reinforced a popular myth (widely disproven by neuroscience and cognitive research) that only some people are capable of thinking and reasoning mathematically. Research consistently suggests that mathematical ability is not a fixed trait but rather a capacity that can be developed with effort, practice, and the right learning environment.

While well-meaning adults often reinforce and normalize this myth as an act of empathy ("I was never good at math either") or a way to highlight diverse learning styles ("It is ok if math does not come easily to you—everyone has their strengths"), the consequences can be devastating for students and their learning. Students who believe that mathematics ability is innate and fixed can face persistent mathematics anxiety, avoid challenges and opportunities to learn mathematics (e.g., opting out of higher-level mathematics classes), and suffer from underperformance (Beilock & Maloney, 2015; Grootenboer & Marshman, 2016). In the United States, the students who fall victim to these repercussions are disproportionately female and students of color (Gutiérrez, 2018). A related myth that can further impact students' mathematical identities is the idea that mathematics is culture-free. Gutiérrez (2018) describes the damage that can occur for students when they are asked throughout their K-12 education to "leave [their] identities at the door" (p. 3), follow what seem like arbitrary rules made by others at the expense of making their own sense of things, and engage in mathematical thinking that is presented as separate from their own lived experiences. Ultimately, not only do students develop negative, rather than positive, mathematics identities, but they also experience a sense of dehumanization.

Responsive teachers work to combat these myths and trends by prioritizing the development of positive mathematical identities for all students. To do this, they shift the messaging in their classrooms from "it's ok, math is just not for everyone" or "let's make it easier, just follow these clear steps" to "you can make sense of mathematics in a way that feels genuine to you" and "I will support you as you grapple with the hard work of sensemaking." This involves clear and consistent declarations of the revised messaging, gently but explicitly challenging claims that perpetuate myths and stereotypes, and calling public attention to students who are working hard to build their own, powerful mathematical ideas. It also involves a shift in the focus of teacher praise. Rather than complimenting students on speed, correct answers, and the reproduction of procedures that have been modeled for them, responsive teachers celebrate when students persist through productive struggle, develop original lines of logical thinking, and share their ideas with others. They also intentionally highlight instances when students engage in important mathematical practices, paying particular attention to uplifting those who tend to see themselves, or are seen by others, as lacking in mathematical competence (Cohen & Lotan, 1997).

Supporting the development of positive mathematics identities also involves intentional work to help individuals feel personally connected to the mathematical work going on in the classroom. This means designing learning activities that offer multiple entry points for students, ensuring that classroom materials represent varied cultures, and using examples and contexts that show the value of mathematics in diverse communities, careers, and everyday life. It also means that teachers provide regular, formative feedback to students about their thinking in order to support ongoing development and also invite students to share feedback about their learning experiences (e.g., expressing how they feel, drawing connections between the content they are learning and their lived experiences, suggesting what might help them learn, and voicing frustrations or anxieties) so that the teacher can proactively address concerns and support each student more effectively.

Prioritizing the development of positive mathematical identities in the classroom has multiple benefits. First, it allows students to embrace the understanding that mathematical ability is not innate and fixed, but rather, that it can be developed through effort, persistence, and the making and revising of mistakes. When students honestly believe this, they adopt a *growth mindset* (Dweck, 2006). Growth mindsets help students to persist through moments of struggle and recognize challenges as an opportunity for growth rather than an indicator of failure. This, in turn, makes students more confident and resilient mathematics learners.

Second, it helps students who have experienced mathematical trauma in the past to confront and heal their wounds (Ashcraft, 2002; Skultety et al., 2023). When teachers acknowledge students' negative feelings about mathematics, provide a space to share painful experiences from the past, and actively support them in rebuilding their confidence, they empower learners to see themselves as capable mathematical thinkers and problem solvers. This helps students overcome potential learning barriers by lowering mathematics anxiety, decreasing mathematics avoidance, and ultimately increasing mathematics performance (Beilock & Maloney, 2015).

Finally, prioritizing the development of positive mathematics identities helps foster the inclusive culture that responsive teaching strives to create. When students are regularly asked to have, revise, and share their ideas—ideas that relate to their prior understandings and experiences—they develop a sense of belonging in their mathematical learning community. They come to believe that they have worthwhile mathematical thoughts and that other students do too. The consistent invitation for students to express themselves through mathematics helps each student to experience feelings of connection and joy when solving problems, and this, in turn, leads to increased ownership, motivation, and passion for learning mathematics (Gutiérrez, 2018). Ultimately, creating a space where students have ownership over their ideas and are allowed and expected to do their own sensemaking creates an environment where all learners can thrive. By valuing student ideas and believing in their ability to learn challenging mathematics concepts, teachers create access to high-level mathematics for all students, including those who have historically been excluded.

When making a pedagogical decision, responsive teachers can honor this principle by asking themselves: *Will this decision help one or more of my students strengthen a positive mathematics identity?*

Guiding Principle 4: Ensuring All Students Have Access to Mathematics

In order for students to make sense of new mathematics, learn collaboratively with peers, and build positive mathematics identities, they must have access to the learning activities taking place in their classroom. This may seem obvious, but while it is easy to embrace the idea of accessibility in the abstract, many people do not think about it concretely if it does not directly affect them.

For example, people often walk in and out of buildings without thinking about what might happen if they could not climb the steps. However, a building without a ramp is inaccessible to someone who uses a wheelchair to move around. While that person certainly recognizes when they are denied access, others may not even notice that a barrier exists. Classrooms are no exception to this phenomenon. If students can access the activities the teacher has designed, they are likely to be able to learn the mathematics they need to learn—in other words, they can get inside the building. If they cannot even enter the building, however, it is unlikely that they will be able to reach the learning goals set in front of them. Unless teachers pay close attention, they may not even notice if some students do not have clear access to the learning activities designed for them.

Historically, some students have been granted more or easier access to mathematics. In classrooms that use a more traditional approach focused on rote learning or the replication of procedures that have been modeled, students who are quick processors or have strengths in memorization often find a clear pathway to success. However, those with different strengths often face barriers that prevent them from engaging in the teacher's planned activities. Additionally, students whose cultural ways of communicating more closely match those of their teacher (or textbook) tend to have an easier time accessing learning activities. Modes of communication matter for expressing and understanding ideas, and mismatches in vocabulary, syntax, and speech patterns, or the contexts, examples, or metaphors used, can cause unintended access barriers for some students.

Much like how the person running up the flight of stairs never stops to think about what it would be like if they needed a ramp that was not there, well-intentioned teachers can miss the fact that some of their students lack access to learning activities. Biases, whether explicit or implicit, that cause teachers to believe that some students do not have the ability or inclination to do mathematics, can also get in the way. Responsive teachers firmly believe that every student has the right to access meaningful and engaging mathematical learning experiences, regardless of their learning strengths and weaknesses or their cultural ways of interacting with the world. Thus, they push themselves to honor their students' diverse backgrounds, experiences, and mathematical beliefs.

This commitment can be carried out in several ways. First, teachers can work to create a culture that values diverse voices and ways of thinking. When teachers intentionally and regularly create space for multiple ways of thinking and varied ways of expressing ideas, students become comfortable sharing their ways of understanding, their questions, and the connections they make between the mathematics in their classroom and their experiences outside the classroom, even if it differs from those of their peers, teachers, or textbooks. Creating this kind of space involves regularly making specific, responsive teaching moves such as asking students to share their reasoning, encouraging reluctant students to continue explaining even as it gets difficult, revoicing partially formed ideas or representing ideas visually, and offering praise when learners take risks.

Second, responsive teachers pay explicit attention to power dynamics and work to uplift voices and ideas that might otherwise get passed over. This requires monitoring and encouraging less confident individuals and empowering individuals from groups that have been historically and systemically underrepresented or discouraged in school mathematics. A particularly challenging part of this work is that, in order to do it, educators need to be critically conscious of their own (often implicit) biases, recognize the impact of negative stereotypes and assumptions, and actively work to dismantle them (Seda & Brown, 2021). This means truly embracing and honoring diverse expressions of mathematical understanding that emerge in the classroom. This can be challenging—it is hard to understand ideas that are different from one's own—but responsive teaching involves a commitment to that hard work, knowing that it will pay off for students who might otherwise be denied access to important learning.

Finally, responsive teachers devote time to helping their students make sense of mathematical tasks before they ask them to begin solving. Unpacking a task is a vital mathematical skill distinct from solving it, and students require support in learning how to do it. Responsive teachers always carve out time to help students do this unpacking work together, making sure they understand the vocabulary and the key contextual features in the task (Jackson et al., 2012), helping students to articulate in their own words both the problem to be solved and the goal, and supporting students to activate prior knowledge that might be of use during problem solving. When responsive teachers preserve time for this unpacking, they ensure that students have the space to struggle productively with the mathematics they should be learning, rather than struggling (usually unproductively) with barriers to understanding the task.

Responsive teachers prioritize access because it provides more equitable outcomes for all students. When access is something that teachers pay attention to, students come to feel safe, comfortable, and valued in their classroom. In addition, the community grows to understand that diverse thinking is valuable in mathematics. From a practical standpoint, more students can and will be successful when teachers commit to providing access.

When making a pedagogical decision, responsive teachers can honor this principle by asking themselves: *Will this decision help to ensure that all my students have access to the important mathematics I am trying to help them learn?*

Learning mathematics is not about replicating specific procedures; likewise, responsive teaching is not about carrying out a predetermined script or set of teaching moves. Instead, it is about responding to one's students, in the moment, to help them make sense of mathematics, build collaborative learning communities, grow positive mathematical identities, and gain access to every learning activity. Learning how to do this requires experimentation, reflection, and a commitment to ongoing growth. The guiding principles discussed above can provide stability and direction, even as specific instructional moves may shift from moment to moment. By consistently returning and attending to these principles, teachers' instructional choices will grow in responsiveness and fundamentally build toward more student-centered, asset-based learning. As we dive into the specifics of how to plan and carry out a responsive lesson, remember that the goal is not perfection, but rather thoughtful decision-making driven by the belief that all students bring valuable ideas to the table that can be built upon to achieve mathematical learning goals.

What Does a Responsive Mathematics Lesson Look Like?

Responsive teaching can occur during any activity that engages students in authentic thinking or analysis. This book focuses on one high-leverage activity—engaging students in genuine problem solving around a single task—as a framework for exploring the responsive teaching process. We use problem-solving tasks to anchor our examples because they offer a commonly used and potentially rich opportunity for students to participate in truly doing mathematics. When students engage fruitfully in problem solving, they see how mathematics can be used to model and make sense of puzzling or intriguing situations. The standard word problems commonly found in mathematics curriculum materials can be transformed into exciting, genuine learning experiences for all students through responsive teaching. Our goal is to illustrate what responsive mathematics teaching looks like in this context, while also inspiring a vision that could extend to other open-ended mathematical activities, such as working out computational problems, playing games, solving puzzles, engaging in number sense routines, centers, or review, and completing projects. We have even worked with educators who have used responsive teaching to help students prepare for open-ended items on standardized tests.

16 ◆ Becoming a Responsive Mathematics Teacher

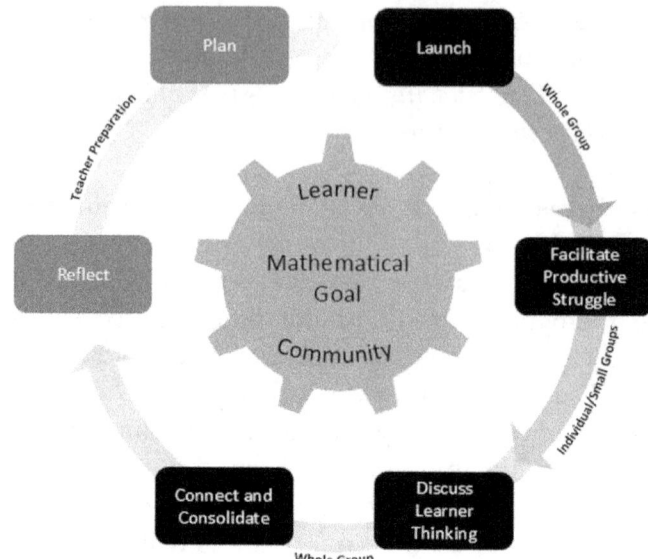

Figure 1.2 Responsive mathematics instructional model. (To access a more detailed version of this instructional model, please visit: www.routledge.com/9781032882222)

The model of responsive mathematics teaching shown in Figure 1.2 (and described in more detail in the following chapters) honors the four principles described above through a cyclical process that involves: planning a lesson around an engaging mathematical task; supporting students in unpacking and solving the task; discussing solutions and strategies; helping students to connect and consolidate new mathematical ideas in light of the solutions and strategies discussed; and finally, reflecting on what students have learned and what they still need in order to continue moving forward. Responsive teaching is inherently iterative, requiring constant reflection and adjustments based on evidence of student learning. The following chapters begin at the start of the in-class portion of a problem-solving lesson (the launch) and progress clockwise through the cycle to provide an accessible overview of the flow of a responsive mathematics lesson. The process, however, must always start with careful planning and preparation.

Planning

Before teaching a responsive problem-solving lesson, teachers need to identify the mathematics to be learned and select a task that allows students to explore the important concepts within that mathematical goal. The task must provide a genuine problem or challenge to solve, rather than a procedure to follow. Using what is known about students from their engagement in previous lessons, teachers may need to adjust the task they choose (by changing numbers, altering contexts, or opening the task up to allow for multiple approaches) and then anticipate the ways that students are likely to approach it, places they may get stuck or confused, and ways they might respond to those challenges. Planning also involves thinking through specific teaching practices for each of the components discussed below in relation to the mathematical goals and the make-up of the community of learners in the classroom.

Launching

The in-class portion of a responsive mathematics lesson begins with a launch, or introduction to the task, during which teachers guide students to unpack the problem situation, identify any constraints, and ponder the unknowns. Through the launch, the teacher ensures that each student has the opportunity and support to make sense of the problem individually, while also guiding the group toward developing a shared understanding of the important parameters of the task. During the launch, the teacher also ensures that students are prepared to begin working on the task independently and productively.

A productive launch involves making space for students to break down the problem, discuss key contextual components, surface prior knowledge (mathematical or contextual), and clarify what a successful solution might look like or must have. Ultimately, the opening of a responsive mathematics lesson sets students up to engage with the task in ways that will lead them to grapple with important mathematics without getting frustrated or lost. This supports their sense of agency and the belief that they can use what they know to make sense of challenging problems.

Facilitating Productive Struggle

Once students understand the problem they are going to tackle, a responsive teacher provides adequate time and space for students to engage in problem solving. Students may begin by working alone or in collaboration with others, but as they solve, the teacher actively circulates to monitor and support their progress. A certain amount of struggle on the part of students is necessary—otherwise, it would turn into a rote exercise rather than solving a genuine problem—but if the struggle becomes too intense, students may shut down or feel defeated. Therefore, when needed, the teacher facilitates productive struggle by supporting students in getting started, getting unstuck, making connections, synthesizing or extending their thinking, or feeling comfortable taking risks. Most importantly, the teacher uses responsive teaching moves to provide support without lowering the cognitive demand on students. This means allowing students to engage deeply with the task by eliciting both their existing ideas and stuck-points and then carefully nudging them forward without taking over the thinking process or telling students exactly what to do. In a responsive mathematics classroom, the goal is for students to do the heavy lifting of figuring out a solution, rather than the teacher.

Discussing Learner Thinking

When students have had adequate time to work productively on the task, the teacher then facilitates a whole-class discussion of learner thinking. By nature, genuine problem-solving tasks will have multiple solution paths, and as long as the teacher has not directed students to use a specific strategy, students will choose methods that they are comfortable with and ready to use. The purpose of the whole-class discussion is twofold: for students to make sense of each other's thinking so that they can be exposed to different ways of solving the problem and for the teacher to help the class connect the ideas that emerge to more formal mathematical concepts.

A successful discussion of learner thinking relies on the teacher having purposefully selected some examples of student work that show diverse problem-solving approaches and then sequenced those strategies in a way that builds toward some key mathematical ideas or concepts. During the discussion, the teacher focuses on uplifting a variety of voices to engage the entire group in developing an understanding of the mathematics in the strategies that are shared. To do this, a responsive teacher uses a variety of discussion or talk moves, such as wait time, asking "why" and "how" questions, and revoicing to validate and clarify student ideas. The teacher also represents student thinking visually, using diagrams, charts, or other tools to make abstract ideas more concrete and accessible. A key component of facilitating these discussions is to make space for a variety of students to share their ideas, being particularly mindful of highlighting and elevating the contributions of students who may not always be perceived by others (or perceive themselves) as mathematically capable, to build positive mathematical identities.

Connecting and Consolidating

The in-class portion of a responsive mathematics lesson wraps up when the teacher provides an opportunity for learners to connect and consolidate their learning of the important mathematics that surfaced through productive struggle and class discussion. This sometimes involves helping students formalize their ideas by explicitly connecting their strategies to key mathematical concepts, generalizing patterns they have discovered, or proving and/or disproving conjectures. It can also involve asking students to apply, revise, or summarize their developing understandings. These endeavors help students uncover the "whys," refine their thinking, integrate new insights, and package their learning so that it can be more easily drawn upon in future lessons.

Attending to the work of connecting and consolidating ultimately deepens student comprehension and ensures that students see how their own ideas fit together with the larger mathematical goals of the lesson, unit, and curriculum. The connecting and consolidating portion of the lesson also helps the teacher by providing an opportunity to collect evidence of students' understanding. Responsive teachers then use the evidence they collect about students' developing thinking to inform the design of subsequent lessons and their future instructional choices.

Reflecting

Once the in-class portion of the problem-solving lesson is over, the responsive teacher always reflects on the extent to which they met their pedagogical and learning goals. Responsive teachers take time after a lesson to review student work, consider the trajectory of the class discussion, and analyze any data they collected (e.g., video recordings of their instruction, observational notes about students or the lesson, or students' written work). The reflection process also involves considering the equity of learner participation, the progress of students' developing mathematical identities, and the state of group dynamics to track how well all voices are being incorporated and assess the inclusivity of the mathematical learning community.

Committing to regular reflection after lessons creates an intentional space in which teachers can examine students' developing understanding, their experiences, their progress, and their challenges. This kind of intentional reflection on the lesson and learning that occurred helps teachers make informed decisions about the next steps in their instruction. When responsive teachers engage in a reflective process, they foster continuous improvement for their students' learning and their own teaching, enabling the preparation of future lessons that meet students where they are and promote meaningful engagement and growth. In this way, the reflection process leads right into the beginning of the next cycle, with the planning of a new lesson.

The Structure of This Book

> *As a new teacher this year, I was completely overwhelmed. I love math and I wanted to make it exciting and meaningful for my students, but I didn't really know where to begin. They didn't seem to like it and honestly, most of them were struggling to understand the things I was explaining to them. I had no idea what to do. I ended up going to a session on responsive teaching. It made sense. I started noticing how many things I was telling my students and how little I was asking them to actually figure out. After a few responsive teaching sessions, I decided I would figure out how to ask better questions. Focusing on questioning gave me somewhere to start to change my teaching. Working toward becoming a more responsive teacher has made me feel less overwhelmed by the idea of teaching math and more in control of my students' learning.*

This book aims to help educators deepen their understanding of responsive mathematics teaching and consider ways that they might shift from traditional conceptions of what teaching mathematics involves to new, more empowering responsibilities. The subsequent chapters provide frameworks, tools, and strategies to enhance opportunities for students to engage actively in sensemaking, build collaborative learning communities, develop positive mathematical identities, and gain equitable access to learning activities. We invite you to reflect on how these approaches can inform your own teaching (or the teaching of others you support) and inspire a shift toward more responsive and inclusive mathematics classrooms.

In Chapters 2–5, we explore each component of a responsive mathematics problem-solving lesson, beginning with the launch and moving clockwise through the instructional model (Figure 1.2), thereby providing an overview of the flow of a single lesson. While a responsive lesson is inherently fluid and adaptable to student and classroom needs, this book follows the natural progression of the model to illustrate how each component informs and builds upon the previous one. Chapter 2 explores the work of launching, Chapter 3 examines what is involved in facilitating productive struggle, Chapter 4 covers how responsive teachers facilitate whole-group discussion of learner thinking, and Chapter 5 overviews the art of connecting, consolidating, and reflecting on evidence of student learning. These chapters include one or more vignettes inspired by our work with responsive mathematics teachers and their students, offering concrete examples of how these components might look and sound in action. These vignettes have been constructed to reflect authentic student voices and teacher decisions, and to illustrate what responsive teaching looks and sounds like at different grade levels and contexts. Each chapter also breaks down the corresponding portion of the instructional model into specific teacher responsibilities, illustrated through an instructional tool. The tools offer actionable steps for teachers and examples of facilitator moves and questions. Additionally, each chapter includes a section guiding teachers on planning for that part of the lesson, including lesson planning templates and potential questions a teacher can ask themselves as they plan the section discussed in that chapter.

Chapters 6–8 zoom out beyond the specifics of the instructional model to highlight the work that responsive teachers do outside of the confines of classroom instruction. Chapter 6 provides a comprehensive guide for teachers to plan a responsive mathematics lesson from start to finish. This chapter is designed to help individual teachers refine their planning process and serve as a valuable resource for grade-level teams and instructional coaches looking to support collaborative lesson planning. Chapter 7 offers a framework for building a classroom community where students feel comfortable and safe engaging in active sensemaking, an important precursor to teaching responsively. It provides ideas for setting norms and instilling routines to foster a safe community that encourages brave mathematical thinking. In addition to supporting individual teachers, this chapter also offers support for educators who design professional learning aimed at helping teachers build collaborative learning communities. Chapter 8 is intended to support teachers, teacher educators, and instructional leaders as they consider how to share, explore, and support the implementation of responsive teaching practices beyond individual classrooms, at the school or district level.

As a reader, you can choose how to engage with this book based on your goals and role as an educator. If you are a classroom teacher, new to responsive teaching and looking to transform your practice, we recommend reading the book from beginning to end. Engaging with the book chronologically will provide a comprehensive understanding of the instructional model, strategies for implementation, and examples of what this work looks like in the classroom. If you are a teacher educator seeking resources for a methods class or professional development, you could explore specific chapters that align with your goals. For instructional leaders with a foundational knowledge of this kind of teaching, consider starting with the later chapters, which provide guidance on building responsive communities and scaling practices across schools or districts. Ultimately, this book is designed to meet you where you are, offering flexible entry points for a range of educators while equipping readers with resources to explore and engage with responsive mathematics teaching.

Reflection Questions

1. Reflect on your own experience as a mathematics learner in relation to the four guiding principles of responsive teaching. How did your learning experiences help you engage in mathematical sensemaking? To participate in a collaborative learning community? To develop a positive mathematics identity? To gain access to the mathematics you were supposed to be learning? In what ways did they fall short of supporting you in reaching these goals?

2. Now, consider your learners' experiences. What opportunities do they currently have to engage in mathematical sensemaking? To participate in a collaborative learning community? To develop

a positive mathematics identity? To gain access to what they are supposed to be learning? What additional or alternate opportunities would you like them to have? How might you actualize those?

3. Where do you see connections between your current teaching practice and the responsive lesson structure described in this chapter? What visions do you have for ways that you might grow or change your teaching practice based on what you have read so far?

2

Launching a Task

Responsive teachers begin problem-solving lessons by introducing the task they have selected for students to engage with. This introduction, or launch, aims to help students unpack the problem they are about to solve, ensuring that they feel confident, inspired, and prepared when they begin to craft a solution strategy. In a successful launch, the teacher and learners collaborate to develop a shared understanding of the task's context and the problem to be solved. The teacher also helps the group define parameters for working on the task and set expectations for the product of their work. Taking the time to launch a task before asking students to solve it engages students actively in the sensemaking process, promotes the development of individual positive mathematics identities and a collaborative learning community, and ensures that all students have access to the activity they are about to engage in.

This chapter begins with a series of vignettes that illustrate how two teachers, Mr. Porter and Mrs. Braxton, each launched a task that they adapted from their textbook in their first-grade classrooms (Figure 2.1). They chose the task because it focused on building relationships around an important concept and first-grade standard: decomposing a teen number in multiple ways.

Because both addends are unknown in Anya's Pennies, there are multiple valid solutions. This kind of open-ended structure presents an engaging challenge for students. It allows them to have repeated opportunities to break apart the number 13 and requires that they make careful sense of what they are being asked to do. For students to be ready to tackle this challenge, they need to feel confident that they understand what is going on in the task and what they should be solving for; in other words, the launch matters for

DOI: 10.4324/9781003536710-2

Anya saved 13 pennies.
She put some pennies in a jar and the rest in her piggy bank.
How many pennies could be in the bank and in the jar?

Figure 2.1 Anya's Pennies.

students' success. As you read through the vignettes describing how each teacher launched this task, pay close attention to the opportunities provided for students to make sense of the task. What do you notice as you compare the two approaches to launching this task?

> ### Mr. Porter's Launch: "Are there any questions?"
> Mr. Porter stands at the front of his first-grade class and reads aloud Anya's Pennies, which he has also projected on the interactive whiteboard. He then reads the task aloud a second time, and asks, "Are there any questions?"
>
> Jasmine responds, "I think there are more in the jar." Mr. Porter pauses her, "Interesting idea Jasmine! Does anyone else have any questions about this problem?" After a period of silence, Naveah calls out, "I know the answer!" Mr. Porter holds out his hand gently toward Naveah and says, "Ok, please keep that to yourself. We don't want to give away the solution."
>
> After another brief pause, Mr. Porter states, "If there aren't any questions I think we're ready to try solving this problem on our own." He makes a final check for raised hands and says, "Alright, it's solving time. Everyone get out your pencils and be sure to show your work!"
>
> A few students get started right away, but many put their heads down or begin playing with items on their desks. Several students immediately raise their hands or call out to Mr. Porter for assistance. Mr. Porter spends the next 20 minutes traveling from desk to desk, explaining to individual students how to solve the task. He walks most students through a solution step by step. After the lesson, while reflecting, he concludes that the task was just too difficult for them.

> ### Mrs. Braxton's Launch: "What is happening in this story?"
> "Alright, everyone, I want you to take a quick look at this picture." Mrs. Braxton shows the class the image from the Anya's Pennies task and asks,

"What do you see?" Kyle announces that he sees a piggy bank, and Kayla adds that she also sees a jar. "I had a piggy bank when I was a kid, and I put money in it to save for a toy. Anyone else save money in either a piggy bank or some other kind of container?" asks Mrs. Braxton. Most students nod.

"Great. We're going to solve a task that has to do with this picture. First, I'm going to read it aloud. I don't want you to try to solve the problem yet. Just listen and pay attention to what is happening." Mrs. Braxton displays the task on the board and reads it out loud. She scans the room, attentive to her students' postures and expressions. "I'm going to read it one more time. This time, close your eyes, listen *really* closely, and try to picture in your mind what Anya is doing."

After the second read, she asks the students to share what they pictured in their minds while she was reading. Alan raises his hand and says, "I pictured Anya dropping coins in the hole in the top of the piggy bank." "Did anyone else picture that?" asks Mrs. Braxton. Most of the class raises their hand. "What kind of money did you imagine?" "Pennies," exclaims Rita. "Thirteen of them!" Mrs. Braxton circles the words *13 pennies* on the board. She probes for additional ideas, and Yanelly adds, "I saw her put some in the piggy bank and some in the jar." Mrs. Braxton responds, "Ah! Yanelly just said something very important! Does anyone think they understand what Yanelly means by *some* in the piggy bank and *some* in the jar?"

After giving the students a moment to think, Mrs. Braxton calls on Marcus. "The pennies get split up," he explains. "How do you know that?" asks Mrs. Braxton. Marcus continues, "because Anya puts some of her pennies in the jar and the rest in the piggy bank." Yannelly and several other students nod in agreement. Mrs. Braxton says, "Okay, so she puts *some* of the 13 pennies in the jar and all *the rest* in the piggy bank." She writes the word SOME on the jar and the words, THE REST on the piggy bank. "Have you ever had to put something in two different places?" Peter shares that he has two shelves at home where he keeps his books. Lyla makes a connection to storing some of her dolls in a toy box and the rest on her shelf.

Mrs. Braxton says, "Okay, I am going to read the question again. This time I want you to think about what we have to figure out. What is our job?" She reads and then asks the students to turn and talk about what they think they are supposed to be figuring out. As the students discuss, Mrs. Braxton walks around to hear their ideas. She invites one pair to share. They explain that they have to figure out how much money Anya puts in the piggy bank and how much she puts in the jar. "Ah! Ok. So, when we find a solution, it will include the number of pennies you think are in the jar and the number of pennies you think are in the piggy bank. Great. Do you think Anya has to use all 13 pennies?" There is a bit of mumbling, but most students are saying yes. Mrs. Braxton affirms, "Yes. All 13 pennies have to have a home—either they

> go in the jar [touches the picture of the jar], or in the piggy bank [touches the picture of the piggy bank]."
>
> "I have one last question for you. Do you think this is the kind of question where there is one answer or more than one answer?" Mrs. Braxton calls on Simon, who says, "There are a lot of answers." "How do you know that?" Mrs. Braxton presses. "Because you could put, like, a lot in the jar and a little in the bank or the other way around, or a lot of different ways." Mrs. Braxton asks, "What do the rest of you think about Simon's idea?" Most students nod. Jamilla calls out, "I can already think of like three ways to do it."
>
> "OK" says Mrs. Braxton, "It sounds like your brains are ready to start solving. Go ahead and get started working on your own ideas, and in a few minutes, I'll give you a signal to start working with a partner. We don't have real pennies, but you can use any materials from your toolbag to help if you need them. Remember that mathematicians try to find answers but also convince others that those answers are true. So be sure to come up with a way to show the rest of us how many pennies you think could be in the jar and how many could be in the bank."

Launching to Facilitate Sensemaking

Launching a task should be a way to initiate the sensemaking process for students so that it permeates throughout the solving. This means being mindful not to demonstrate how to approach the task (or solve a similar problem), which would result in students spending their time replicating the teacher's strategy rather than making sense of it for themselves. Although seeing a solution strategy modeled might help students get to a correct answer, they would not develop the understanding and mindsets needed to solve new or different problems in the future. Both Mr. Porter and Mrs. Braxton avoided that pitfall by allowing students to solve the task using a strategy of their choice. However, there were some key differences in how they launched the task that had an impact on the students' learning opportunities.

By reading the task aloud, both teachers ensured access for students who might struggle to read it independently. Mr. Porter read the task aloud once to his students. Mrs. Braxton, on the other hand, first primed her students to understand the context by allowing them to briefly reflect on the picture of the piggy bank and the jar, and then hear the task read aloud multiple times, providing guidance for what to focus on. Try to picture in your mind what Anya is doing.") She then invited her students to share their thoughts, giving her important information about their prior knowledge as well as potential areas of confusion.

The additional moves that Mrs. Braxton made also provided her students with increased opportunities for sensemaking. By giving her students a brief opportunity to talk about the picture, she prepared them to make connections to the context before considering the problem to solve within that context. By offering specific guidance on how students should listen (close their eyes and try to visualize), she allowed her students to develop clarity about the action occurring in the task. And finally, by asking students to reflect on what they saw, Mrs. Braxton gained an understanding of how students were beginning to make sense of the task, and the entire class had the opportunity to benefit from the insights shared by their peers.

An additional difference between the two launches is the nature of the questions that the two teachers used to engage their students in making sense of the task. After reading the task aloud, Mr. Porter asked his students if they had any questions. While this open-ended prompt is likely aimed at clarifying any confusion before sending students to begin problem-solving, it requires students to articulate their questions before they have had a chance to make sense of the task. Mr. Porter, like many well-intentioned teachers, assumed that the lack of student response meant that everyone understood the task, its context, and the problem being posed. This assumption led him to allow students to begin working toward solutions, only to find that most were actually confused about what they were being asked to do.

Mrs. Braxton, on the other hand, asked a variety of questions, all of which served to help students unpack the context and the problem itself. She asked questions designed to ensure that students could identify the different objects (piggy bank, jar) and quantities (13 pennies) in the task and that they could understand Anya's actions with those objects. She identified possible points of confusion and asked specific questions designed to bring clarity (e.g., "Do you think Anya has to use all 13 pennies?"). Other questions were designed to help the group build a shared understanding of the task (e.g., "Does anyone think they understand what Yanelly means by *some* in the piggy bank and *some* in the jar?"). She also used questioning to help students connect the action Anya was performing in the task to their own lives to make the problem they were being asked to solve feel more familiar (e.g., "Have you ever had to put things in two different places?"). Finally, she ended her launch by asking questions that ensured her students were clear about what they should be doing and how their work time would look.

The distinction between the vignettes reflects two very different approaches toward developing student understanding. Mr. Porter's approach assumes that students either understand independently, with little effort, or that understanding can be developed through answering student-generated questions. Mrs. Braxton's approach, on the other hand, assumes that some initial confusion is a natural part of problem solving and that a teacher can leverage potential points of confusion to help the whole class ultimately feel more prepared to solve problems. By encouraging students to engage in practices like picturing the scenario, drawing on their prior knowledge and experiences, and listening to and building on the insights of their peers, Mrs. Braxton used her launch to facilitate understanding through individual and collective sensemaking of the task. By helping her students draw on what they knew to negotiate a common understanding, she ensured each student had an entry point to begin solving. Her students were ultimately more successful in solving Anya's Pennies than Mr. Porter's students, not because they had different mathematical abilities, but because they were encouraged and supported to make sense of the task before they began trying to solve it.

Why is Launching a Task Important and What Makes It Effective?

A successful launch, like Mrs. Braxton's, takes time and careful preparation. Responsive teachers work hard to facilitate a dialogue that allows students to reach a consensus about the answers to two critical questions: "What is going on in this task?" and "What are we trying to figure out?" To do this, students need thinking time, time to turn and talk, time to hash out ideas in the whole group, and, most importantly, time to have their own ideas and describe them in their own words. This is a commitment. While some teachers may be tempted to skip or shorten the launch to preserve time for students to work on the task, the careful work done to reach a group consensus is essential to students' success and understanding. How a task is launched influences how students engage with it during problem-solving, shapes the whole-class discussion, and ultimately affects what mathematics students learn (Jackson et al., 2013; Stein et al., 1996).

Strong launches—those that are neither *underlaunches* (like Mr. Porter's) nor *overlaunches* (when teachers provide too much support by modeling or suggesting how to solve the problem)—help students prepare to problem solve in several ways. First, they provide the time and space needed for learners to slow down and perform vital sensemaking prior to focusing on finding the solution. Learners, and their teachers, are often tempted to jump right to finding an answer rather than taking the time to think about what information is given, what is happening, and what a solution to the task might look like. Encouraging students to put the brakes on and make sense of a task ensures that they enter the quest for a solution with all the facts straight and ready at their fingertips. Note that unpacking a problem in this way is not the same as highlighting keywords or phrases for students to help them decide what operation to use to solve the problem. The strategy of isolating words and quantities from the context of the problem, while used by many well-meaning educators, is ultimately both counterproductive and ineffective. Many tasks, such as Anya's Pennies, do not have any keywords, and even if they do, they can often lead students to use the wrong operation (Karp et al., 2019). More importantly, focusing on keywords encourages students to put their sensemaking aside and "just grab the numbers and compute" (Hyde, 2006, p. 3).

Launches also provide an opportunity for students to engage in visualization of the problem and its context, an essential component of problem solving (Paivio, 1986). Successful problem solvers construct mental models of problem situations (Hegarty et al., 1995), asking themselves questions like, "Is this a problem where I'm finding the total or the part? Are some quantities changing over time? Have I solved a problem like this before?" They then draw on this model of the situation to develop a plan for solving. Asking students to imagine the situation, act out the situation, or make connections to familiar contexts or experiences are all effective ways to support their sensemaking and development of a mental model.

Another reason launches are important is that they set students up to engage successfully in whole-class discussions about their solutions after solving the problem. Unpacking the task by eliciting students' prior knowledge and engaging them in collaborative sensemaking of the context, text, and mathematics helps to develop a shared understanding of the task. This ensures that students are all solving the same problem and that they all have an entry point to begin finding a solution. In overlaunches, teachers tend to try to achieve these outcomes by simply explaining important information and leading students toward a specific solution path; in a responsive launch, teachers create opportunities for students to make sense of the task themselves, in conjunction with their peers.

Figuring out how to strike this balance—preparing students to be ready to solve without doing all the difficult thinking for them—is key to a successful launch. Jackson et al. (2012) highlight four components of a successful launch of a complex task: discussing the key contextual features, identifying the key mathematical ideas, developing shared language, and maintaining the cognitive demand. This means taking the time to elicit and learn about the prior knowledge students have of the scenario in the task and helping them make sense of the important mathematical relationships, without suggesting a strategy or solution pathway. For example, in preparing to launch Anya's Pennies, a teacher needs to attend to the following considerations: Do students know what pennies are? Have they ever seen a piggy bank? Is there any other language that might be confusing or unfamiliar? Will they be confused about what it means that Anya is "saving" pennies? Students could use counting, addition, or subtraction to solve this task, but understanding that there is a total amount (13 pennies) that is being split up between two parts (jar and piggy bank) is critical to finding a pathway to multiple solutions and ultimately seeing the relationship between addition and subtraction. Confusion around any of these contextual, language, or mathematical factors may impede many students from getting started with the task, and ultimately, from reaching the mathematical goal.

A RESPONSIVE LAUNCH	
Involves …	Does NOT Involve …
<ul><li>Providing a space for students to deliberately make sense of the task before solving</li><li>Drawing on students' prior knowledge and experiences to collaboratively unpack key contextual and mathematical elements of a task, what is happening in a task scenario, and what learners are being asked to solve for</li><li>Clarifying mathematical terms and phrases that are necessary to make sense of the task</li><li>Setting expectations for problem solving: where students will work, who they will work with, what tools they can use</li></ul>	<ul><li>Jumping right into having students solve a complex task</li><li>Assuming students already understand the task and context, or that the understanding is not important for problem solving</li><li>Asking students if they have any questions</li><li>Highlighting key words or phrases to signal an operation or strategy to use</li><li>Directing students to a specific strategy or process to use to solve a task</li><li>Walking through a sample solution or similar problem before sending students off to solve</li></ul>

Launching a Task: The Teacher's Role

While learners need to do the heavy cognitive lifting during the launch, the teacher plays a pivotal role in ensuring that all students have made sense of a task before moving on to trying to solve it. We have found it helpful to think about the teacher's role in a launch as consisting of three primary responsibilities: (1) establishing individual understanding, or ensuring that each student has the opportunity and support to make sense of the problem on their own, (2) establishing collective understanding, or supporting the class in developing a shared understanding of the task and its parameters, and (3) building a bridge to solving, or preparing students to transition to working independently and productively. These three responsibilities are detailed in the following sections, along with examples to illustrate how they might be used in different classroom contexts.

The First Responsibility: Establish Individual Understanding of the Task

The primary goal of establishing individual understanding is to give all learners time to engage with the problem independently. When teachers prioritize individual processing time over a teacher-led explanation of the task, it sets the expectation that all learners can and should digest the task they are about to solve and begin to make their own sense of what is happening. The Launch Tool presented in Table 2.1 outlines the work a responsive teacher can do to help students achieve this goal.

The first way teachers can support students in individual sensemaking is to provide *multiple ways to process the task*. This often means giving students time to read or hear the problem more than once. Teachers may read the problem out loud for younger students, as both teachers did in the opening vignettes. For older students, teachers can first give students time to read independently and write notes, saying, for example, "Your only job right now is to read the problem and try to make sense of it yourself. Feel free to write

Table 2.1 Launch Tool, Responsibility #1

Responsibility #1: Establish Individual Understanding of the Task	
Give **multiple ways to process the task** (e.g., hearing it read out loud, reading silently, choral reading, different voices, taking notes).	• *Listen carefully. I'm going to read it twice.* • *Your only job right now is to read the problem and try to make sense of it yourself.* • *Feel free to write on the problem to help you make sense of it.* • *Rami, will you read the problem out loud?*
Ask learners to **visualize the problem** and describe what is happening in the situation.	• *What is happening in this situation? What's going on here?* • *Try to make a picture in your mind of what is happening in this task.*
Have learners **describe the task in their own words.**	• *Can someone tell us what is going on in the problem in their own words?* • *What are we being asked to figure out?*

on the problem to help you make sense of it." A combination of reading and hearing the problem can provide access points early in the problem-solving process through multiple learning modalities (reading, seeing, and listening).

It is also essential to encourage learners to *visualize the problem.* Mrs. Braxton did this when she said, close your eyes, listen *really* closely, and try to picture what Anya is doing." This move helps students create a mental image of the action in the task. Visualization can help learners make sense of abstract situations that they might otherwise struggle to comprehend. It can also help them slow down and ensure they are not rushing straight to a solution without first understanding all the information given in the problem.

Once students have had multiple opportunities to see, hear, and visualize, it is important to check the pulse on individual understanding by having learners *describe the task in their own words.* For example, by asking, "Can someone tell us what is going on in the problem?" the student who responds will need to articulate their developing knowledge and understanding, and by doing so, actively process the key elements of the task. This, in turn, helps other students by providing an additional inroad to understanding the task. Hearing a peer describe a situation makes it accessible in a new way and more familiar language. This move also helps the teacher gain a sense of how individuals are perceiving the problem. It may surface partial understandings, misconceptions, or missed information that the teacher can flag as needing to be further unpacked during the forthcoming discussion. In this way, it establishes the grounds for the collective understanding that should be built before students go off to solve the task.

The Second Responsibility: Establish Collective Understanding of the Task

After supporting individual sensemaking, the next responsibility of the teacher is to establish a collective understanding of the task. The teaching moves illustrated in the Launch Tool in Table 2.2 can be used to structure a dialogue where the group engages in sensemaking together, making space for students to speak to each other, grapple with and build on each other's ideas, and reach a consensus on what the task is all about. Teachers can also highlight or insert critical information orally or by making notes, annotations, or drawings on the board.

An important way to establish collective understanding is to elicit or *make connections to learners' prior knowledge or experience* and then work to fill in gaps in knowledge. A simple way to do this is to ask students to share personal stories about their experiences with key contextual features of the task. Mrs. Braxton illustrated this kind of move when she asked her students about their experiences with piggy banks and times when they put things in two different places. Connecting to learners' lives and frames of reference

Table 2.2 Launch Tool, Responsibility #2

Responsibility #2: Establish Collective Understanding of the Task	
Elicit and/or **make connections to prior knowledge and experience** and fill gaps as needed.	• Who has cooked with a family member before? Did you have to measure any ingredients? What tools did you use? • This problem uses the term regular polygon. We learned about them last week. Talk to your partner about what it means for a shape to be a regular polygon. • Have we seen a problem like this before? How is this one similar or different?
Provide opportunity for **clarification** of the task and vocabulary (scaffolded or open-ended questions)	• What do you think it means when it says a "fair share"? • Is this the kind of problem that could have more than one solution, or are we looking for a single correct solution?
Record group sensemaking of problem.	• List important information/constraints the group agrees to on the board.
If needed, ask **explicit questions** without specifying an equation, strategy, or operation for solving.	• It asks us to find the largest rectangle. Could the answer be a square? Why or why not?

affirms and honors their personal experiences, and highlighting those connections in a group setting fosters a communal sense of sharing and belonging (Ladson-Billings, 1995; NCTM, 2014). It can also be helpful to facilitate connections to recent classroom experiences by prompting students to recall important concepts or ideas that emerged from the discussions of prior tasks (e.g., "Remember we learned about regular polygons last week," or "Who can remind us of where we have seen this before?"). By supporting connections to prior collective knowledge, the teacher surfaces the mathematical foundations for the group to refine and build upon continually.

Another important part of establishing collective understanding is providing opportunities for *clarification* of essential vocabulary or other elements of the task. Teachers can anticipate specific terminology or contexts that might be less familiar or confusing for learners and then use open-ended questions to determine how much scaffolding or intervention is needed to address potential confusion. Mrs. Braxton demonstrated this by asking her students, "Does anyone think they understand what Yanelly means by *some* in the piggy bank and *some* in the jar?" Mrs. Braxton knew that understanding the meaning of *some* is critical to solving the task. Instead of providing a definition, she waited until a student used the word and then asked an open-ended question designed to unearth the meaning. This was a critical and timely move. It allowed students to grapple with and make sense of the scenario, giving them ownership over their learning. As a teacher, it may seem more efficient to tell or show something, rather than let students struggle through it, but in the end, taking that kind of shortcut prevents students from experiencing the most critical parts of the sensemaking journey.

Another key component of developing collective understanding is to record group sensemaking of the task strategically. Mrs. Braxton illustrated this when she did things like circling the words "13 pennies," labeling "SOME" on the picture of the jar, and "THE REST" on the image of the piggy bank. Collecting this kind of key information in a common, accessible space (e.g., board or chart paper) serves several purposes. First, it provides a helpful reference for learners when they begin working toward a solution; they know they can look up at the board if they get stuck. Second, it allows the teacher to track what gets unpacked during the launch and decide what else needs to come out. Later in this chapter, we illustrate how teachers can plan for the information that needs to come out in the launch by crafting a *launch board vision*. This plan can then guide the construction of the board or chart during the launch discussion to ensure essential elements are not missed.

Although being responsive often involves open-ended questioning and following the students' lead, guiding students in or away from a specific direction is sometimes necessary. Responsive teachers use their judgment to determine when to ask *explicit questions* that draw students' attention to an essential element of the task that has not otherwise come up during the conversation. For example, Mrs. Braxton realized that it was vital that her students understand that Anya's Pennies is a task with multiple solutions. Still, since that had not come up naturally in the conversation, she brought it to their attention directly: "Do you think this is the kind of question where there is one answer, or more than one answer?" Mrs. Braxton knew that addressing this concept would allow her students to engage more fully with the mathematics behind the task, so she used explicit questioning to ensure it was discussed during the launch.

Establishing collective understanding is about eliciting and capitalizing on the group's ideas and experiences to come to a consensus on what the task is all about. While there are no hard and fast rules about time allocation, this portion of the launch often takes the most time, as it involves hearing from many voices and letting those voices converse and grapple to build an understanding of the task. Once this collective understanding is established, the teacher can shift to getting students ready to begin pursuing a solution path.

The Third Responsibility: Building a Bridge to Solving

After developing individual and collective understanding in the launch, the teacher's final responsibility is to build a bridge to solving the task. The third responsibility, as outlined in Table 2.3, involves setting clear expectations for what will happen as students go off to work on the problem, what the final product or solution should look or sound like, what tools they can use, and what to do if something goes awry. This is also an important time for a final check-in to assess student readiness to engage with the task.

Before sending students off to begin working on a task, it is essential to *clarify* the components of a complete solution. This does not mean that teachers should suggest a specific strategy or format that students should follow, but rather, that they help students understand how to know if a solution is complete. Good problem-solving tasks often ask students to justify their answer. The launch is a good time to ensure students are clear on what that

Table 2.3 Launch Tool, Responsibility #3

Responsibility #3: Build a Bridge to Solving	
Clarify the components of a complete solution.	• Can someone remind me what we are trying to figure out in this problem? • So you have two jobs. First—to find out how much money he started with. Second—to have some kind of work that shows your thinking and proves your solution.
Set expectations for work time, considering student groupings, work locations, and length of time.	• Take a few minutes to start solving the problem yourself. In a few minutes, I'll ask you to start talking with someone else about your ideas. • In about 15 minutes, I'm going to ask each group to share what they are finding.
Provide access to available tools and resources (both physical and human)	• Think about using the counters or the base ten blocks up here if they might help you. • If you have a question, ask your group mates first, and then if you are still unsure, you can call me over.
Assess individual and class readiness to engage in productive struggle on the problem.	• Consider: Are most people ready to start solving? • Consider: Is there anyone who seems like they may need extra support understanding the problem or getting started?

might look like: drawings, models, equations, written representations, etc. If students are being asked to find multiple solutions, look for patterns, or prove that they have found all the possible answers, this section of the launch provides time to make that responsibility clear and concrete. Mrs. Braxton attended to this when she stated that complete solutions would include various combinations of pennies in the bank and corresponding pennies in the jar, as well as some justification for the claims made.

Teachers also need to *set expectations* for what student work time will look like. This includes parameters for who students will work with, where they can be in the classroom space, and how long they will have to complete their task. Sometimes, a teacher might want students to start working independently before giving them an opportunity to collaborate (e.g., "Take a few minutes to start solving the problem yourself. In a few minutes, I'll ask you to start talking with someone else about your ideas"). When students work in small groups, the teacher may assign roles to keep all the group members working productively. It can also be helpful to give time parameters (e.g., "In fifteen minutes, I am going to ask each group to share their thinking so far") while being mindful to avoid implying that everyone will be finished solving in a given amount of time.

Another component of transitioning students to active problem solving is *providing access* to available resources, without prescribing the use of a particular tool. This may involve suggesting potential materials that could be used (e.g., manipulatives, calculators, graphic organizers, etc.) or other people in the classroom that could be resources, including other students and adults. Students should know who they can go to for support, and when they should do so (e.g., "If you have a question, ask your group mates first, and then if you are still unsure, you can call me over.") This promotes autonomy and collaboration, positions students as mathematically competent, and frees up the teacher to facilitate productive struggle, the next component of responsive mathematics teaching.

Finally, before ending the launch, it is important *to assess individual and class readiness* to engage in productive struggle. This reflective move constitutes a judgment call and requires the teacher to ask themselves: Based on what has come out in the launch discussion, do most learners seem ready to start solving this task? If the answer is no, more unpacking is likely necessary. If the answer is yes, but a few individuals may need more support, the teacher can prioritize checking in with these students once the class begins to work on the problem. The vignettes at the start of this chapter show two different ways of handling this in-the-moment reflection. Mr. Porter's assessment of class readiness was brief and shallow, which resulted in his having to intervene with many students during solving time. Mrs. Braxton, on the other hand, used her thorough unpacking of the task to build a sense of where most of her students were with their understanding. As a result, she had a good idea of who was ready to start working independently, who might need a little support getting started, and how she might begin to facilitate productive struggle.

Planning to Launch a Task

Pulling off an effective launch is challenging but well worth the effort. As described in Chapter 1, responsive mathematics teaching involves both adaptivity and anticipatory skills. Careful preparation and planning and continually referencing the guiding principles (prioritizing mathematical sensemaking, promoting collaborative learning communities, supporting a positive identity, and ensuring that all students have access) can help avoid under- or overlaunching in a responsive problem-solving lesson.

Planning to launch a task includes three main components, each of which is illustrated in Mrs. Braxton's plan to launch Anya's Pennies, shown in Table 2.4. The *Launch Board Vision* maps out the aspects of the task that the launch

Table 2.4 Mrs. Braxton's Launch Plan for the Anya's Pennies Task

Planning for Launching a Task	
Launch Board Vision	
What We Know	**Vocabulary/Language**
• 13 pennies total • Jar and a piggy bank • Some in each [Diagram: SOME and THE REST combining to 13]	• "Some in the jar"—at least 1 penny, but not all the pennies • "The rest in the piggy bank"—all the leftover pennies • Piggy bank/jar—places to store money
Goal	**Theories & Questions**

• Figure out different combinations of:
   ○ how many pennies could be in the jar
   ○ how many pennies could be in the piggy bank
• Proof for your claim
	• Do we have to use all 13 pennies? (Yes)
	• Could there be more than one answer? (Let's try it and find out!)

(Continued)

Table 2.4 Mrs. Braxton's Launch Plan for the Anya's Pennies Task *(Continued)*

Make Sense of the Task (Individually & Collectively)

- Project task, but cover up the text, so students can see the pictures of the jar and piggy bank.
- Reveal text. Read the task aloud and point to the pictures of the jar and the piggy bank while reading.
  - *What do you see?*
- Read the task to the students multiple times. On the final read, encourage visualization:
  - *Close your eyes. Picture what Anya is doing.*
  - *Can anyone tell us what they saw in their mind?*
- Make sure the following topics are discussed and recorded (see Launch Board Vision):
  - *How many pennies does Anya have altogether?*
  - *Where are the places she can put her pennies?*
  - *She puts "some in a jar." What does that mean to you? Or what might that look like?*
  - *She puts "the rest in the piggy bank." What does this mean?*

Build a Bridge to Solving

- Confirm what a solution entails:
  - *How will you know if you have answered the problem?*
  - *Solutions will have two quantities—a number of pennies in the jar AND a number of pennies in the piggy bank.*
  - *If you find one solution and you still have time left, see if you can find another one!*
  - *Make sure you are recording your ideas on your paper so we can share them.*
- Time and Materials
  - *You'll have 5 minutes to work on your own and then I will ask you to work with your partner.*
  - *We don't have pennies, but you can use any of our basket of materials or our chart "Ways We Can Add and Subtract."*

discussion should address and drafts a visual representation of how that information could be organized and represented for the class. The *Make Sense of the Task* section of the plan helps the teacher prepare questions to ensure each learner can develop an understanding of the task and that the class can develop a common understanding. Finally, the *Build a Bridge to Solving* section involves creating a plan for communicating the expectations as the students transition from the launch discussion to independent or small group work time.

Launch Board Vision

The launch board vision allows the teacher to think through what needs to come out during the launch and consider ways to make that information accessible and useful for students. Recording information on the board (or chart paper, interactive white board, etc.) as students unpack the problem is an essential component of a launch because it emphasizes the relevant details and serves as a visual resource that learners can refer to as they begin solving. Thinking about what this will look like ahead of time creates a map in the teacher's mind for what to elicit during the discussion and how to organize and chunk this information visually, as it emerges.

The teacher's board may not end up looking exactly like the vision. Still, both the vision and the board itself should, in some way, include four key components: (1) *What We Know* (the constraints of the problem), (2) *Vocabulary* (words and phrases that matter to understanding the task and the context), (3) *Goal* (a summary of what students are supposed to figure out), and (4) the *Questions/Theories* the teacher anticipates students may bring up. Some teachers use the names of these components as headings on the board, but it is not necessary to include them or arrange them in any specific order.

What We Know

This section of the board vision involves thinking through the constraints and context of the task that students must consider before they begin solving. The information in this section will differ depending on the task's complexity. Mrs. Braxton wanted to ensure her students understood that there were 13 total pennies and two places the pennies could end up—the jar and the piggy bank. She decided to visually represent the jar and piggy bank as distinct shapes to support students' understanding that the coins can be in two separate places.

Vocabulary

The second consideration for planning the launch board vision is to anticipate the language or vocabulary in the task that might need clarification. Sometimes, mathematical terms must be translated into age-appropriate definitions in the students' language. In other cases, specific phrasing should be clarified to help the learners understand key mathematical ideas in the problem situation. For example, Mrs. Braxton wanted students to unpack the phrase "some in the jar" to realize that at least one penny is put in the jar, but not all the pennies can be there. In the opening vignette, she highlighted this language when a student used it and then asked the class to think about what it meant. Because she planned for this ahead of time in her board vision, it was easier for her to recognize the opportunity when it came up during the discussion and remember that she wanted to record it on the board.

Goals

Another critical component of the launch board vision is to think through the overall goal students should have when solving the task. Clarifying this on the board helps students get started and provides a valuable reference for anyone needing guidance during the problem-solving process. Mrs. Braxton thought it was important for her students to know that their goal was to figure out how many pennies could go in the piggy bank and how many would be in the jar, given that there were 13 pennies in all. Because she planned to record this, she primed students to reflect on it, stating, "Okay, I will read the question again. I want you to think about what we have to figure out this time. What is our job?" She also felt it was important to remind students that strong solutions include justification as well as answers. Including this on the board can serve as a touchpoint for the teacher to reference if a student believes they are finished but are missing elements of proof or a component of the solution.

Theories/Questions

The final portion of developing a launch board vision involves anticipating potential questions and theories that might emerge from students and thinking through various ways to respond. As outlined in Mrs. Braxton's plan, a teacher might plan to answer a question with a definitive response ("Yes, you have to use all 13 pennies") and at other times they may decide to put a pause on a particular idea until students have the opportunity to explore it for themselves (e.g., "There might be more than one answer, let's find out"). Thinking through these responses in advance can help reduce the teacher's decision-making load during the lesson.

In the classroom, it can be helpful to have a designated space on the board to record students' wonderings and conjectures that might arise during the launch discussion. Having a landing spot for theories can also help teachers respond when a student offers a comment that suggests a specific strategy or solution during the launch. In such cases, the teacher can use the theories/questions section of the board to write down the idea as a possible pathway to pursue, highlighting the fact that there are also other ways to solve (e.g., "It sounds like Mary is thinking about making a table. You might decide to try that too, but remember that there are many different ways to solve this problem, so choose something that makes sense to you.") Many teachers find that having this designated area to capture questions and theories is a way to acknowledge students' thinking without giving too much away or influencing other students' problem-solving approaches.

Making Sense of the Task

In addition to articulating the key information to draw out during the launch discussion and anticipating a way to visually arrange these ideas when documenting them publicly for student reference, it is also essential to plan out specific moves and questions that will help to surface, clarify, and unpack those ideas during the launch. Teachers need to think through how they will expose students to the task, which might involve some combination of showing pictures, reading the text independently, and hearing it read aloud, sometimes from multiple voices. Students can also be encouraged to take notes or mark up the task, which can be especially helpful for older students or complex problems. Mrs. Braxton, for example, planned to project just the pictures in the problem first, then project the text of the problem, read it out loud twice, and then read it a third time with a guided visualization exercise.

Next, it is helpful for the teacher to generate questions that can be used to structure the whole group discussion about the task. This often includes questions that will allow learners to describe what is happening in their own words ("Can anyone tell us what they saw in their mind?"), open-ended questions that are likely to prompt students' sensemaking ("She puts 'some in a jar'. What does that mean to you?"), and more explicit questions that can be used to elicit ideas from the launch board vision ("Where are the places she can put her pennies?"). Not all these questions will likely be needed, as much of the information will come from learners' retelling of the task and the teacher building from those ideas. However, planning a list of questions allows the teacher to be prepared to elicit information or considerations more directly if they do not come up organically.

Build a Bridge to Solving

This last part of planning the launch consists of articulating how to help students make the transition to individual, partner, or small group work. This involves specifying the essential parts of a solution, the structure of the work time, and the resources available for students. Making sure that students know and understand what the problem is asking and what their solution should look like can help organize students' attempts at finding solutions and help students who believe they are finished more accurately assess if they are actually "done." When teachers plan what this criterion looks like in advance, they are better prepared to prompt students to talk about it and record it effectively on the board. It is helpful for teachers to consider what a valid solution looks like (e.g., in Anya's pennies, two numbers are needed—the number of pennies in the jar and the number of pennies in the piggy bank), if the problem has more than one solution, and what constitutes a viable proof or justification.

When planning, teachers should also consider how and where students will work, the structure of collaborative work, how to prepare students to work with others, and where students will physically be during work time. For instance, a teacher might plan for students to turn and talk to a partner next to them, or they might set a specific time when students will move to a different table to work in small groups. It is also essential to plan for the materials that will be made available and when and how students should access those materials.

Comparing the Plan with the Execution

Take a moment to compare Mrs. Braxton's plan for her launch of Anya's Pennies with the actual execution of her launch, as described in the vignette. You might notice that while she did not follow her plan exactly as a script, most of what she planned came up during the launch. She used many of the open-ended questions she designed to elicit her students' ideas and then built on those ideas in ways that allowed the class to arrive, on their own, to the conclusions she had specified ahead of time. Because she carefully considered all the necessary components in advance, but remained committed to having her students do the hard work of making sense of the task, she could be responsive to her students in the moment, thus preparing them to approach the task productively.

A Delicate Balancing Act

The launch is an invitation for students to begin a process of sensemaking—an opportunity that must be intentionally protected and cultivated. Ultimately, facilitating this opportunity involves pursuing a delicate balance. The responsive teacher supports and guides students to help them understand the task they are about to solve without giving too much away.

It can be tempting to rush through the launch to give students more time to work or to get through the lesson more efficiently. This usually results in an *underlaunch* that leaves students ill-prepared to solve the task because they have not yet made sense of the problem. Providing too much support to make things easier for students can also be tempting. When teachers tell students how to interpret the problem or model how to solve a similar problem, this results in an *overlaunch*, in which the opportunity for struggle is largely removed.

When executed well, launches serve as equalizers that give all students an entry point into a task and the tools they need to get started. They help students to slow down—combating the inclination to rush to operate on quantities—and provide a pause button that helps them focus on the process rather than looking for a quick answer. Additionally, they ensure that all students are solving the same task, as they have developed a shared understanding of the situation and what is being asked of them. When teachers launch a problem effectively, the entire class is primed to engage in the sensemaking required for problem-solving.

Taking the time for students to do this is well spent, because it prepares students for a more productive work time and gives them valuable skills they can apply to future problem-solving situations. Students learn how important it is to read through or listen to a task, visualize the context, and determine what they are being asked to figure out before they choose an operation or strategy. Additionally, when students feel they understand what is going on in a task, they will likely be motivated to persevere through problem-solving challenges.

Resisting the urge to shape the essential sensemaking for the students is another challenge. This includes not suggesting a way to start, hinting at or directing students to a specific strategy, providing a number sentence, or working through a sample solution together. When teachers do these things, it often results in all students solving the problem in the same way, compromising the opportunity to engage them in a rich and productive whole-class discussion of different approaches. More importantly, it takes the critical parts of problem solving away from students, and they will spend their time trying to understand the teacher's way of making sense of the task rather than developing their own understanding. In a responsive mathematics lesson, the process of making sense is facilitated by teachers but not performed by them, maintaining the cognitive load and protecting students' autonomy.

It is also worth resisting another common temptation during the launch: choosing a few willing or confident students to demonstrate their understanding. This is antithetical to the goals of providing an entry point for all students and welcoming all students into the process of sensemaking. The launch is a time to build new understanding, make connections from prior knowledge and the content or context of the task, and foster a shared understanding of the class. By doing so, we reduce barriers to access and lay a foundation for equity.

To avoid turning a lesson into a performance, it is important to create opportunities for all students to visualize, verbalize, annotate, and reflect on their understanding. Continually asking questions during the launch phase—rather than telling, showing, or suggesting—can help prevent common pitfalls and ensure students engage in sensemaking. The teacher's role is not to provide answers for the students or to send them off to work without preparation. Instead, the goal is to support individual and collective sensemaking, building a bridge to successful problem solving.

Reflection Questions

Teacher Responsibilities	Guiding Principles
1 Establish individual understanding of the task. 2 Establish collective understanding of the task. 3 Build a bridge to solving the task.	1 Prioritize mathematical sensemaking. 2 Promote collaborative learning communities. 3 Support a positive mathematical identity. 4 Ensure all students have access to mathematics.

1. How does each of the teacher's responsibilities of launching a task described in this chapter address the guiding principles of responsive teaching?
2. Consider the following task (or another problem-solving task you have used recently):

> **Colored Pencils**
>
> There are 6 tables in Mrs. Potter's art classroom. There are 6 students sitting at each table. Each student has a box of 10 colored pencils.
>
>   a How many colored pencils are at each table?
>   b How many colored pencils do Mrs. Potter's students have in total?

    a What would it look like to launch this task responsively?
    b What would it look like if the teacher overlaunched the task?
    c What would it look like if the teacher underlaunched the task?

3. What ideas are you taking away from this chapter that you want to try in your instruction?
4. As you think about integrating these ideas into your instructional context:

    a What is already in place that you can build on?
    b What challenges do you foresee?
    c What can you do to try to overcome those challenges?

3

Facilitating Productive Struggle

After launching a low-floor, high-ceiling task, the next component of teaching a responsive mathematics problem-solving lesson is actively supporting students as they grapple with the task, facilitating their productive struggle. We begin this chapter with two vignettes that describe contrasting ways a teacher might respond to a student struggling to solve a given task during independent or cooperative work time. Both took place in second-grade classrooms after the teacher had launched a task involving equal groups of ten, as shown in Figure 3.1.

This task can be challenging for second-grade students because many of them are still working on unitizing, or thinking about a group of ten as both as a collection of ten ones and one group of ten. At the same time, the task is

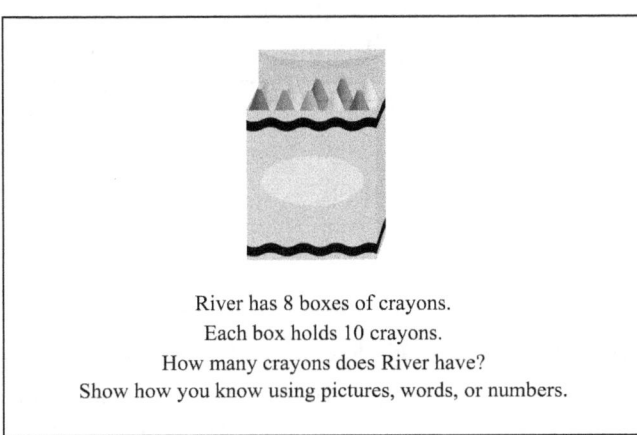

River has 8 boxes of crayons.
Each box holds 10 crayons.
How many crayons does River have?
Show how you know using pictures, words, or numbers.

Figure 3.1 River's Crayons task.

DOI: 10.4324/9781003536710-3

accessible by being open to multiple strategies—students can draw out eight boxes of ten crayons and count by ones, skip count by ten eight times, draw on known facts to add in chunks, or even recognize that eight tens are 80. To develop a workable strategy, however, students need to understand the situation of equal groups described in the problem.

After introducing this task to the whole class, utilizing some of the launch strategies described in Chapter 2, Ms. Allen and Ms. Gonzales began to circulate in their classrooms to see how students solved the task. The two vignettes that follow describe the different ways that each teacher responded to a student who appeared to have misinterpreted the problem as an additive situation (8 + 10), rather than an equal groups situation (8 groups of 10).

Ms. Allen's Classroom: "Draw me 8 boxes with 10 crayons in each."

As students begin working on the task at their desks. Ms. Allen circulates to monitor student progress and answer questions. Tanisha has written 8 + 10 = 18 on her paper. Ms. Allen looks over her shoulder and asks, "You think there are 18 crayons altogether?" Tanisha looks up at the teacher, raising her eyebrows as if unsure. Ms. Allen points to the problem text at the top of Tanisha's paper and reminds her, "There are eight boxes of crayons, right? And each box holds 10 crayons. What does that word each mean?" Tanisha shrugs, and Ms. Allen explains, "Each box has 10 crayons, so can you draw me a box with 10 crayons?"

Tanisha draws 10 lines while counting to herself silently. Ms. Allen watches her and smiles. She praises Tanisha's drawing, pointing out that Tanisha has drawn one box with 10 crayons. Ms. Allen reminds Tanisha that she needs 8 boxes like the one she's just drawn, reiterating that each box must have 10 crayons. Ms. Allen leaves Tanisha to work on her own with these parting words, "Draw me 8 boxes with 10 crayons in each and then you can tell me how many there are all together, ok?"

Ms. Allen circulates to other students, and Tanisha finishes drawing her boxes and counting. When Ms. Allen returns a few minutes later, Tanisha proudly shows her the answer of 80. Ms. Allen responds, "Yes, there are 80 crayons, not 18! I knew you could do it." Tanisha grins, pleased that she has gotten the correct answer to the problem.

Ms. Gonzales Classroom: "What would it look like if you drew all the crayons?"

As the students work on the task, Ms. Gonzales circulates, monitoring their progress. She passes by Ana's table and notices that Ana seems to have an incomplete understanding of the task. She sees that Ana has drawn eight crayons and has the equation 8 + 10 = 18 written on her whiteboard. Ms. Gonzales stops and asks Ana, "Can you tell me a little about your drawing?" Ana explains that she drew eight crayons, but cannot explain why when pressed by her teacher.

Ms. Gonzales redirects her to the problem and has Ana read it aloud. She then poses the question, "What are there 8 of?" Ana responds that there are 8 boxes of crayons, but she still seems unsure how to make her picture represent the task. "What else do we know?" the teacher asks. Ana responds, "Every box has 10 crayons." Ms. Gonzales then asks Ana if she can draw one box of crayons. Ana adds a square around the 8 crayons she has already drawn. Ms. Gonzales asks, "How many crayons are in that box?" As Ana counts up to 8, she has an "aha" moment, adding two more crayons to the box to have 10 crayons. Sensing that Ana is moving in a more productive direction, Ms. Gonzales says, "I think you're onto something here. Your drawing is a great starting point. What would it look like if you drew all River's crayons? Why don't you work on that while I check in with other groups?"

The teacher continues circulating and talking to other students before returning to check on Ana's progress. She sees the picture on Ana's board (Figure 3.2).

"Can you tell me about what you've drawn?" Ms. Gonzales asks. Ana explains that the squares show the boxes of crayons, and the lines inside them are crayons. The teacher asks, "Is that all the crayons River has?" After thinking quietly, Ana says that River has 80 crayons total and explains her reasoning by counting by 10s as she points to each square in her drawing. "Nice job revising your thinking!" Ms. Gonzales praises Ana and invites her to share her work with the group when they discuss the task.

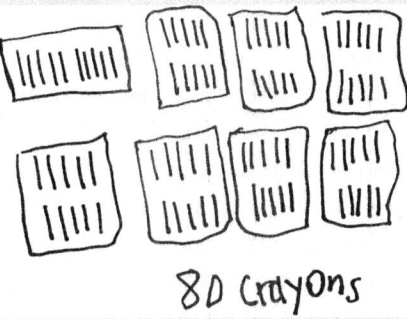

Figure 3.2 Ana's work on River's Crayons task.

These two vignettes describe similar storylines. In both cases, a teacher encounters a struggling student and offers support that helps the student arrive at a correct solution to the problem. However, the differences between the two vignettes illustrate how traditional ways of managing student struggle differ from a responsive approach to facilitating productive struggle. In the first vignette, Ms. Allen spoon-feeds her student, Tanisha, a lot of important information about the problem and ultimately provides her with a strategy to solve it. Most of the hard thinking is done by Ms. Allen; she provides the definition of "each" and tells Tanisha what to draw and how to use the drawing. In the second vignette, Ms. Gonzales asks her student, Ana, questions to elicit the same information that Ms. Allen told Tanisha (there are 8 boxes of crayons and 10 crayons in each box) and cultivates a learning experience in which Ana can figure out a viable solution strategy on her own.

In Ms. Gonzales's responsive approach, the work of figuring out the problem situation is gently, but squarely, placed on the student. This gives the teacher valuable information about how the student is making sense of the task while at the same time empowering the student to make her own connections between the various elements in the task (the boxes and the crayons). It also guides Ms. Gonzales to ask questions tailored to Ana's thinking. Once Ms. Gonzales' questioning helps Ana have her crucial "aha" moment (realizing that there are multiple boxes of crayons, each with the same number of crayons), she finds a way to keep Ana thinking and moving forward with her strategy. She gives Ana a job, asking what it would look like if she drew all the crayons, to see if Ana can apply the approach she has already used to find the total amount of crayons. Notably, she does not tell Ana how to do this, leaving her to grapple with figuring it out.

Although both students feel a sense of accomplishment at the end of the story, Tanisha is pleased that she got the correct answer, reinforcing a misconception that mathematical success is about getting it right. On the other hand, Ana has ownership over her work; although she also arrived at the correct answer, more importantly, she engaged in sensemaking about representing equal groups. For her, success was about developing a strategy that she could use to solve a problem independently. In the process, Ana realized that she could count by tens instead of counting individual crayons, moving closer to Ms. Gonzales's mathematical goal for this lesson: helping students unitize and use groups of ten to solve problems.

As teachers, we may think that our job is to guide students toward the mathematical goal by breaking things down to avoid student confusion. This is especially tempting because breaking ideas down for students by getting them to engage in answering a series of low-level questions can be a quicker way to lead students to a correct solution. But it is a short-term win. While teachers like Ms. Allen are typically well-meaning and invested in their students' success, prioritizing efficiency and avoiding frustration inadvertently removes valuable learning opportunities for students. As discussed in the next section, confusion and struggle are essential to learning. Thus, facilitating students' productive struggle is a central and ongoing pursuit of a responsive teacher.

What is Productive Struggle and Why is It Important for Learning?

Over a century of research tells us that struggle is not something to avoid, but rather is something to be leveraged as a vital part of learning. Theorists as far back as Dewey (1910) spotlight the importance of giving students opportunities to grapple with "perplexity, confusion, and doubt" to spark new thinking and deeper understanding. As Piaget explains (1960), *disequilibrium*—a state in which learners struggle because their existing ideas have been challenged or destabilized—is a necessary precursor to taking up new, more sophisticated ideas in meaningful ways. When learners are in disequilibrium, they may feel a sense of discomfort, but this discomfort provides a motivation to learn—an internal drive to return to the state of equilibrium, in which things make sense. As learners make sense of new information and situations, their ideas evolve and change, a process that Piaget calls *accommodation*. Hiebert and Grouws (2007) explain how intentionally engaging students in struggle is a central feature of instruction, promoting this mental restructuring. Giving students opportunities to encounter problems without an "immediately apparent" solution path and creating space to grapple with and bring their own resources to bear on such problems is essential to advancing deep and meaningful understandings of mathematics (p. 387).

If you have ever taught a child to ride a bicycle, you have experienced the fine line between providing too much and too little support as someone learns something new. Hold on to their seat for too long, and they do not learn the balancing skills necessary to ride on their own; hold on too briefly, and they fall off the bike, get frustrated, and threaten to give up. Facilitating productive struggle is about holding onto that seat for just the right amount of time. Walking students through a predetermined problem-solving path is the pedagogical equivalent of leaving training wheels on too long. Like a novice cyclist who must learn to balance, pedal, and steer simultaneously by persevering through the wobbling that can feel a bit uncomfortable, students, too, need to pedal through the wiggle of new mathematical ideas, grappling with uncertainty to come to new understandings.

When students engage in productive struggle, they do not just focus on producing a correct answer but try to make sense of the task and devise a potential solution path (Warshauer, 2014). They ask questions, model or write down their ideas, clarify their thoughts by talking with peers, evaluate their progress, and revise their strategies. Most importantly, they persevere and persist rather than giving up. It is through this kind of grappling that students make connections between their existing knowledge and new ideas and develop deeper and longer-lasting *relational understanding* (Skemp, 1976).

In one important study of middle school classrooms, student gains in conceptual understanding were highest when they were given the opportunity to solve challenging tasks that required them to reason mathematically and connect procedures with concepts (Stein et al., 1996). In another study that compared mathematics instruction in different countries, high-achieving classrooms were characterized by students engaging in struggle to make connections between procedures and concepts (Stigler & Hiebert, 1999). In lower-achieving countries (including the United States), even when challenging problems were presented, teachers tended to model a strategy or show a worked example. By doing so, the teachers reduced the challenge of the task and removed the opportunity for students to struggle.

Not all struggle, however, is productive. If struggling leads to substantial frustration or a tendency to shut down when things are too difficult, then it can become unproductive. According to Vygotsky (1978), learners need to struggle within a *zone of proximal development*, a space where tasks or activities are challenging but can be accomplished with support or *scaffolding*. Without this support, overly challenging tasks that place too high a level of cognitive demand on the student can provoke anxiety and lead to negative self-perceptions. If students are not able to make sense of a task at all or get too stuck to start or continue, the unproductive struggle becomes problematic. When students experience repeated unproductive struggle without resolution, they may internalize negative perceptions about their ability to learn and do mathematics (Grootenboer & Marshman, 2016).

PRODUCTIVE STRUGGLE	
What It Is …	**What It Is Not …**
• Making sense of a task by drawing on prior knowledge and developing understanding • Engaging with others to ask questions and clarify ideas • Experimenting with different solution paths and evaluating progress • Persevering through discomfort • Recognizing mistakes and dead ends as important and valuable parts of the problem-solving process • Evaluating whether an answer makes sense in the context of the problem	• Using keywords or prescribed methods to develop a solution path • Overlooking peers as resources and thought partners • Executing steps in a prescribed solution path • Giving up when challenge is encountered • Avoiding mistakes and being embarrassed or discouraged by them • Assuming learning is complete because an answer has been found

Facilitating Productive Struggle: The Teacher's Role

The teacher plays a critical role in shaping and supporting students' struggle so that it is productive. When teachers respond by telling too much or leading students directly to the correct answer (as Ms. Allen did with Tanisha in the first vignette), the struggle is alleviated at the expense of the opportunity to engage in reasoning and sensemaking. Alternatively, teachers can make specific moves that support, rather than remove, the struggle. To begin, it is important to create the conditions for learners to encounter struggle. This involves providing learners with the opportunity to legitimately grapple with tasks (independently or collaboratively), encouraging them to pursue their own strategies, and building a space in which learners think, process, and plan before they are expected to produce a solution (see Chapter 2 for more on how the launch of a task can create these conditions).

Once students are actively grappling with a task, teachers can monitor their progress, circulating the room to listen, observe, and look for signs of struggle. The goal of this monitoring is to identify students who need support to initially engage in productive struggle, sustain productive struggle, or transition from unproductive to productive struggle. When encountering a student who needs such support, the teacher can intervene by asking questions, providing time or encouragement, and acknowledging the importance of perseverance through struggle (Warshauer, 2015). Intervening effectively is complex but rewarding work that requires preparation, practice, and ongoing refinement.

Facilitating students' productive struggle requires that teachers make sense of and respond to emerging student ideas in real time. This capacity to make "in-flight decisions" to adapt one's teaching to what learners know, think, and can do at any given moment (Borko & Livingston, 1989) is what makes the facilitation of productive struggle complex. In our work with teachers, we have found that having a framework of potential moves to draw upon can be a helpful way to guide and inform this in-the-moment instructional decision-making. To understand and enact the work of facilitating productive struggle, it can be helpful to think about two main responsibilities of the teacher: (1) to understand a learner's idea and point of struggle and (2) to help the learner move forward with their idea. Similarly, Smith and Stein (2018) propose that teachers should be prepared to pose questions to both uncover what students know and understand and move students toward the mathematical goals of the lesson. In the following sections, we describe each of these multifaceted responsibilities in more detail and introduce a tool to support teachers to carry them out.

The First Responsibility: Understand a Learner's Idea and Point of Struggle

Being responsive while facilitating productive struggle is fundamentally about following the learner's line of thinking. This means that a teacher needs to surface the learner's existing ideas as well as any points of struggle they encounter. Doing so requires taking a stance of genuine curiosity toward student thinking rather than simply making sure a student is on-task, monitoring how far they have gotten, or fixing their errors (Munson, 2018). The teacher who is genuinely curious about student thinking asks authentic questions—ones to which the answer might not be known ahead of time or might be illuminating, or even surprising.

The Facilitating Productive Struggle Tool (Table 3.1) breaks the work of understanding learners' ideas and struggles into three types of moves, each serving a different purpose. Typically, the first step is to use *eliciting moves* to draw the learner's ideas out. Simply put, this involves inviting a student to share their thinking about how they are approaching the task and their reasoning. For example, the teacher might say, "Tell me about what you are doing" or ask, "How are you thinking about this?" At this point, it is important for the teacher to listen carefully and try to make sense of the learner's response, being mindful not to make assumptions or statements about what the student might be thinking, or "fill in" their thinking for them (Shaughnessy et al., 2021).

Once the student has had a chance to explain, the teacher will likely need to follow up with *clarifying moves* designed to probe the learner's thinking further and deepen the teacher's understanding of their reasoning. Clarifying moves should invite the learner to unpack their ideas in specific ways. For example, a teacher might prompt for further information (e.g., "Can you say more about that?") or for clarification of a specific idea, (e.g., "What do you mean when you say 'the bigger one'?"). Once the teacher thinks they understand the learner's idea, they can verify that their understanding is accurate by rephrasing the learner's idea and asking something like, "Do I have your idea right?"

Eliciting and clarifying moves often work in tandem, with an eliciting move followed closely by a clarifying one. In the opening vignette, for example, Ms. Gonzales used an eliciting move when she asked Ana to tell her about her drawing, and then followed up with a clarifying move, asking her why she drew eight crayons. These two types of moves may also work cyclically. In many cases, teachers first elicit and clarify the learner's line of reasoning and then continue to elicit and clarify the point of struggle that the learner is encountering. This might begin with an eliciting question like, "So, where are you stuck?" and continue with a clarifying statement like, "Ah! I see. So, you know how many crayons are in two boxes, but you're having trouble figuring things out if there are more boxes?"

A blend of eliciting and clarifying moves is often enough to draw out both the learner's existing thinking and their point of struggle. Sometimes,

Table 3.1 Facilitating Productive Struggle Tool, Responsibility #1

Responsibility #1: Understand a Learner's Idea and Point of Struggle	
Eliciting Moves draw out or surface the learner's idea	
Invite learner to share their thinking	• Tell me about what you are doing! • What's your idea? • How are you thinking about this? • Where are you stuck?
Clarifying Moves deepen understanding of the learner's thinking	
Ask learner to elaborate	• Can you say more about that? • Tell me more about how your diagram works.
Rephrase learner thinking and verify	• I think what you're saying is _____. Did I understand your idea right? • So, you started here [pointing to learner's work]?
Clarify an important idea, ambiguous phrases, or vocabulary	• What do you mean when you say, "the bigger one?" • When you say, subtract it, what is the "it" you are referring to?
Igniting Moves help the learner get started or articulate an idea	
Offer support getting started	• Would you like help getting started? • Let's read the problem again.
Draw out prior knowledge	• Tell me everything you know about squares.
Redirect learner's attention to key information	• What do you know? What are you trying to figure out? • When the problem says, "the amount doubled," what does that mean to you?
Prompt learner to articulate where they are stuck	• What's confusing right now? • Is there something you don't know/understand that you need to know/understand?
Normalize struggle	• I see you are feeling stuck now, but I know you can figure this out. • Let's work together to get you started. • Feeling confused is a normal part of the learning process. I'm here to support you.

though, the learner is either not able to articulate their thinking or is stuck, such that they have not been able to generate an initial idea. In cases like these, the teacher can use *igniting moves*. These moves are designed either to help the learner articulate a complex, nascent idea or get started with the germ of an idea. Igniting moves commonly begin with the offering of broad, open-ended support that has the potential to let a student make key realizations about the problem context or question. Oftentimes, this involves returning to the task by suggesting something like, "Let's read the problem again."

If it seems like the student already understands the problem context and question, a teacher might alternatively try to spark an idea in a more targeted way, either by drawing out prior knowledge ("Tell me everything you know about …"), or by redirecting the student's attention to key contextual information in the task ("What do you know? What are you trying to figure out?"). In Ms. Gonzales's case, in the second vignette, she uses both kinds of igniting moves (broad and targeted), first redirecting Ana back to the problem and asking her to read it aloud, and then asking her a question to help her focus on an important piece of contextual information: "What are there 8 of?"

Sometimes, teachers may encounter students who have slipped into unproductive struggle and are feeling frustrated. In these cases, igniting moves can also be helpful. A teacher might begin by normalizing a learner's feelings of frustration and their need for support. One way to approach this is to provide explicit statements that reinforce a sense of positive self-efficacy (e.g., "I see you are feeling stuck now, but I believe in you and know you can figure this out"). Another way is to provide assurance that the teacher is there to support them until they feel less frustrated (e.g., "Let's work together to get you started"). Students' belief in their own capacity as mathematicians substantially impacts their endurance for problem solving and their tolerance for wading through confusion (Grootenboer & Marshman, 2016). Sometimes, simple words of confidence from a teacher can buoy a student just enough to get them back to a point of productive, rather than unproductive, struggle.

Teachers might also address a frustrated student with another kind of igniting move—a prompt designed to help a student articulate what is making them feel stuck (e.g., "What's confusing right now?" or "Is there something you don't know that you need to know?"). When a teacher uses this kind of igniting move, they help the learner to take ownership of their own cognitive processes. Understanding and taking control over the process of thinking through a challenging task, also called metacognition, is important for problem solving, learning, and growth (Flavell, 1976; Polya, 1957). Reinstating control over one's ideas, even if it is only articulating what is confusing, can be empowering and vital for making the shift from unproductive to productive struggle.

Eliciting, clarifying, and igniting moves all involve taking a stance of genuine curiosity to draw out learner thinking to understand how they are approaching the task and where they might be stuck. To see how these moves look and sound in the classroom context, let's look into Mr. Cooper's third-grade classroom as they work on the following task:

There are 36 crackers in a box. The crackers are to be shared equally among friends. What are all of the different ways that friends can share the 36 crackers? How do you know that you found all of the different ways?

(Boaler et al., 2018, p. 78)

Note that this task has multiple solutions and is open to many different strategies, such as physically making equal groups with concrete objects, trial and error, repeated addition, multiplication, division, or knowledge of factors.

Eliciting, Clarifying, and Igniting Lamar's Thinking

Lamar was working with a set of small cubes to help him solve the problem. Mr. Cooper watched for a bit as Lamar separated the cubes into piles, noticing that not all the piles had the same number of blocks (see Figure 3.3).

"Can you tell me what you're doing?" Mr. Cooper asked curiously. Lamar replied, "I'm doing 10." Mr. Cooper pushed Lamar to explain what he meant: "You are doing 10 of what?" Lamar clarified that he meant he was trying to make 10 piles. Mr. Cooper then asked Lamar, "Are they even?" to help Lamar determine whether each of his piles had the same number of blocks. Lamar thought for a moment, counted a few of the groups, and answered that they were not. Immediately after answering, he quickly swiped all the blocks into one big pile and declared, "Now I'm going to try 8 piles."

Mr. Cooper quietly watched while Lamar spread 8 of his blocks out in a circle. Lamar whispered out loud, "one, two, three, four, five, six, seven, eight" as he moved each one to be the start of a pile and then started to deal out the rest of the cubes one by one. While Mr. Cooper knew that making 8 groups, like the previous attempt to make 10, was not going to lead to a correct solution (given that 8 and 10 are not factors of 36), he also recognized that Lamar was using a viable strategy by dealing out the cubes one by one to ensure that the groups would be equal. He decided to let him continue with this idea, waiting to see if he was going to need more support.

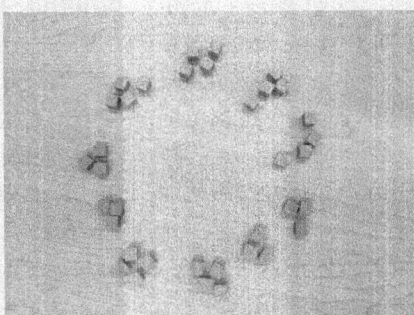

Figure 3.3 Lamar's initial work on the cracker task.

In this example, Mr. Cooper's use of eliciting, clarifying, and igniting moves helped to draw out Lamar's way of making sense of the problem and redirect him toward an important condition of the task, the need for equal groups. When Mr. Cooper noticed that Lamar was making unequal piles, rather than correct him, he elicited Lamar's thinking by asking, "Can you tell me what you are doing?" He then used a clarifying move to ensure that he understood Lamar's idea of "doing 10" by asking, "You are doing 10 of what?" Finally, he used an igniting move to help Lamar situate this idea in the context of the problem—the fact that the friends were sharing the crackers equally—by asking "Are they even?"

It is important to note that as Mr. Cooper attended to Responsibility #1 (understanding Lamar's idea and point of struggle), he helped Lamar maintain ownership of his ideas and solution strategies. This approach primed Lamar to keep persevering toward a solution. At this point, Mr. Cooper was ready to shift to Responsibility #2 of facilitating productive struggle: helping his learner move forward with their idea. In the next sections, we will explain the kinds of moves that a teacher can use to carry out this responsibility, and then we will return to Mr. Cooper and Lamar's story to find out what happened next.

The Second Responsibility: Help the Learner Move Forward with Their Idea(s)

Once a teacher has surfaced a learner's thinking and identified a point of struggle, the teacher is ready to support the learner in moving their line of thinking forward, toward the mathematical goal. Attending to this responsibility requires that the teacher first pause and make an internal assessment about what to do next. Teachers must carefully interpret what they have uncovered about the learner's ideas to identify whether they are ready to struggle productively or need more help. If the learner is ready to struggle productively on their own, the best move for the teacher to make is often to walk away, allowing the learner to grapple independently. If the learner needs continued support, the teacher must decide whether they have a potentially workable strategy started but need an intervention to help them continue to utilize it, or if there is an issue or gap that needs to be proactively addressed before the learner can reasonably begin to employ a strategy. Munson (2018) describes this type of intervention as providing "nudges" to move or grow student thinking. The responsive moves, summarized in the second part of the Facilitating Productive Struggle Tool shown in Table 3.2, can help a teacher to provide both kinds of support.

If a learner seems to have components of a viable strategy or idea, but encounters bumps in the road as they try to employ it, the teacher can use *sustaining moves* to help the learner continue moving forward with that line

Table 3.2 Facilitating Productive Struggle Tool, Teacher Responsibility #2

Responsibility #2: Help the Learner Move Forward with Their Idea(s)	
Sustaining Moves help the learner move forward with their line of reasoning	
Echo or clarify specific parts of learner's idea	• Looks like you figured out that even numbers won't work.
Use the learner's words or language to prompt them to apply to an idea	• I heard you say you can double one & half the other. Can you use that thinking to help?
Draw attention to potential next steps	• What would be helpful to know next? • You figured out how many times 2 will fit into 10. What do you need to do now?
Assign or specify a next step	• Why don't you try finding the next numbers in the pattern?
Supporting Moves help bridge factors that are standing in the way of progress	
Offer a simpler version of the task	• What if we think about how many hands are under the table first, instead of the number of fingers?
Provide a fact or bit of needed information important	• One yard is equal to three feet.
Offer a tool to lift some but not all of the cognitive load	• Why don't you use a calculator? • Would counters help you to keep track?
Pressing Moves surface breaks in logic or misconceptions, oversights, or over-generalizations	
Ask learner about a situation they have not yet considered	• I wonder what would happen if you used a negative number? • Do you think this will always work?
Highlight a break in learner's logic	• It looks like you were first converting everything to fourths but then you changed to fifths.
Pose a question to surface errors or incomplete understandings	• Are these the same or different?

(Continued)

Table 3.2 Facilitating Productive Struggle Tool, Teacher Responsibility #2 *(Continued)*

Consolidating Moves nudge learners to move their thinking toward a more complete solution	
Draw attention to missing parts of solution	• It looks like you used your model to find a number of friends that will work! How many crackers are each going to get? • How can you prove that you have found all the solutions?
Prompt connections between learner's work and the task	• So, have you figured out which plan he should choose? • Based on the towers you built, what are all the ways you could make ten?
Suggest a way for learner to synthesize their ideas	• It looks like you have done a lot of hard thinking. Why don't you put it together and try to answer the original question? • How would you convince someone that your answer is correct?

of reasoning. Sometimes this is as simple as echoing specific parts of the learner's ideas (e.g., "Looks like you figured out that even numbers won't work") or using the learner's own words or language to prompt them to apply an idea (e.g., "I heard you say, 'double one and half the other.' Can you use that thinking to help?"). Often, just hearing their ideas reflected back helps learners make needed connections to persevere. Teachers might also nudge stalled learners forward by drawing their attention toward potential next steps. They could do this either by asking them a question (e.g., "What would be helpful to know next?") or assigning them a next step (e.g., "Why don't you try using your strategy to find the next few numbers in the pattern?"). If a teacher decides to assign the next step, it is crucial to leave room for the student to continue thinking and reasoning, rather than giving them a rote procedure to follow.

There are also times when students have ideas that can be built upon, but gaps in their understanding pose roadblocks that make it hard for them to move forward strategically. In this case, *supporting moves* can help bridge the gaps or address the factors that are standing in the way of progress. This might involve offering a simpler version of the task to try first (e.g., the same scenario but with simpler numbers), providing a fact or essential bit of information (e.g., sharing with the learner that one yard is equal to 3 feet), or offering a tool to lift some, but not all, of the cognitive load (e.g., a chart, a graphic organizer, a set of counters, or a calculator). Supporting moves are intentional, proactive attempts on the teacher's part to give the learner something they need, that they are missing, to allow them to continue thinking on their own. Nuance is required when employing supporting moves to keep learners in their zone of proximal development (Vygotsky, 1978). The teacher must fill a learner's gaps enough to make forward motion possible, without giving so much that the working and thinking are done for them.

Sometimes learners are impeded from moving forward because of incomplete understandings, oversights, or over-generalizations in their thinking. In this case, a teacher can facilitate productive struggle by using *pressing moves*. In contrast to supporting moves, which involve providing concrete information or tools, pressing moves are designed to help learners recognize their own errors. They can include asking the learner about a situation they have not yet encountered (e.g., "I wonder what would happen if you used a negative number?"), encouraging a student to consider generalizing the claim they are making (e.g., "Do you think this will always work?"), explicitly highlighting a break in their logic (e.g., "It looks like you were converting everything to fourths here, but then you changed to fifths?"), or posing questions to surface errors or misconceptions (e.g., "Are these the same or different?"). When teachers utilize pressing moves, they empower learners to realize the limitations of their logic and take charge of improving it.

Sometimes learners are not stuck, but rather, believe they are finished with a task, even though their solution is incomplete or could be extended to address an important mathematical idea. In this case, teachers can help learners move forward by providing a nudge or spark to move their thinking toward a more complete solution. These *consolidating moves* allow the teacher to draw attention to missing parts of a solution (e.g., "How can you prove that you have found all the solutions?"), prompt a connection between the learner's work and the parameters of the task (e.g., "Based on the towers you built, what are all the ways you could make ten?"), or suggest a way of synthesizing ideas (e.g., "It looks like you have done a lot of hard thinking, why don't you put it together and try to answer the original question?").

Let us return to Mr. Cooper's work with Lamar to see what sustaining, supporting, pressing, and consolidating moves look like in a classroom setting. When our story ended, Mr. Cooper patiently watched Lamar as he tried to make 8 equally sized groups with 36 blocks to solve the Sharing Crackers problem.

Sustaining, Supporting, Pressing, and Consolidating Lamar's Thinking

Lamar moved 8 blocks into a big circle on his desk, each representing the beginning of a group. Lamar proceeded to give a second block to each group, and then a third. He shifted some groups so they did not run into each other and gave each group a fourth block. As he started giving each group a fifth block, he realized he would run out of cubes. He stopped, leaving the four leftover cubes in the center (Figure 3.4).

"Oh, it doesn't work," Lamar said, deflated. He made a move like he would push all the blocks together again. Mr. Cooper quickly extended his hand over Lamar's blocks, saying, "Wait! Let's look at your work and see if it can help us. How many groups do you have?"

Without looking at the blocks, Lamar replied that there were 8 groups of 4. "Are you sure?" Mr. Cooper pressed. This prompted Lamar to look down and start counting the groups quietly. He got to 8 and then hovered his hand over the pile of remaining blocks in the center, realizing he had four left. "Oh! I have another group!" he exclaimed.

"So, what do you have now?" Mr. Cooper asked. "9 groups of 4," Lamar replied, to which Mr. Cooper asked, "And what do the 9 and the 4 mean?" Lamar enthusiastically responded, "Nine friends will get four crackers each!" Before moving on to monitor other students, Mr. Cooper validated Lamar's persistence and encouraged him to apply his strategy further: "Great job, Lamar! You stuck with that, and now I think you have a working solution. Make sure you write that down and then see if you can use your approach to find another one."

Figure 3.4 Lamar's revised work on the cracker task.

In the second half of Lamar's episode of productive struggle, Mr. Cooper built upon the knowledge he gained about Lamar's thinking when he attended to the first responsibility (understanding Lamar's idea and point of struggle) to attend to the second responsibility (helping Lamar move forward with his ideas). He used sustaining, pressing, and consolidating moves to help Lamar advance his thinking toward a viable solution, and the mathematical goal for the lesson—understanding the concept of multiplication as repeated addition of equal groups.

When Mr. Cooper realized that Lamar had overlooked the fact that his extra blocks in the center made another equal group of four, he applied a sustaining move to assist Lamar in preserving and utilizing the helpful model he had built. Mr. Cooper used a gesture and a directive to stop Lamar from destroying the model ("Wait! Let's look at your work and see if it can help us"), and instructed Lamar to closely examine the groups he had made ("How many groups do you have?"). In doing so, he scaffolded Lamar to extend a useful train of logic that Lamar was ready to abandon. When Lamar replied, "8 groups of 4," answering Mr. Cooper's question without using his model, Mr. Cooper enacted a simple, but powerful pressing move ("Are you sure?"), which helped Lamar to notice the crucial oversight he was making. Whether students express correct or incorrect thinking, it is important to use this move to focus on justification rather than signaling that correction is needed.

Once Lamar recognized that his model was showing a potential solution to the task, Mr. Cooper used consolidating moves to nudge Lamar's initial thinking toward a more formalized conclusion. He first helped Lamar to definitively articulate the solution illustrated by his model by asking, "What do you have now?" He then ensured that Lamar was connecting the equal groups in his model to the context of the problem by asking him what the 9 and 4 meant. This move ensured that Lamar's answer was backed by a conceptual understanding that would ultimately help him internalize the mathematical goal of Mr. Cooper's lesson.

Mr. Cooper's enactment of Responsibility 2 (helping the learner move forward with their ideas) involved making intentional moves that supported Lamar in advancing his own, slightly flawed thinking until it was stronger and more accurate. Notably, Mr. Cooper allowed Lamar to make a mistake and then provided scaffolding to help Lamar figure out how to build off his mistake to come to a correct solution that made sense to him. Mistakes, reworking, and revision are vital components of the mathematical learning process. By helping learners embrace and utilize rather than avoid mistakes, teachers can emphasize the power of articulating, exploring, and reflecting on ideas, even if those ideas turn out to need revision. This positions students as competent, capable problem solvers, preparing them to feel increasingly confident to persevere through struggle independently.

Responding to a Range of Struggles

Mr. Cooper's interaction with Lamar illustrates how a teacher might facilitate productive struggle for a learner who has an idea for a strategy but is stuck executing it. However, this type of struggle is not the only kind of struggle third-grade students might have when solving the 36 crackers task. As with any class or task, there are a range of ideas that learners might have and a range of ways that those learners might get stuck. This means that Mr. Cooper, like all responsive teachers, needed to be prepared to respond flexibly to various challenges when facilitating productive struggle. The following two examples help demonstrate the adaptability a responsive teacher needs to have to support diverse learners' thinking and struggles.

> ### Supporting Cara to Get Started
> As Mr. Cooper walked away from Lamar, he noticed Cara across the room, with a puzzled look on her face. It did not seem like she had gotten started working, so he approached her table and asked how things were going. "I don't get it," Cara exclaimed. "What's confusing you?" Mr. Cooper asked her. "It doesn't tell me how many friends. I can't figure out how many crackers if I don't know how many friends," Cara explained. "Oh, I see how that could be confusing," Mr. Cooper replied. "Why don't we pick a number of friends that it could be and try it?" Cara thought momentarily and announced that she thought there could be two friends. Mr. Cooper then asked, "If two friends shared the crackers, how could you figure out how many each friend would get?" Cara's eyes lit up, and she started writing on her paper. Noticing that Cara seemed prepared to struggle independently, Mr. Cooper said, "Why don't you work on that, and I will come back to check on you in a bit?" Cara continued intently writing on her paper as Mr. Cooper left to monitor the rest of the class.

Unlike Lamar's situation, in which the learner had a strategy but needed support applying it, Cara needed help getting through a roadblock to begin to think of a strategy in the first place. She was hung up on something that was confusing her about the question itself. While Mr. Cooper still used an eliciting move to figure out what Cara was thinking, as he did with Lamar, his method of addressing her struggle was different. For Cara, Mr. Cooper employed a supporting move in which he asked questions that helped her to narrow the scope of the problem so that she could find an entry point—something Lamar did not need. As Mr. Cooper continued monitoring the rest of his learners, he encountered further diversity in their thinking and struggles.

> **Pressing Zoe and Reggie to Make Meaning of Their Solutions**
>
> Walking away from Cara's table, Mr. Cooper noticed Zoe and Reggie engaged in a heated discussion. He approached their table and asked, "What are you guys working on?" "We found a bunch of solutions," Zoe said, pointing to a list on her paper, "but we can't decide if the flipped ones count as one or two answers." "What do you mean by 'flipped' ones?" Mr. Cooper asked. Reggie replied, "Like you could have four and nine or nine and four." "Ah!" Mr. Cooper said, recognizing that Reggie was currently focused only on the numerical solutions, but not the meaning of those quantities in the context of the problem. He pointed to 9 and 4 on their list of solutions and pressed, "What do these numbers mean? Maybe it will help you decide if you put the numbers in the context of the problem." Zoe said, "Well, nine friends get four crackers each."
>
> "Or ..." Reggie said loudly, "... or four friends can get nine crackers." "Do you think those are the same or different?" Mr. Cooper asked. "They are different," Reggie said. "Do they both work?" Mr. Cooper wondered. Reggie and Zoe looked at each other and nodded: "Yes!"
>
> "I think you have discovered something exciting!" Mr. Cooper said. "Why don't you see if this pattern applies anywhere else in your list of solutions? I will leave you to discuss this, and maybe you can share what you figured out with the class during our discussion."

In this instance of facilitating productive struggle, Mr. Cooper attended to yet another way learners can get stuck. While Lamar was having trouble applying a viable strategy and Cara was having trouble finding an entry point into the task, Zoe and Reggie struggled to make sense of the correct solutions they had generated to make a generalization. Mr. Cooper's initial move with Zoe and Reggie was the same—to elicit the learners' thinking ("What are you guys working on?" and "What do you mean by the 'flipped' ones?"), but once he knew what Zoe and Reggie were struggling with, he customized his response to help them move forward. Specifically, he used a series of consolidating moves to help the two learners connect their numerical answers back to the context of the problem—a move that Cara did not need, and Lamar was not ready for until Mr. Cooper had supported him through several other bumps in the road.

Given how distinct these four students' struggles were, it may sound obvious that Mr. Cooper would respond in different ways. Still, it is vital to understand that he only knew how to respond to them because he spent time asking about, listening to, and analyzing his learners' thinking. Mr. Cooper took Responsibility #1 (understanding the learner's idea and point of struggle) seriously so that he could use what he learned about the learners' ideas to inform the choices he made to accomplish Responsibility #2 (helping the learner move forward with their ideas).

When learners get stuck, it is the teacher's job to assess the situation and support progress toward the mathematical goal in a way that is rooted in the learner's current thinking. Many well-meaning teachers, faced with struggling students, provide one-size-fits-all supports, step-by-step rote directions, or easy answers. Often, this happens because the teacher either never asks what the learners were thinking in the first place or dismisses imperfect thinking and quickly replaces it with a standardized approach. In contrast, responsive teachers honor learners' existing thinking and avoid the temptation to take on too much of the cognitive load. In the next section, we explain how teachers can prepare themselves to be responsive to a range of learners with diverse thinking and thus resist the temptation to rely on the fast, easy, one-size-fits-all approach.

Planning for the Facilitation of Productive Struggle

Planning and preparing are key components of responsive teaching, and it is vital in learning to facilitate productive struggle. Preparing to facilitate productive struggle involves anticipating potential learner thinking and potential teacher responses. First, teachers should anticipate different ways that learners might engage their prior mathematical understandings and the variety of strategies that they might use to solve the task. Next, teachers need to anticipate possible ways students might get stuck as they grapple with the problem. Finally, teachers should develop potential instructional responses to each anticipated form of struggle. In this section, we highlight the work teachers can do ahead of time to be prepared to support diverse learner thinking as their class is working through a task.

Anticipating Student Thinking

An essential part of planning, which often gets bypassed, is for teachers to solve the tasks themselves. Without a firm handle on a given task's mathematical possibilities, concepts, and challenges, teachers will be ill-prepared to support their learners in problem solving and struggling productively. A meaningful way to build a nuanced understanding of any task is for teachers to solve it in a way that makes sense to them, ensuring that they can produce and justify a solution. Once the teacher has engaged with the task as a learner, the next step is to anticipate ways different learners will likely approach the task. When doing this, teachers should consider what they know about their specific learners' prior knowledge and experience with relevant concepts and strategies.

When anticipating learner thinking, it can be helpful to consider the features or characteristics of the task. Some tasks lend themselves to *multiple solution paths*, meaning students can use different strategies to arrive at a solution. The River's Crayons task at the beginning of this chapter is an example of a task with multiple solution paths. Learners might count out crayons by ones, skip count by tens, or recognize that 8 tens are 80 to arrive at a solution. For this type of task, teachers should generate as many different strategies and representations as possible that are likely to be used by their learners.

> Giving teachers time to plan together can be valuable in the process of anticipating learner thinking, as multiple teachers will likely be able to anticipate a wider variety of strategies than one teacher alone. Experience can also inform the anticipation process. If someone has taught the task before, they are likely to have a better idea of the variety of ways students will approach it. See Chapter 8 for more on collaborative planning.

On the other hand, some tasks have *multiple correct solutions*. While learners may still use various strategies to solve this type of task, they will also have the opportunity to look for patterns or relationships among the various solutions and justify that they have found all of them. The Sharing Crackers task described in Mr. Cooper's class is an example of a task with multiple solutions. In this task, a pattern emerges among the factors, or whole-number divisors, of the total number of crackers. Anticipating learners' thinking on a task with multiple solutions includes identifying diverse strategies that generate varied solutions and unearthing the mathematical concepts that those solutions help the learner understand. Tasks like these often include additional extension questions to help guide the learner toward these conclusions or generalizations, such as "How do you know that you found all the different ways?"

Anticipating learner thinking also involves identifying potential difficulties or challenges learners may face. Partial or incomplete understandings may lead a learner down a path to an incorrect solution or may result in the learner getting stuck. Both situations are good opportunities for teachers to facilitate productive struggle. During this part of the planning process, teachers should also note possible challenges that learners might face due to misunderstanding the context, vocabulary, or situation in the task. These can and should be proactively addressed in the launch (described in Chapter 2), but some learners may need to revisit specific aspects of the task privately with the teacher even after a successful launch.

Preparing Potential Responses and Scaffolds for Student Thinking

After anticipating learner thinking, planning can shift to preparing potential teacher responses to the predicted learner struggles. We recommend drawing from the categories in Responsibility #2 of the Facilitating Productive Struggle tool to assist in this process. If a learner is not struggling productively during the lesson, the teacher will need to do an in-the-moment, internal assessment of where the learner is and how best to help them move forward. A teacher's planning should help them identify potential challenges so that they can intervene in response to those challenges more efficiently and effectively.

There are typically three main types of struggles to plan and prepare for, although this may vary depending on the task. First, teachers need to be ready to address learners who *cannot get started* on the task. Second, teachers need to be prepared to support learners who *get started solving but then get stuck* at some point along the way. Finally, teachers must prepare to support *learners who have found a solution and/or believe they are finished with the task* when further work is required or possible. Even if a student has found a solution, if the task has a high ceiling, there should still be ways to engage these students in further exploration, consolidation, or formalization of mathematical concepts or ideas.

Let us consider an example of how Ms. Gonzales, who supported Ana's struggle in the opening vignette, planned out responses to potential student struggles to monitor and address various needs efficiently. Table 3.3 shows Ms. Gonzales' filled-out planning tool. (The complete *Responsive Math Teaching Planning Template* is discussed in more detail in Chapter 6.) Ms. Gonzales wrote out specific questions she could ask in response to different types of student thinking, using the Facilitating Productive Struggle Tool for support. In this approach, the idea is not to create a script that the teacher reads from but rather to practice and front-load the decision-making. Taking the time to develop a potential response to likely types of student thinking allows the teacher to spend more mental energy engaging with the student instead of needing to assess thinking and respond on the fly.

Planning for Learners Who Are Struggling to Get Started

When planning potential responses for learners who do not have a way to get started, teachers may want to generate questions to help learners think about specific aspects of the tasks, what they know, or what they are being asked to figure out. For many learners, questions that help them make better sense of the task (usually forms of *igniting* moves) will be enough to get them started. In Ms. Gonzales' plan, she wrote out two such questions, one to direct learners to re-read the text of the task and another to prompt them to retell the story of the task in their own words. It can also be helpful to plan *supporting*

Table 3.3 Ms. Gonzales' Plan for Facilitating Productive Struggle on the River's Crayons Task

Planning for Facilitating Productive Struggle

Students Who Can't Get Started

- Ask them to reread the task
    - *"Can you read the task for me?"*
- Ask them to retell the story in their own words
    - *"Can you tell me what's happening in the problem?"*
- Suggest that they try representing one box of crayons with a drawing or manipulatives
    - *"What would one box of crayons look like?"*

Students Who Get Stuck

- Ask them to explain their work so far and determine where they are stuck or have a misunderstanding.
    - If the student has drawn only one box of crayons: *"What would your drawing look like if you showed ALL of River's crayons?"*
    - Redirect to the problem if needed (reread/retell)
- If the student has represented the problem incorrectly (wrong number of boxes/wrong number of crayons in each box):
    - *"How many boxes of crayons does River have? Where can I see that in your work?"*
    - *"How many crayons are in River's crayon boxes? Where can I see that in your work?"*
- If the student has added 8 + 10 instead of thinking about groups of 10:
    - Determine if the student understands the problem—have them reread and retell the story
    - *"How many crayons are in one box? Is there a way you can show me that on your paper?"*
    - Pose a simpler version of the task with manipulatives—*"What if there were only two boxes of crayons? Can we figure out how many crayons River would have?"* (Offer student cubes or markers.)

Students Who Are Finished

- Pair them with a student who solved the task differently and ask them to explain their strategies to each other (student who counted by 1's with a student who was able to skip count by 10's)
- Ask them if they can represent their answer with an equation
- Pose an extension question that goes above 100: *"What would happen if River had 12 boxes of crayons?"*

moves for students who remain stuck even after they have made sense of the task, such as concrete tools, graphic organizers, or an alternate version of the task. Ms. Gonzales anticipated that she might suggest drawing out one box of crayons to help students who seemed to have trouble visualizing the scenario.

Planning for Learners Who Begin Solving and Get Stuck

Another typical type of struggle occurs when a learner begins to solve but gets stuck or confused at some point. Anticipating a variety of strategies that students can use to solve the task is key to preparing for this particular student struggle. Each strategy can be considered for potential challenges, confusion, or common errors. *Clarifying moves* can be planned to help determine the specifics of a learner's confusion, followed by *supporting and/or pressing moves* to help a learner better understand their ideas and/or determine errors in their thinking. Scaffolds that organize or help visually display a learner's thinking may also help students see a better way forward using their approach. In Ms. Gonzales' plans, she anticipated that some students might only draw one box of 10 crayons, not realizing that there were 8 boxes. Alternatively, she suspected that some might confuse the number of crayons in each box and the number of boxes. Finally, she also anticipated Ana's error of adding the quantities in the problem together, ignoring or not understanding the important idea that there are 10 crayons in each box.

For this last scenario—the one that ended up applying to Ana—she planned a series of moves, starting with an *igniting move* in which she imagined herself asking the learner to reread and retell the story. She planned to follow that up with a *pressing move*, asking "How many crayons are in one box?" to surface the key concept of grouping. Finally, she planned to use a *supporting* move to help the learner focus on a manageable part of the task: "Is there a way you can show me that [one box] on your paper?" In Ana's case, the combination of these moves was sufficient to support her in productively moving forward with the task. You can see that Ms. Gonzales had also planned an additional *supporting move*, offering a simpler version of the task ("What if there were only two boxes of crayons?"), in case further help was needed, but she ultimately decided that employing that move was unnecessary for Ana. This illustrates how carefully Ms. Gonzales tailored her response to what she learned about her specific learner in real time.

Planning for Learners Who Think They Are Finished

Finally, teachers will encounter learners who say they are finished or are unsure what to do next. In some instances, more work is needed; learners might still need to find further solutions, display and/or explain their thinking, or make a clear mathematical argument. In these situations, teachers can plan for *consolidating moves* that will redirect students to uncompleted aspects of the task. Learners may be finished with the initial assignment and need a challenge connected to the original task to keep stretching their thinking. Ms. Gonzales planned to ask students who correctly solved the task and showed proof of their reasoning to see if they could represent the solution with an equation. She also planned to pair students up with another student who used a different strategy so that they could explain and compare their solutions. In this case, she thought students who drew out all the crayons one by one might benefit from seeing how a peer could count by tens.

When a learner has completed a task, and a teacher uses a *sustaining move* to get the learner to extend their thinking (by solving a related, but more complex problem), the teacher helps the learner re-engage in productive struggle. At the same time, other students have more time to continue working at their own pace, solving the original task. Ms. Gonzalez planned to provide the option of solving the same task for 12 boxes, knowing that this would extend the patterns of multiples of ten beyond 100.

Handling the Unexpected

The anticipatory work that a teacher does should help them be responsive to their learners. Scripting out possible questions and listing potential supports on the lesson plan helps to reduce some of the complexity of the decision-making that occurs in a moment of responsiveness. It allows teachers to have a toolbox of moves for different scenarios at the ready. That said, it is never necessary for teachers to read directly from their planning document as they facilitate productive struggle. Often, the work of anticipating prepares teachers to be able to generate the questions they want to ask spontaneously.

On the other hand, if a teacher is unsure how to respond to a learner in a given moment, there is nothing wrong with a teacher checking her notes briefly and using one of the prepared questions verbatim, assuming the question makes sense, given the learner's struggle. The most important caveat to the planning process for responsive teachers is that all the prepared supports must be held in store until it is clear that specific learners need them. Teachers must actively resist the temptation to provide them preemptively to any or all students, thereby reducing the cognitive load and opportunity to work through productive struggle.

No matter how well teachers anticipate their learners' thinking, they are still likely to encounter strategies or errors that were not anticipated. This is to be expected; human thinking is diverse, and each learner brings prior knowledge and experiences to bear on any task to be solved. When teachers prepare for several different strategic approaches and a host of likely points where learners might get stuck, they are more likely to have the time and mental energy needed to make sense of and respond effectively to the few unanticipated strategies or errors that come up. A learner's thinking may seem unfamiliar at first, but teachers can still use the planned responses to help clarify and move that thinking forward. Regularly engaging in planning to facilitate productive struggle also builds the capacity for anticipating how learners might approach tasks and the ability to respond to surprising or unanticipated ways of thinking, in the moment. This preparation also allows teachers to support diverse learners and continuously engage them in productive struggle, addressing the age-old problem of what to do when some learners are finished while others have barely gotten started.

Stepping Back and Slowing Down to Move Forward

As the examples in this chapter illustrate, facilitating productive struggle is primarily about unearthing, making sense of, and responding to learners' unique thinking. At the heart of this process is the recognition that all students can solve challenging problems, bringing resources that can be built upon. It also involves combatting often well-intentioned desires to jump in and provide thinking for learners by preventing or taking away confusion, errors, or false starts. In this way, facilitating productive struggle is as much about figuring out what not to do as it is about figuring out what to do. It is essential to resist the temptation to lead learners toward predetermined strategies, signal a particular solution path, make assumptions about what students are thinking or their abilities, or define success as the correct answer or solution. In addition, it means not providing one-size-fits-all support for all learners, without taking time to assess what they need. Rather than removing all potential obstacles or difficulties, the goal is to provide support tailored to a specific learner when and where it is required.

Learners and teachers alike often find discomfort in this place of struggle. We are all accustomed to, and usually rewarded for, helping others by providing clear directions, throwing a lifeline, or clearing up confusion. But as teachers, we must be mindful of students' capacity to engage in problem solving and reasoning. Allowing students to make sense of challenging tasks means intentionally limiting our voices, our preferred ways of making sense, or what may seem to us like the most efficient or elegant solution. It requires stepping back to understand, build on, and ultimately lift up the learner's point of view. By doing this, we allow learners to experience the challenging work of struggle and the joyful rewards of getting through that struggle to formulate their own solutions.

Importantly, this also means adopting a stance that recognizes that all students are capable of making sense of mathematics and that our job as teachers is to figure out how they are making sense and build on the resources they are bringing. At the same time, we need to be aware of how biases and stereotypes can creep in and affect how we interpret student thinking. Being responsive to student thinking requires both recognizing learner assets and confronting our own deficits, continually considering how our interpretations might be shaped by assumptions about what students can and cannot do that serve to reinforce and reproduce patterns of inequity in the teaching and learning of mathematics.

> **Facilitating Productive Struggle**
> - IS NOT asking questions that lead learners toward a predetermined strategy
> - IS NOT pointing out keywords that signal a particular solution path
> - IS NOT providing one-size-fits-all supports to avoid potential struggle
> - IS NOT providing simpler tasks based on the assumption that a problem will be too hard
> - IS NOT defining student success in terms of getting the correct answer

Finally, the work of facilitating productive struggle takes time. It may seem counterintuitive that stepping back and slowing down can help move student learning forward. We may feel we can move things forward more efficiently by providing a strategy or hinting at the answer. This can be particularly tempting when it feels like time is limited, there is too much content to cover, or students are expressing confusion. Students, in fact, often feel these same pressures and may look to us to provide shortcuts or strategies. As the following teacher reflected after working on these skills for over a year, dedicating the time and energy to facilitating productive struggle supports the learner experience in the long run.

> I used to think I didn't have time to teach like this because I was so concerned about getting through lessons and covering everything. It was easier and quicker just to show them how to do it and provide the steps. I realized, though, that teaching like that was like building on a foundation of sand. I'm not gonna lie—facilitating productive struggle is hard and I still don't always know how to respond to every student's work, but at least I'm not spoon feeding them and doing all the thinking for them. When in doubt, I ask questions about their work. Learning to facilitate productive struggle has been a productive struggle for me as a teacher, but I'm getting there.

Reflection Questions

Teacher Responsibilities	Guiding Principles
1 Understand a learner's idea and point of struggle 2 Help the learner move forward with their idea(s)	1 Prioritize mathematical sensemaking 2 Promote collaborative learning communities 3 Support a positive mathematical identity 4 Ensure all students have access to mathematics

1. How do each of the teacher responsibilities of facilitating productive struggle described in this chapter address the guiding principles of responsive teaching?
2. Imagine that you are having students solve the River's Crayons task in Figure 3.1. A student has drawn one box of crayons with ten crayons in it and is stuck on what to do next.
    a What would it look like to facilitate this student's productive struggle responsively?
    b What would it look like to give too much support to this student?
    c What would it look like to give too little support to this student?
3. What ideas are you taking away from this chapter that you want to try?
4. As you think about integrating these ideas about facilitating productive struggle into your instructional context:
    a What is already in place that you can build on?
    b What challenges do you foresee?
    c What can you do to try to overcome those challenges?

4

Discussing Learner Thinking

Once a teacher has facilitated students' productive struggle on a cognitively demanding task, the next step is to facilitate a discussion of students' solution strategies to surface and explore the relevant mathematics. This chapter focuses on an extended example of a discussion in a second-grade classroom to illustrate what it looks and sounds like to discuss learner thinking responsively. The discussion we explore throughout this chapter took place after the teacher, Ms. Farrell, launched a task called Chickens and Goats (see Figure 4.1) and then facilitated students' productive struggle as they formulated a variety of solution strategies.

When responsive teachers discuss learner thinking, they do so with a mathematical goal in mind—a skill, relationship, or concept they will work to surface through the students' discussion of their ideas. In the Chickens and

June is peering under her neighbor's fence. Her neighbor has chickens and goats in their backyard, but June can only see the animals' legs. She counts 14 legs in all. How many chickens could her neighbor have? How many goats?

Prove that your solution(s) are correct using mathematics.

Figure 4.1 The Chickens and Goats task.

DOI: 10.4324/9781003536710-4

Goats task, students need to identify combinations of multiples of 4 (goat legs) and multiples of 2 (chicken legs) that add up to 14 (total number of legs). Ms. Farrell selected this task to allow her second-grade students to explore the concept of equal groups and its relationship to skip counting within the context of a complex task. Working fluently and flexibly with equal groups is a building block for understanding multiples and developing multiplicative reasoning. The following few sections will illustrate how Ms. Farrell facilitated a class discussion centered around an analysis of three student solutions to the Chickens and Goats task to help students develop an understanding of grouping and counting by equal groups to find a total.

An essential part of discussing learning thinking is *selecting and sequencing* the strategies that the class will explore together (Smith & Stein, 2018). As Ms. Farrell circulated to facilitate students' productive struggle, she made note of several solution strategies that she wanted the class to discuss. The strategies she selected are shown in Figure 4.2.

Before inviting the students to investigate these strategies collectively, Ms. Farrell sequenced the pieces of work so that the class would be able to make sense of each student's train of logic and build up to the idea of using repeated addition and skip counting to combine equal groups. She decided to start with Matthew's work because she thought it would be accessible to all students in the class. She reasoned that making sense of a concrete model would offer an easy entry point because it clearly shows all the goat legs and chicken legs that he used in each solution. Making sense of Matthew's strategy would also set students up to connect to other, more abstract strategies

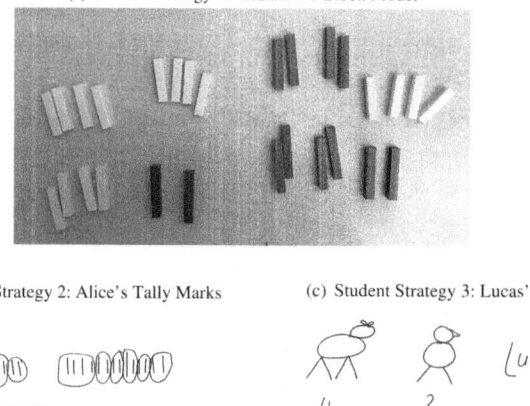

Figure 4.2 Selected student solutions for discussion.

that used multiples of two and four to solve the problem, rather than physical representations of each leg.

The vignette that follows illustrates the first part of discussing learner thinking as it unfolded in Ms. Farrell's room.

Making Sense of Matthew's Model

As Ms. Farrell gathers her students on the rug, she projects the photos that she took of Matthew's block model so that all students can see it on the board.

Ms. Farrell:	Alright y'all! It's time to look at some solutions. Settle into your spots and bring your eyes up to the board. We are going to start by making sense of a model that Matthew built. The first thing I want you to do is just see what you see. Take a minute to look at Matthew's model. [Ms. Farrell waits in silence for about 30 seconds.] What do you notice about Matthew's model? [Several students raise their hands.] Anya?
Anya:	Well, I see red blocks and yellow blocks.
Ms. Farrell:	Ok! Great. Did anyone else notice that? [Many students nod; two students raise their hands.] Let's hear more about the red and yellow blocks from Brianna and Richard. Brianna, tell us what you noticed.
Brianna:	I think the colors are the animals.
Ms. Farrell:	I wonder what Brianna means when she says the colors are animals. Richard, you look like you want to connect to Brianna's idea.
Richard:	Yeah. That's what I thought too. Like the, the yellow ones will be the goats, and the red ones will be the chickens.
Ms. Farrell:	Brianna, is that what you meant when you said "the colors are the animals?" [Brianna nods.] Let's make sure we are all understanding Brianna's and Richard's idea about Matthew's model. Turn to your talk partner and discuss. Could the yellow blocks represent goats, and the red blocks represent chickens? Why or why not?

As the students talk to each other, Ms. Farrell scans the classroom, listening in on different conversations.

Ms. Farrell:	Ok. Rhys and Jada, I overheard you talking about something interesting. Can you share it with us?

Rhys:	Yeah. We said yellow is goats 'cause there are four. And red is like chickens 'cause chickens have two.
Ms. Farrell:	Chickens have two what?
Rhys:	Two legs.
Ms. Farrell:	Ah! Matthew, are we getting your model right? Do the yellow blocks represent goat legs and the red blocks represent chicken legs?

[Matthew smiles and nods.]

Ms. Farrell:	Ok. Now that we know that, let's take a close look at the photo on the left. (Figure 4.3.) What do you all think is going on here? [Ms. Farrell waits about 20 seconds] Sam, you look excited about something. What is it?
Sam:	He's right! It's a solution.
Ms. Farrell:	Can you say a little more about why you think Matthew is right and has found a solution? Everyone else, as Sam is talking, see if you are convinced by his argument.
Sam:	Well, there are three goats. So … one, two, three FOUR, five, six, seven, EIGHT, nine, ten, eleven, TWELVE. Then there's one chicken with two legs. So there's 14!
Ms. Farrell:	Is anyone following what Sam is saying? Could you explain it in your own words?
Alice:	Sam said Matthew made three groups with 4 yellows. It's the three goats. That's 12 legs. Then he made a group, one group, of 2 reds. It's the one chicken. 12 plus 2 is 14.

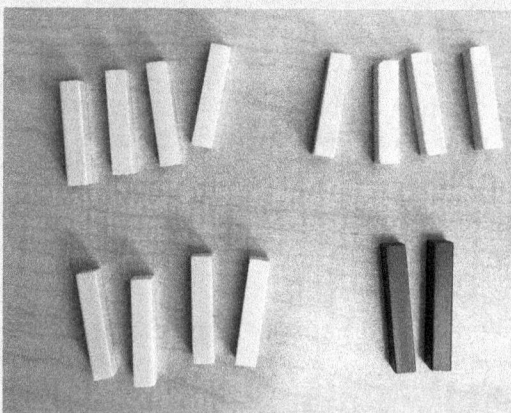

Figure 4.3 Ms. Farrell focuses students on a portion of the displayed work.

Ms. Farrell:	What do the rest of you think about what Sam and Alice are claiming? Has Matthew found a solution to this problem?
Matthew:	Can I say why yes? [Ms. Farrell nods.] I found a solution because I got 14 legs in all: 12 goat legs, 2 chicken legs.
Ms. Farrell:	So what is Matthew's solution to this problem?
Alice:	3 goats and 1 chicken. [Alice begins to point at the groups of 4 yellow blocks] Those are goat 1. Those are goat 2. Those are goat 3.

As Alice is talking, Ms. Farrell annotates Matthew's work on the board to show the three groups of 4 and 1 group of 2 so that students can see both the number of groups or goats and the number of legs in each group (Figure 4.4).

Ms. Farrell:	Matthew, can you tell us how you built this model to find this solution?
Matthew:	I made a lot of groups of 4 with the yellow blocks. Then I counted them.
Ms. Farrell:	Counted them how?
Matthew:	Like 1, 2, 3, 4 …
Ms. Farrell:	Ah, so you counted by ones. And then how did you know to stop making groups of 4?
Matthew:	Because it was going to be higher than 14. [Matthew gets up and points at the yellow blocks in the picture one-by-one.] I said 1, 2, 3, 4 [pause] 5, 6, 7, 8, [pause] 9, 10, 11, 12. Four more was 13, 14, 15, 16 [extends one

Figure 4.4 Ms. Farrell's annotations on Matthew's work.

	finger with each number]. That's too many. So then I put red blocks for 13 and 14. And it was one chicken.
Ms. Farrell:	Great! It sounds like you fit as many groups of 4 into 14 as you could, and then when you couldn't fit anymore in, you fit in a group of 2! Thanks for letting us look at your work and for helping us make sense of your strategy, Matthew. Does anyone have any questions for Matthew? Yes, Emiliano?
Emiliano:	What's the other part—with the lots of red and a little yellow?
Matthew:	Another solution.
Ms. Farrell:	Ah! So this part [Figure 4.5] shows a different possible number of goats and chickens? [Matthew nods.] Great. Why don't you all turn to your talking partner and see if you can make sense of Matthew's second proposed solution? You and your partner have two jobs. First, figure out how many chickens and goats Matthew claims there could be in this solution. Second, see if you agree or disagree with his claim. Turn and talk now.

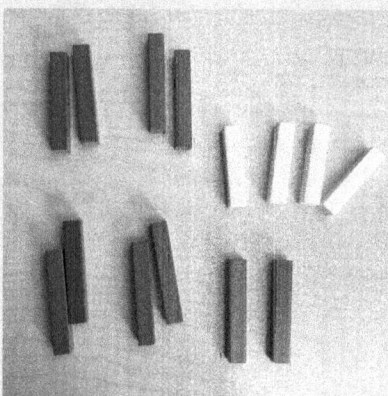

Figure 4.5 Matthew's second solution.

In this example, Ms. Farrell facilitated a discussion with her class centered on making sense of and evaluating Matthew's solution strategy. This positioned Matthew and his ideas as mathematically valuable, and the rest of the class as viable sensemakers of a new mathematical idea. Ms. Farrell's focus as she facilitated was to support the class in collaboratively unpacking the logic behind Matthew's solution strategy. It is important to note that she placed the responsibility for doing this on the shoulders of all the other students—not on Matthew. Rather than asking Matthew to show and tell, Ms. Farrell asked a series of intentional questions to help the other students engage with his model to make sense of it. She also worked hard to ensure that the sensemaking was collective, asking questions and giving directions to weave the ideas of various students together and build comprehension of the key ideas behind Matthew's approach. Ms. Farrell's focus on collective sensemaking ensured that everyone in the class could understand Matthew's claim about possible solutions to the task.

Once she felt sure that the class understood what Matthew did, Ms. Farrell pushed them further by asking them to evaluate the validity of his conclusions. She placed the students in charge of determining if Matthew's answer was correct and asked them to consider how they might use mathematical reasoning to defend claims they agreed with. Assessing the soundness of Matthew's logic is essential to understanding the mathematics behind his thinking and equips all students in the class with two important resources: (1) an alternative problem-solving approach to the one they used (thereby broadening their toolbox of strategies) and (2) the understanding of grouping they will need to understand the increasingly abstract strategies that Ms. Farrell will have them discuss next.

Some classroom discussions look quite different from the one illustrated in this vignette above, primarily focusing on the teacher's ideas of formal mathematics. These discussions are usually well-meaning efforts by teachers to provide clarity or to cut to the chase by focusing only on a single strategy the teacher has deemed most efficient. Unintentionally, though, teacher-centered discussions tend to lead to shallow levels of understanding for only some members of the classroom community. In contrast, the discussion that Ms. Farrell facilitated prioritizes sensemaking of student thinking, which helps all students engage actively in understanding a variety of problem-solving strategies. This helps every student in the class to build slowly but surely toward a more formalized understanding of the mathematics behind the task in a developmentally appropriate and highly engaging way. As discussed in the next section, student-to-student discourse and collective sensemaking are critical for deeper learning.

Why is Discussing Learner Thinking Important for Learning?

In a responsive discussion of learner thinking, the responsive teacher begins by purposefully selecting and sequencing pieces of student work or other representations of students' strategies as a focus for the discussion (Smith

& Stein, 2018). The teacher then engages the class in a cycle of inquiry about each piece of work/strategy to: (1) make collective sense of the work/strategy and then (2) leverage that sensemaking to ensure that students develop understanding and ownership of the mathematical concepts and procedures at the heart of the task, moving everyone's thinking forward.

When facilitated successfully, the discussion contributes directly to students' learning and development and is key in nurturing equity in mathematics classrooms—essential goals for any mathematics lesson. Responsive discussions that achieve these goals have specific designs and aims that can differ significantly from discussions that are more typically found in mathematics classrooms. At its core, discussing learner thinking is an intentional, structured effort on the teacher's part to support students in understanding each other's mathematical thinking.

Perhaps the most pressing reason to devote the time and effort to discuss learner thinking is that when students make sense of each other's ideas, they build a fuller and deeper understanding of the mathematics they are exploring. When students have opportunities to engage in meaningful discourse with each other, their learning of mathematics is enhanced (Boaler, 2008; Chapin & O'Connor, 2007). We know that people learn in and through interaction with others, and more specifically, by using language to convey meaning (Vygotsky, 1978). Explaining one's ideas to others leads to deeper understanding for the explainer (Carpenter & Lehrer, 1999; Franke et al., 2007) and making sense of others' ideas is beneficial to the listener (Boston & Wolf, 2006; Hiebert et al., 1997).

When students talk with each other about their mathematical ideas in an intentional and supported way, they have opportunities not only to reorganize and firm up their own thinking but also to encounter new ways of understanding things. Exposure to alternative forms of reasoning expands students' sense of what is mathematically possible and increases the number of tools each student has at their disposal for making sense of mathematical ideas. Most importantly, discussion of diverse thinking allows students to see connections between different approaches (Kazemi & Hintz, 2014). These types of connections between strategies help students to be able to see the same mathematics happening at a concrete level (action-based), a representational level (image-based), and an abstract level (language-based) (Bruner, 1966). As a result, discussing learner thinking helps each student to deepen and refine their own understanding. This moves individuals closer to grasping ideas at an abstract level and prepares them to be able to figure out what to do in the future in specific mathematical situations, how to do it, and why it should be done.

In addition to benefits for individual learners, when students engage in making sense of each other's thinking, they also develop shared understandings as a

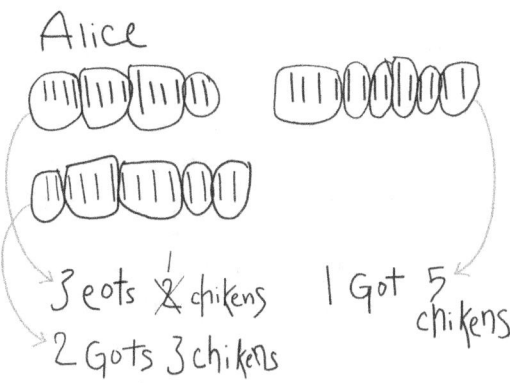

Figure 4.6 Alice's tally marks with Ms. Farrell's annotations.

community, creating resources that can be drawn on in future discussions and building relationships that support risk-taking (Yackel & Cobb, 1996). As students examine a peer's piece of work and, through discussion, negotiate an understanding of "what's going on here," they generate language and ideas that represent a collective comprehension of the mathematics being learned. For example, as the discussion continued in Ms. Farrell's class, making sense of a second student strategy for the Chickens and Goats problem allowed the class to develop an important communal idea.

Ms. Farrell started by projecting Alice's solution (Figure 4.6) and facilitating a discussion of her strategy, annotating Alice's work throughout the conversation. Once the class had made sense of Alice's approach of using tally marks to represent three solutions (3 goats and 1 chicken, 2 goats and 3 chickens, and 1 goat and 5 chickens), Ms. Farrell decided to have them investigate a key claim that Alice made about the number of possible solutions.

Ms. Farrell:	Interesting. Alice is making a claim that her work shows ALL the possible solutions to this problem. I wonder why she might think that? What do you think?
Ms. Farrell pauses for about 20 seconds and motions for hands that shoot up to go down while others are thinking.	
Eric:	I think she might be right. There are no more numbers of goats there could be.
Ms. Farrell:	Let's consider what Eric is saying. I want to make sure you all get his idea. Does anyone think they understand it? Eric said, "There are no more numbers of goats there could be." Leon?

Leon:	I think he means like there's a line with 3 goats, a line with 2 goats and a line with 1 goat. Can there be any more? Nope. Just 1, 2 or 3.
Ms. Farrell:	What a great question Leon. Can there be any other number of goats than the three scenarios that Alice has shown? Chat with a partner. [Students chat for about a minute and then Ms. Farrell brings them back together.] Matthew, you look excited!
Matthew:	Yeah, this is the same as my model. I mean, three is the most goats you can fit in. If you count 4 more after 12, you go over. Go over 14, I mean.
Ms. Farrell:	Ok, so it sounds like you, and Alice, are claiming that the highest number of goats possible is 3 goats. What do the rest of you think of that? Are you convinced? [Everyone nods.] Amazing! That's an important thing for us to have figured out together. So, Alice and Matthew have us convinced that the maximum, or most, number of goats possible for this problem is 3, because if we add one more, we go over the total number of 14 legs that we were given in the task.

Shared understandings often extend beyond a single lesson. In subsequent weeks, as students were tackling a problem about using the fewest coins to make 65 cents, a student connected this problem with the group's earlier experience with the Chickens and Goats task, commenting, "This is like the goat problem. Remember? We had to see how many of the big ones fit in and then you could do the little ones once the big number didn't fit any more." Not only do the creation of these shared understandings help individuals to grasp important mathematical concepts, but they bring the entire mathematical learning community together to build both resources and a sense of trust and unity.

Discussions like the one in Ms. Farrell's classroom impact students' affective as well as cognitive development, helping them to build positive identities as mathematics learners, a guiding principle of responsive mathematics teaching (see Chapter 1). Engaging students in discussions about their own and their peers' ideas is motivating (Middleton & Jansen, 2011) and builds confidence (Hiebert et al., 1997). As a result, students are more likely to feel positively about their study of mathematics and their own potential to engage successfully as mathematicians (Grootenboer & Marshman, 2016).

Being trusted to decide what does and does not make sense—a main component of responsive discussions—also builds positive mathematical identities. Mathematics teachers often serve as the gatekeepers of sensemaking in mathematics classrooms, deciding if an answer is correct or incorrect, when explanations are sufficient, and when confusion needs to be cleared up (Franke et al., 2007; Secada & Berman, 1999). Engaging students in making sense of each other's thinking and inviting the community to question proposed ideas to decide if those ideas are sound or not, shifts that dynamic. Mathematical authority is shared across the learning community, and students grow to see themselves as capable of understanding and evaluating mathematical ideas independently (Battey et al., 2016; Cobb et al., 2018).

When discussing learner thinking, teachers can build positive mathematics identities by intentionally *assigning competence* to students who perceive themselves or are perceived by others as less capable (Cohen et al., 1998). This can take the form of public commentary on mathematical thinking and reasoning (e.g., "It's so important that James noticed how the pattern grows by two each time. That helps us see how multiples of two work!") or by purposeful selection and discussion of a piece of student work, even if it is not complete, or contains a small error. These moves reinforce students' capacity to make sense of things and contribute to the learning community, while simultaneously working toward the mathematical goals.

In addition to contributing to students' cognitive and affective development, effective facilitation of the discussion of learner thinking can also address larger social justice goals. Teachers actively combat entrenched inequities in mathematics classrooms by engaging students as competent sensemakers who can build toward formalized mathematics from their own and their classmates' ideas. Discussions of learner thinking can be an important place for teachers to provide equitable opportunities for all students to engage productively with mathematical ideas (Boaler, 2015; Tate et al., 2014).

When discussions are not responsive, there is often a mismatch, or a gap, between students' existing ideas and the strategies or concepts the teacher wants the students to understand. This gap is often more pronounced for students whose cultural knowledge and ways of knowing may be dismissed because they do not neatly match dominant, typically white, middle-class ways of knowing (Muhammad, 2020). On the other hand, when the teacher focuses on collectively uncovering the connections between different strategies that students propose, students begin to stitch together relationships between their own ways of knowing and others' ways of knowing—including formalized versions of mathematics. When teachers intentionally include all students in a mathematical discussion, they push back against stereotypes and assumptions about who can do mathematics and who can contribute worthwhile thinking. This helps the group to build an equitable learning community and helps individual students to become habituated to the idea that diversity in thinking is valuable and useful.

DISCUSSING LEARNER THINKING	
Is ...	Is NOT ...
• A discussion centered on student work (including rough ideas, more polished ideas, and unfinished or slightly flawed work with potential). • Organized intentionally by the teacher via strategic selection and sequencing of work to help students develop specific mathematical understandings. • Collaborative sensemaking in which learners actively try to understand each other's ideas. • Intentionally inclusive of all students and their ideas and attempts to understand. • Aimed at supporting students in understanding a variety of problem-solving strategies/approaches, connections between strategies, and the whys behind the hows.	• A discussion centered primarily on teacher ideas or a best or "prize" piece of student work. • Open-ended discussion with little teacher facilitation, or discussion organized around randomly elicited strategies (e.g., "who would like to share?"). • Teacher modeling or student show and tell. • A space that privileges preferred or advanced student thinking. • Aimed at ensuring that students can effectively replicate one, formalized mathematical strategy.

Overall, discussing learner thinking helps the responsive teacher to attend to three important learning goals: deepening and strengthening students' mathematical understanding; improving students' confidence and mathematical self-concept; and disrupting entrenched biases that lead to inequitable learning in classrooms. The next section explains in more detail how responsive teachers can actively facilitate the kinds of discussion that will achieve these goals.

Discussing Learner Thinking: The Teacher's Role

Collaborative sensemaking that fosters deep mathematical understandings, positive mathematics identities, and more equitable learning is unlikely to happen if students are merely left to contribute to and monitor their own discourse. While student ideas are at the center of meaningful classroom discussions, it is the teacher who provides the structure needed to knit a cohesive discussion together and connect the meat of the discussion to the mathematical goals for the lesson. Discussing learner thinking requires artful and careful facilitation that is carried out in response to the solutions students generate and the ideas they have about each other's work.

To help make this kind of responding-in-the-moment facilitation more manageable, we present a framework of clearly defined responsibilities and potential moves. There are four main responsibilities for the teacher to attend to during discussing learner thinking: (1) determining which student ideas the discussion will focus on; (2) bringing a learner's strategy out into the open for discussion; (3) helping other learners to actively engage with and understand the strategy; and (4) leveraging the discussion of the strategy to surface important mathematics. In the sections below, we describe each of these multifaceted responsibilities in more detail and introduce a tool to support teachers in carrying them out.

The First Responsibility: Determine Which Student Ideas the Discussion Will Focus On

Before jumping into a discussion of mathematical ideas, a responsive teacher needs to determine which student ideas should be the focus of the discussion. As outlined in Table 4.1, this responsibility involves both selecting and

Table 4.1 Discussing Learner Thinking Tool, Responsibility #1

Responsibility #1: Determine Which Student Ideas the Discussion Will Focus on
Identify 2–4 Pieces of Work or Strategies to Discuss
Select pieces of work or strategies that: • provide opportunities to examine, highlight or showcase the mathematics to be learned. • show a variety of approaches. • are clear or organized enough to be made sense of by others (with some effort on the part of the students and intentional facilitation on the part of the teacher).
Decide How to Order the Work or Strategies Within the Discussion
• Begin with a piece of work or strategy that is likely to be accessible for most learners (e.g., a simpler visual model or a concrete approach like guess and check or testing real numbers). • Save more complex or abstract strategies for later in the discussion. • Arrange the strategies so that they build on each other in some way (increasing level of sophistication, increasingly abstract, closer and closer to a specific understanding or procedure, etc.).

intentionally sequencing the examples of student work or strategies to investigate as a class (Smith & Stein, 2018).

The process of identifying and selecting two to four pieces of student work begins while the teacher is circulating through the room to facilitate learners' productive struggle on the task. When selecting pieces of work, the teacher should consider several things. First, it is important to select work that provides opportunities to highlight or showcase the important mathematical ideas in relation to learning goals. For example, when Ms. Farrell was preparing to facilitate a discussion of the Chicken and Goats problem, her goal was for students to develop an understanding of the relationship between equal groups and skip counting. She decided to select work from Matthew, Alice, and Lucas (see Figure 4.2) because each could be connected to that goal. There were other legitimate solutions that she did not select for the discussion (see Brianna and Javi's solutions in Figure 4.7). Despite containing interesting mathematics, these pieces of work were less aligned with Ms. Farrell's mathematical goal for the class.

Brianna used a strategy of finding combinations of 14 and then deciding which of those potential solutions were possible. Javi modeled a chicken and a goat and then counted repeatedly by ones, touching each leg in his model until he found numbers of chickens and goat legs that added up to 14. Although both students came up with correct solutions, neither piece of work clearly showed groups of twos and fours, and thus were not going to help Ms. Farrell's students think about seeing the equal groups as units.

When identifying strategies or pieces of work, it is also important to make selections that illustrate a variety of problem-solving approaches. Too often, mathematics instruction perpetuates the myth that there is one right or best way to solve a task, when in actuality, most problems can be solved in many ways. Creating an environment where multiple solution paths are welcomed

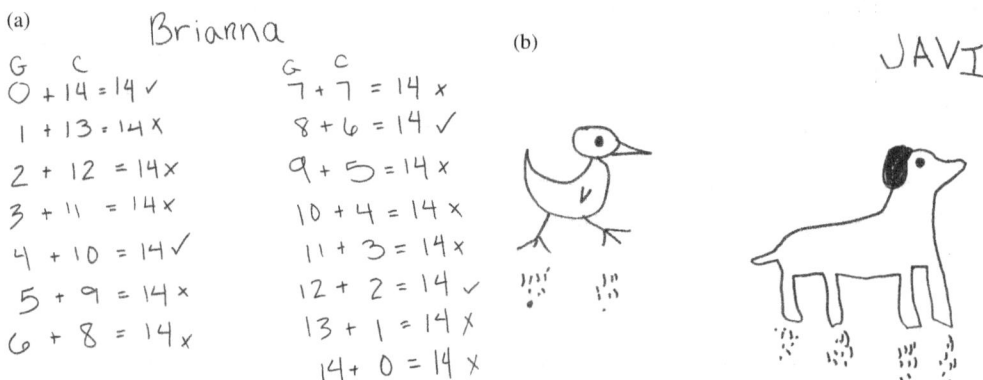

Figure 4.7 (a) Brianna and (b) Javi's solutions to the Chickens and Goats task.

helps students become familiar with a broad set of tools that they can use to tackle problems. Having a toolbox to rely on also encourages risk-taking and experimentation, empowering students to try out new or tentative approaches. Making sense of mathematical ideas as they play out in different ways provides an opportunity for learners to make deeper connections. Keeping in mind both the goal of connecting equal groups to skip counting and a desire to showcase a variety of approaches, Ms. Farrell selected Matthew's physical model, Alice's method of using tally marks, and Lucas's table of multiples. Each of these strategies was unique, allowing learners in the class to access three different ways of combining equal groups to solve the problem.

Ms. Farrell also carefully sequenced the work for discussion so that the strategies built on each other in a way that could support deeper conceptual understanding for all her learners. She decided to begin with Matthew's concrete model because it provided an accessible way for students to see and understand one possible solution. Ms. Farrell planned to discuss Alice's work next because her tally marks visually modeled both the total of 14 legs and the more abstract idea of different units or groups of two and four in each combination. The circled sets of tally marks related to Matthew's block model, while also providing a bridge to Lucas' more abstract and unfinished solution involving multiples. Without seeing Alice's work first, students may have had a harder time seeing those groups in the quantities represented by Lucas' table. By displaying the strategies side-by-side, Ms. Farrell could use questions to help students see the relationship between skip counting and the multiples of that number, and the idea that each multiple contains a set of equal groups. This concept of unitizing or grouping quantities into units and treating the units as single entities (e.g., one group of four), is at the heart of number sense, place value, and multiplicative reasoning (Hulbert et al., 2023).

The Second Responsibility: Get a Learner's Idea or Strategy Out in the Open

Once a teacher has identified student work to discuss, the next step is to determine how to get that problem-solving approach out into the open so that others can begin to make sense of it. How a teacher chooses to give the class access to a student's work depends on the classroom setup, the technologies available, and the way the student has presented their idea. As Table 4.2 shows, *displaying moves* involve figuring out how to make the ideas visually accessible to others.

Table 4.2 illustrates four main ways that teachers can display student thinking so that all students can see and interact with it. The first method is to use technology to display the actual written work. This can be done by using a device that projects images of documents or by taking a picture of the work and sending it to an interactive display or whiteboard. Oftentimes,

Table 4.2 Discussing Learner Thinking Tool, Responsibility #2

Responsibility #2: Getting a Learner's Strategy or Idea Out in the Open
Use Technology to Project Learner Work on a Screen, Monitor, or Board   • A good option when the work is drawn or easily moveable.   • Take a photo of learner work and share the photo on a screen, interactive whiteboard, or digital platform.   • Use a device that captures and displays images or concrete models on a screen in real time (e.g., a document camera can show a model made from base-10 blocks or students' written work).
Arrange a "field trip"   • A good option when the work cannot easily be moved or replicated.   • Invite all learners to gather around a model or piece of work so that everyone can see it (e.g., *Let's take a field trip over to Marissa's table so we can see the model she and Andrew built using the base-10 blocks.*)   • Ensure that everyone can see the work by proactively arranging the way students sit/stand.
Ask a Learner to Replicate Their Work   • A good option for classrooms with fewer technology resources.   • Prior to the discussion, ask a student to replicate part or all of their written work in a designated space visible to all (board, chart paper, etc.).
Invite Learners to Share or Physically Model Their Thinking   • Helpful if a student used a strategy that does not appear on a piece of paper or in a physical model.   • Draw a representation of the strategy while the student is explaining.   • *Aondrea—you used an interesting counting strategy. Can you show it to us? Everyone, while Aondrea counts for us, listen to what she does with her voice, and look at what she does with her fingers so we can talk about it afterwards.*

it is helpful to show only a portion of the work so that the class can focus on a piece of the strategy. When students build physical models with manipulatives, such as base-10 blocks or counters, teachers can either take a photo of the model to display or invite the rest of the students to travel over to the model and discuss the work while gathering around it.

Some students may have an idea or strategy that is worthy of discussion but not represented visually. This can be the case with students who are not yet proficient with writing, students who have not translated an idea into a visual form, or students who are using an idea that is better represented by verbalization (e.g., a counting strategy that involves emphasizing certain numbers to show a pattern). In these instances, teachers can help the rest of the class gain access to the idea by inviting students to share their ideas (e.g., "Ada, I noticed that you were moving counters around on your desk. Can you show us what you were doing?") and focusing the other students on what to pay attention to as they are looking and listening (e.g., "Watch what Ada is doing with her counters and see if you can figure out why she is making the groups she is making."). Recording a written representation of the learner's strategy while they verbalize it will help make it accessible to other classmates and provide a basis for further discussion. This can be an important way for the teacher to model how to represent mental strategies (e.g., if a student counts on, the teacher can record the starting number and sequence.)

During Ms. Farrell's class discussion, she had to consider how to help other students access the three strategies shown in Figure 4.2. Since Matthew built a physical model, Ms. Farrell projected a photo of his work on the interactive whiteboard. Alice and Lucas' solutions were on paper, so she used her document camera to project them. Providing clear and accessible visual representations of student work enables teachers to facilitate meaningful engagement with ideas and strategies for all students.

The Third Responsibility: Help Others to Engage with the Idea/Strategy

Once a teacher has ensured that all students have access to the strategy being discussed, the next step is to help the class actively engage with the work and the underlying ideas. A common practice when discussing student work is to ask the student whose idea is being discussed to tell the rest of the class about their thinking. However, in this kind of show-and-tell sharing, the rest of the students tend to listen respectfully but passively, hearing their classmates' explanations without putting effort into following and understanding the ideas. In other words, students miss out on the opportunity to genuinely make sense of each other's ideas.

Rather than asking the author of the idea or strategy to talk about their work, teachers can use the responsive moves outlined in Table 4.3 to help the community of learners collaboratively unpack the strategy being shared. While this is happening, the author of the strategy usually listens and fields occasional questions but largely remains silent as others discuss their ideas.

Helping students actively unpack their classmates' strategies often begins with *directing* moves that explicitly guide students to make sense of the work displayed. Because following other people's thinking can be complex, particularly with rough-draft or disorganized work, teachers can help students focus by priming them to intentionally examine an aspect of the work. These moves help students to look and listen attentively at specific things (e.g., "As you look at Tomas' diagram, pay attention to his color coding"). For particularly

Table 4.3 Discussing Learner Thinking Tool, Responsibility #3

Responsibility #3: Help Other Learners to Engage with the Strategy or Idea	
Directing Moves focus learners on making individual sense of a strategy or idea	
Direct students to make sense of someone else's work	• Your job is to look at this work and try to make sense of it.
Prime students to listen and look intentionally	• Jane is about to explain where she thinks Anya got the 5 from. Listen carefully and see if you follow her reasoning.
Draw learners' attention to a particular portion of displayed work	• Cover up, circle, box, or highlight a portion of the work being displayed to focus. learners' attention or reduce cognitive load. • Verbally direct learners to pay attention to a particular part of the work (e.g., *To start, I just want you to look at Jose's table, on the left*).
Eliciting Moves draw out learners' ideas about the strategy/idea being investigated	
Invite students to share their thinking	• *What do you see when you look at Risa's work? Nothing is too small--let's just start pointing out what pops out to us.* • *What do you notice? What questions do you have?*
Increase participation and diversify voices	• *What other ideas do people have about Matthew's work?* • *Ashley, you look like you have a question about Kat's equation. Will you share it with us?*
Clarifying Moves help ensure that ideas on the table are clear to everyone	
Ask students to elaborate	• *Can you say more about that?* • *Tell us more about the pattern you see in the output column of Jada's table.*
Repeat what a learner has said, verbatim, to draw attention to it, or ensure that others heard it clearly	• *Interesting Alex. So you think that the problem is asking about "how polluted the coffee got by the milk." I wonder what Alex means by "polluted?"*
Ask other students to rephrase what they heard to generate an opportunity for everyone to hear an important idea in an alternate way and/or have additional time to process the idea	• *Who thinks they understand what Erica said? Can you try to explain it in your own words?*

(Continued)

Table 4.3 Discussing Learner Thinking Tool, Responsibility #3 *(Continued)*

Ask about ambiguous phrases or vocabulary	• When Mia says, "subtract it," what is the "it" she is talking about? • What do you think Sam means when he says, "the bigger one?"
Rephrase what a learner has said to clarify it to other learners and then verify that you have their idea right	• *I think what Deb is saying is that the number we are looking for needs to be divisible by 3 AND 4. Am I getting your idea right Deb?* • *It sounds like Colin is telling us that the zero matters in this case. Is that right Colin?*
Illustrating Moves make one learner's thinking visible to others through the creation of new visuals	
Create an original visual as a student is describing their thinking to help others make sense of the ideas	• Write equations or expressions. • Produce and label a picture, diagram, or model. • Write down words, phrases and/or sentences that students use so that they are easily accessible to and rememberable by others.
Replicate or call attention to gestures that clarify mathematically significant ideas	• *Amanda was just going like this with her arm to show what she meant by "horizontal."* • *Watch Jose again while he shows how much bigger he thinks ½ is than ¼.*

complicated work, teachers can explicitly draw learners' attention to a designated portion by covering up parts that are not vital or giving verbal directions (e.g., "To start, I want you to look at Jose's table—it's on the left side").

Once students have had a chance to look and/or listen intentionally, *eliciting* moves can be used to prompt them to share their initial thoughts. This involves inviting students to begin commenting on the work (e.g., "What do you think is going on here in Risa's work?") and then continuing to draw in other students' ideas to collaboratively build toward understanding (e.g., "Does anyone want to build on what Melanie noticed?"). During these early phases of sensemaking, it often helps to assure students that it is okay if they are not immediately comprehending the entire strategy (e.g., "Start by sharing things you see or notice, and we will put the pieces together until we get it.") Encouragement like this builds students' confidence and allows them to practice the important mathematical disposition of "mucking about" with ideas until understanding develops (Duckworth, 1987).

After this initial sensemaking phase, some learners will have "aha" moments about how the strategy works and will share these thoughts with the rest of the group. This happened in the discussion of Matthew's work when Brianna claimed that "the colors are animals." When a student has this kind of epiphany about how the strategy being discussed works, it is important for the teacher to use *clarifying moves* to ensure that all students understand the conclusions being drawn. A teacher might ask the student who has had the realization to elaborate (e.g., "Can you say more about that?") or repeat what that student said to give others a second chance to hear it. They might also ask others to rephrase what they heard the student say to provide the class with an opportunity to unpack the idea further or have more time to process it (e.g., "Does anyone think they understand what Brianna means? Could you explain it to us in your own words?"). When the student having the epiphany has made an unclear statement, the teacher may press the student or others to be more specific (e.g., "Rhys, you said, 'Chickens have two.' Chickens have two what?").

Teachers can also help the class follow emerging understandings visually by using *illustrating* moves. This usually involves the teacher drawing or writing something on the board, or directly on or next to the work, to help the rest of the group understand something. Teachers might also gesture to build visual clarity by using their hands, bodies, or eyes to physically show an idea a learner is trying to communicate (e.g., "So when Amanda says 'horizontal,' she means the part of Kisha's drawing that goes this way.").

Although the sensemaking responsibilities are firmly on the learners in this type of discussion, the teacher plays an active and crucial role. It is the teacher's job to ensure that the whole class understands the different strategies presented in student work, as well as additional ideas that emerge about those strategies through the discussion. The types of instructional moves highlighted in this section are tools a teacher can employ to support students as they make sense of each other's ideas. Without this collective understanding, carrying out the fourth responsibility of surfacing important mathematics will be much more challenging.

The Fourth Responsibility: Leverage the Discussion to Surface Important Mathematics

The teacher's final responsibility in discussing learner thinking is to move beyond making sense of how a strategy works to ensure that the mathematics behind the strategy is explicit and clear to all students. Responsive teachers do this by intentionally attending to the concepts and skills at the heart of their mathematical goal while they discuss a particular piece of student work. Using the moves outlined in Table 4.4, the teacher can pull the mathematical ideas directly out of the learner's work through the discussion.

Table 4.4 Discussing Learner Thinking Tool, Responsibility #4

Responsibility #4: Surface Important Mathematics Behind Each Strategy	
Focusing Moves draw learners' attention to mathematically significant concepts and relationships within strategies	
Annotate learner work to call attention to key portions of the learner's mathematical thinking or connections between the work and the problem context	• Add arrows, words, labels, pictures, etc. to a piece of learner work to make key mathematical ideas stand out. • Layer color coding on to a learner's equation(s), list, model or table to help everyone see key relationships.
Point at a learner's work in ways that highlight mathematically significant ideas	• So what does this 5 [point to the 5] have to do with the 10?
Pressing Moves prompt students to unpack ideas to surface logic or underlying concepts, or misconceptions, errors, or inconsistencies within the strategy	
Ask students to further unpack an idea or strategy to illuminate the concepts behind it	• How does this equation connect to the area model Dwayne drew?
Ask why a strategy works	• Why do you think Tiffany's method works?
Ask a question that challenges a strategy or provides a counterexample [Note: challenging correct strategies is as helpful as challenging those that are not]	• What will happen if we try 10? • Does this calculation include the $12 they started with?
Linking Moves engage students in questioning, commenting on, or adding on to an idea to make sure that understandings are shared across the class	
Encourage students to ask questions about each other's thinking	• What questions do you have for Joe about his strategy?
Invite students to build on an idea	• Would anyone like to add on to that?
Point out connections to other students' thinking, or to key mathematical concepts	• Emily and Kira both used skip counting to help solve the problem. • Jenna's work is showing us how convenient it is to make a ten when we are adding.

(Continued)

Table 4.4 Discussing Learner Thinking Tool, Responsibility #4 *(Continued)*

Ask students to reason about an idea or strategy	• *Do you agree? Disagree? Why?* • *Kya just said, "all squares are rectangles, but not all rectangles are squares." What do you think about Kya's conjecture?*
Support students in extending a mathematical idea to be able to see patterns or make a mathematical concept explicit	• *How would we use Moira's strategy if there were 36 stickers rather than 24?* • *Build a table to apply the strategy and involve learners in filling it out.*

When teachers use *focusing* moves to surface important mathematics, they draw learners' attention to mathematically significant concepts and relationships within strategies. One common way to do this is to physically point at a portion of the work being discussed and then ask questions that prompt students to reason about that portion of the mathematical logic (e.g., "So you're saying, this 5 doubles to get this 10. What does that doubling represent in the context of the problem?"). Often, teachers also annotate the work being discussed in such a way that makes the mathematical logic explicit. This may include adding notation such as arrows, words, labels, or color coding. The purpose of focusing moves is to help all learners zoom in on the mathematically rich ideas in the student work.

Once students are paying attention to the right things, teachers can continue to surface important mathematics by using *pressing* moves. Pressing moves help students dig deeper to surface logic, underlying concepts, misconceptions, or inconsistencies within the strategy. Teachers can do this by explicitly asking students to further unpack an idea (e.g., "You said James is multiplying by ⅓, but that he divided by 3 to do it. Can you tell us more about that?") or asking why a strategy works (e.g., "Why does it work to do what Steph said and just 'ignore the zeros and put them back in later'?"). Pressing moves can also be used to help students notice a limitation to a strategy and revise their understanding to be more mathematically accurate (e.g., "Will Amina's rule still work if we start with a fraction?"). Using pressing moves ensures that students move forward from understanding how a strategy works to understanding why it works and is mathematically significant.

Linking moves engage students in questioning, commenting on, or adding on to ideas. When teachers use these moves, they help the community of learners collaboratively weave connections that ensure that explicit mathematical understandings are shared across the class. They might do this in an open-ended way by encouraging students to ask questions (e.g., "What questions do you have for Max about his strategy?"), inviting students to build on an idea (e.g., "Can someone try to pick up where Natalie left off to continue her application of Max's strategy?"), or asking students to reason about a strategy (e.g., "Do you agree? Disagree? Why?"). Alternatively, teachers can be more targeted and explicitly point out connections to other students' thinking and key mathematical concepts (e.g., "So, both Emily and Kira used 'skip counting' to help solve the problem"). Sometimes, teachers may need to support the class in extending a learner's work to help the important mathematics bubble up to the surface. In these cases, teachers can use linking moves to help patterns emerge by asking students to apply the logic inherent in a strategy (e.g., "Gary says Cat's strategy is based on the idea that both the cookies and the amount of money doubled. Can we use Cat's thinking to figure out the cost for any other numbers of cookies?").

Overall, the work of surfacing important mathematics involves first evaluating how well students are making sense of a key mathematical idea and then responding in such a way that advances this understanding for the whole class. Responsive teachers weave focusing, pressing, and linking moves together to nudge the class collectively toward a firm grasp on the important mathematical concepts they hope to surface from the discussion. The section below illustrates what this might look like in a real classroom.

An Example of Real-Time Surfacing of Important Mathematics

This portion of the discussion in Mrs. Farrell's classroom picks up just after the class has identified that Lucas' table contains the same three solutions that Alice came to with her with her tally marks. Together, the students are able to connect the numbers in Lucas' table to see that 14 legs can be made from 4 goat legs and 10 chicken legs, 8 goat legs and 6 chicken legs, and 12 goat legs and 2 chicken legs. As the class comes up with these combinations, Ms. Farrell annotates the table with the diagonal connecting lines so that all students can see where the solutions were in the table (Figure 4.8).

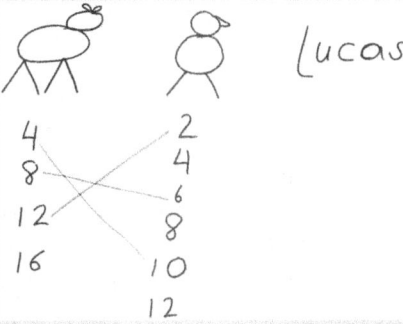

Figure 4.8 Lucas' table with Ms. Farrell's annotations.

Ms. Farrell:	Ok. We found the three solutions in Lucas' table, but I want to make sure we all understand what's going on here. Let's think about this question: How do the numbers in Lucas's table connect to the goats and the chickens in the problem?

[Ms. Farrell waits about 30 seconds while students think.] Mia, what are you thinking?

Mia:	The numbers in the table are the number of legs.
Ms. Farrell:	Can you give us some examples?
Mia:	Like 4, 8, 12, and 16, those are all different numbers of goat legs there could be. And then like 2, 4, 6, 8, 10, and 12 are all numbers of chicken legs there could be.
Ms. Farrell:	Ok! So, where are the actual goats themselves in this table? Or the chickens?
Josiah:	What do you mean?
Ms. Farrell:	Thanks for asking, Josiah. Mia said these numbers [points at the table] are all possible numbers of legs. But I'm wondering how we can figure out how many goats and chickens each of these numbers would represent. For example, right here it shows 8 goat legs. How many goats is that?

Most children call out: "TWO!"

Ms. Farrell:	Wow, it sounds like a lot of you agree on that. I want you to think quietly for a minute. How do you know that? [After waiting 20 seconds or so, Ms. Farrell points toward Simon.]
Simon:	That's two goats because 4 + 4 is 8. [Ms. Farrell nods toward Sarah, who is raising her hand.]
Sarah:	Yeah. It's like there are 2 fours inside the 8. They are hiding.
Ms. Farrell:	Interesting! Do folks understand what Sarah means when she says there are 2 fours hiding inside the 8?
Alice:	Yes. It's like 8 has 4 + 4, like Simon said. But 12 is three goats because it's 4 plus 4 plus 4. You need three. And 16 is four of them. [As Alice talks, Ms. Farrell begins annotating on Lucas's table to show the "hidden 4s"].

Ms. Farrell:	Thanks, Alice! Is there something hiding in the numbers on the other side of Lucas's table? I mean—is there something inside this 2, this 4, this 6 … [pointing at the numbers in the chicken column of Lucas' table.]
Matthew:	Yes! The twos are hiding there. Those are chicken legs. So it's like 4 is 2 twos and 6 is 3 twos. And you could just keep going. They're all twos. [Ms. Farrell continues to annotate the table as Matthew is talking.]
Ms. Farrell:	I want to teach you a new math word that connects to Lucas's table. These numbers here, the ones that are hiding the 4s: 4, 8, 12, 16, are called multiples of 4. Each one is made up of a certain number of 4s. And these numbers here, the ones that are hiding the 2s, 2, 4, 6, 8, 10, 12, are called multiples of 2 because each one is made up of a certain number of 2s. [Ms. Farrell annotates the table to add this information (Figure 4.9).]
Ms. Farrell:	Do these numbers remind you of anything? 2, 4, 6, 8, 10, 12? 4, 8, 12, 16?
Brianna:	It's like when we skip count!
Ms. Farrell:	Exactly! When we skip count by a certain number, we are saying the multiples of that number. Lucas solved this problem by listing the multiples of 4 and the multiples of 2. The multiples of 2 and 4 were the number of legs of each kind of animal. And the hidden numbers—the number of 4s or the number of 2s inside each of these numbers, helps us to see how many animals are represented by each one. Lucas can use all that information to figure out combinations of chickens and goats that work. Amazing job making sense of Lucas' work and connecting it to skip counting and multiples.

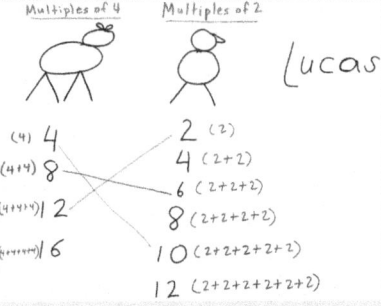

Figure 4.9 Ms. Farrell's annotation of Lucas's Table.

Using Protecting Moves Throughout the Discussion

One more type of responsive teaching move permeates all four responsibilities involved in discussing learner thinking: moves that protect learner thinking. Throughout the discussion, Ms. Farrell does substantial, deliberate work to help the students feel safe taking the kinds of risks they need to take to try out emerging mathematical ideas in a public setting and firm up their understanding of those ideas. She begins by asking open-ended questions, to which a large range of responses would be reasonable. When asking more challenging questions, she often offers students wait time to process their thinking, and/or the opportunity to try their ideas out with a talk partner before sharing their thoughts in front of the whole group.

Ms. Farrell also normalizes the complex work of sensemaking throughout the discussion by explicitly noting the hard work students need to put in to make sense of each other's thinking (e.g., "let's think hard about how Alice might know that") and empathizing with the kind of initial confusion that can come with interpreting others' work (e.g., "it's ok if Lucas' table is not totally clear to you yet. Let's work together and eventually we will make sense of it."). In addition, at several points during the discussion, Ms. Farrell checks in with students to see if she and the class have gotten a student's idea right. Doing so recognizes that people's initial attempts to make sense of things might not be correct (even teachers) and honors students as capable mathematical thinkers whose ideas are worth understanding and exploring. These intentional efforts by Ms. Farrell to cultivate a discussion space in which every student feels safe, valued, and respected are vital to the work of discussing learner thinking. See Chapter 7 for more on the use of *protecting* moves to establish a healthy culture in the mathematics classroom.

Planning to Discuss Learner Thinking

Advance preparation is important for deciding which student ideas the discussion will focus on, how to get each of those ideas out in the open, how to help others to engage with the ideas, and how to surface the key mathematical ideas. Much like preparing to facilitate productive struggle (discussed in Chapter 3), planning for discussing learner thinking starts by anticipating the different ways learners are likely to approach and solve a task and then considering how those various approaches could be used to connect to the mathematical goal. In addition, teachers need to think through how they will help students make sense of the work that is shared and discussed.

Planning for the discussion of learner thinking takes place in two phases. The first happens before the lesson, and the second occurs after the students have solved the task, but before the discussion begins, once the teacher has access to the students' solution strategies. If a problem is solved and discussed on the same day, the second phase of planning happens in real time, mid-lesson. Experienced responsive teachers often find they can effectively manage this, despite the compression of time, provided they have planned for it ahead of time. Sometimes teachers have students solve the problem one day and then discuss it the following day, giving themselves time to examine student work carefully, select and sequence a few strategies for the whole group investigation, and deliberately plan how they will help students understand and unpack each piece of work. Teachers new to responsive teaching may benefit from this slowed-down approach of splitting the lesson over two days because it preserves time for thinking, processing, and decision-making without the time pressure.

We now explore how to effectively plan the discussion of learner thinking, using the example of Ms. Farrell's lesson plan for her class's investigation of the Chickens and Goats task. As is often the case, Ms. Farrell anticipated some, but not all, the strategies that her students used. Discussion facilitation involves both preparation and skillful improvisation in response to the student strategies that emerge in the moment, always with an eye toward the mathematical goal of the lesson.

Anticipating Student Approaches and Solution Strategies

The first part of this preparation involves understanding the different ways students might approach the task. Since the discussion is built around carefully sequenced selections of student work, anticipating the ways students might solve the task enables the teacher to more fluently decide which work to highlight and in what order. This starts with the teacher solving the task in multiple ways and potentially asking others to do so to capture as much variation in strategies as possible.

Once a variety of possible solutions have been generated, it can be helpful to categorize and name the strategies and then identify which of those strategies support the mathematical goal of the lesson. For example, Ms. Farrell hypothesized that her students might use the following types of approaches:

- Starting out with 14 items and then grouping them into twos and fours until all items are used (using either physical objects or drawn objects like tally marks)
- Using an additive approach, starting with one type of animal and then filling in with the other type (e.g., adding 4 + 4 + 4, then filling in with 2) or simply adding 2s and 4s in random order until they reach 14
- Using a subtractive approach, starting from 14 and deducting 2s and 4s until they reach 4
- Using a guess and check approach, drawing or modeling sets of animals, and then counting to see whether they total 14 legs

- Using a replacement model, starting with one solution and then making swaps to generate more solutions (replacing one goat with 2 chickens or vice versa)
- Listing the multiples of 4 and the multiples of 2, and looking for combinations to make 14

After generating these possible approaches, Ms. Farrell decided that three types of strategies would be most useful for her students to unpack: a grouping model, ideally showing sets of animal legs, an additive strategy or building up to 14 using 2s and 4s, ideally using skip counting; and a listing of multiples approach. She selected these three because each would have the potential to help her build toward her goal of an understanding of the connections between skip counting and equal groups.

Ms. Farrell also thought about how she might intentionally sequence these strategy types to allow all students to enter the conversation and support them in building more abstract understandings. She decided to look for either a physical model or a drawing where she could help students make the connection to skip counting and multiples. Note that in the actual discussion, Ms. Farrell ended up using both a physical model and a drawing since both offered valuable opportunities to make this connection.

Preparing to Help Students Make Sense of the Selected Pieces of Work

After deciding on the types of strategies to look for, teachers then need to consider how they will share each piece of work and support students in unpacking and understanding each strategy. The excerpt from Ms. Farrell's plan shown in Table 4.5 illustrates how she mapped out possible questions to ask to unpack each type of strategy.

Planning to Make the Work Accessible

In addition to thinking about categories of approaches students might use, teachers also need to think about how they will share different kinds of student work with the class. Ms. Farrell decided to use a document camera and/or photos shown on her interactive whiteboard so that all students could see each of the strategies well enough to evaluate them during the discussion. She could have also asked those students to replicate their work on chart paper or the board, or gathered students around a desk to view a physical model.

Planning to Help Students Make Sense of the Shared Work

Teachers also need to consider how they will support the rest of the students in unpacking each type of strategy. This involves generating questions or prompts that will unearth the underlying logic of a strategy. For example,

Table 4.5 Planning How Students Will Make Sense of the Work

Planning for Discussing Learner Thinking

Student Work to Share
 	
• Grouping strategy: Physical model or drawing that shows groups of 4 and groups of 2
• Additive strategy: Solution that uses skip counting (maybe starting with one type of animal then shifting to the other)
• Listing strategy: Listing multiples and using addition to find combinations that work
 	
Making the Work Accessible
 	
• Take a photo of physical models and project (or put model under document camera if small)
• Use document camera for other work
 	
Help Students Make Sense of Work Shared
 	
• Physical model or drawing
   ○ Ask students to make connections between the model and the task.
      • What do the cubes/tally marks represent?
      • Where do you see the goats? Where do you see the chickens? How do you know?
      • Does this represent a solution to the problem? Why or why not?
      • Are these all the solutions?
   ○ Use annotation to show goats and chickens (different color for each)
• Skip Counting
   ○ Focus students on equal groups:
      • What do 4's represent?
      • What do the 2's represent?
      • Where are the goats and chickens?
      • Does this represent a solution to the problem? Why or why not?
   ○ Bridge between the models above and skip counting work:
      • How does this connect to the drawing/model in the first solution?
   ○ Have students interrogate whether this is all of the possible solutions and why:
      • Are these all the solutions?
      • How do you know there cannot be another solution?

(Continued)

Table 4.5 Planning How Students Will Make Sense of the Work *(Continued)*

- Multiples
  - Make sense of the numbers in the list:
    - *What do the numbers on this list represent?*
  - Connect to skip counting
    - *How does this strategy connect to the others?*
    - Use colored markers to show connections (find the same solution across all three strategies)
  - Make sense of the list:
    - *How do we know how many goats or chickens there are?*
    - *How did/could _____ use this list to find combinations of goats and chickens that work?*
    - *Do the solutions shown here work? Are there others? How do you know?*
    - Incorporate the word "multiples"

Ms. Farrell anticipated her class might need help connecting the various solutions to the problem context—to see the goats and chickens in each solution strategy. She considered how annotation could help students make connections between different student strategies (i.e., how she might use color to highlight the same combination of goats and chickens across all three strategies).

An equally important goal is to help the class understand the mathematical insights that can be gained from each strategy. To do this, teachers can generate questions that are likely to bring out key mathematical concepts or vocabulary (e.g., multiples in Ms. Farrell's plan). As the vignettes illustrate, Ms. Farrell did not always end up asking the exact questions that she articulated in her plan. Rather, the plan for discussing learner thinking serves as a roadmap to ensure that the facilitation of the discussion draws out key mathematical ideas, while still being responsive to student noticing and questions that arise in the moment. Although the discussion may look different than planned, the plan anchors and steers the discussion, helping the teacher more efficiently choose strategies and representations and use questioning to advance student thinking toward the mathematical goal of the lesson.

Building a House of Bricks: Why It's Worth the Time

Responsive mathematics teaching takes time—time to launch a task, time for students to grapple with the task and experiment with different solution paths, and, as described in this chapter, time to engage students in a meaningful discussion that helps them make connections between solution strategies and important mathematics concepts. Teachers sometimes express that they cannot afford to spend that much time focusing on a single task, or that they feel compelled to rush the discussion or narrow it to a single best strategy for the sake of expediency. The guiding principles of responsive teaching in Chapter 1, however, remind us of the critical importance of giving students space for *sensemaking* and *engaging in a collaborative community*. Those priorities lie at the core of discussing learner thinking and justify the dedication of significant class time to a single task and to the discussion of student work.

A robust discussion about a single high-quality task can foster a richer conceptual understanding than a dozen similar practice problems or workbook pages. Less truly can mean more when a teacher skillfully manages the discussion to engage students in sensemaking and then gradually builds a bridge from their current understanding to a more sophisticated grasp of key mathematical concepts. This slowing down is akin to building the house of bricks in the fairy tale, *The Three Little Pigs*. Student learning may take longer to construct, but it is far more durable than the house of straw that is built from surface-level understanding or fleeting facility with procedures. Giving students time to productively struggle with tasks, as described in Chapter 3, is the building's foundation: it serves as a starting point for conceptual understanding. The discussion is the building's brickwork: a solid structure constructed through the time spent making sense of strategies and ideas. The connection between these ideas and the key mathematical goals becomes invaluable support for future learning.

A well-executed discussion can also generate communal resources that the class can draw from and build upon in future discussions—shared language, strategies, and experiences that can serve as a reference point for other mathematical conversations, making future lessons easier to grasp. These resources serve as mortar, further reinforcing student understanding and uniting individual ideas into a cohesive whole.

In addition to taking time to execute, facilitating discussions of learner thinking may also be one of the most challenging parts of responsive teaching because it involves both careful planning and skillful improvisation. Teachers new to responsive teaching often find that students come up with strategies they do not anticipate, requiring improvisation that can be hard to navigate in the moment. It can also feel difficult to know how to surface the important mathematics from the work that students produce. Novice responsive teachers can develop and hone discussion facilitation skills gradually—initially starting with some stock questions such as, "Is this a viable solution? How do you know?" or generic moves like asking one student to restate what another has shared, and then gradually adding in more moves, refining the ability to see and draw out connections among students' strategies and to important mathematical ideas. However, it is crucial to resist the temptation to move things along more expeditiously by focusing on a single or best piece of student work, conducting the discussion as a show-and-tell with little space for sensemaking, or demonstrating a teacher-preferred, efficient approach to students. Doing so may get to the solution more quickly, but it deprives students of the opportunity to talk about and make sense of mathematical ideas and, in turn, reorganize and distill their understanding.

Opting for the slower and arguably messier route of building discussions around students' work—replete with false starts, errors, and flaws—normalizes the trial, error, and revision inherent in mathematics, reframes mathematics as a subject with multiple access points, and affirms the value of diverse thinking. When done well, responsive discussions of learner thinking encourage risk-taking and experimentation by cultivating a mathematical community where ideas are jointly owned, examined, and unpacked together with safeguards in place to protect and build positive mathematics identities (see Chapter 7 for more on cultivating a responsive mathematics community). Effective discussions of learner thinking also help build a mathematical community in which all students are positioned as competent with worthwhile ideas. Equally important, however, is to ensure that all students understand the important mathematical ideas and can draw on them to make future lessons easier to grasp. This explicit focus on connecting, consolidating, and reflecting on the lesson is the focus of the next chapter.

Reflection Questions

Teacher Responsibilities	Guiding Principles
1 Determine which student ideas the discussion will focus on	1 Prioritize mathematical sensemaking
2 Get a learner's idea or strategy out in the open	2 Promote collaborative learning communities
3 Help others engage with the idea/strategy	3 Support a positive mathematical identity
4 Leverage the discussion to surface important mathematics	4 Ensure all students have access to mathematics

1 How do each of the teacher responsibilities of discussing learning thinking address the guiding principles of responsive teaching?

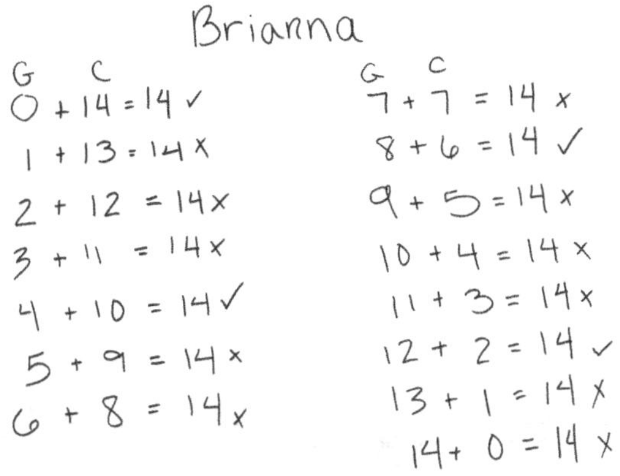

Brianna

```
 G   C                      G   C
 0 + 14 = 14 ✓              7 + 7 = 14 ✗
 1 + 13 = 14 ✗              8 + 6 = 14 ✓
 2 + 12 = 14 ✗              9 + 5 = 14 ✗
 3 + 11 = 14 ✗             10 + 4 = 14 ✗
 4 + 10 = 14 ✓             11 + 3 = 14 ✗
 5 + 9  = 14 ✗             12 + 2 = 14 ✓
 6 + 8  = 14 ✗             13 + 1 = 14 ✗
                           14 + 0 = 14 ✗
```

Figure 4.10 Brianna's work on the Chicken and Goats task.

2 Consider Brianna's work on the Chickens and Goats task (Figure 4.10).

   a What would it look like to facilitate a discussion of her ideas responsively?

   b What might it look like if a discussion of Brianna's work was not facilitated responsively?

3 As you think about discussing learning thinking into your instructional context:

   a What is already in place that you can build on?

   b What challenges do you foresee?

   c What can you do to try to overcome those challenges?

4 What are you taking away from this chapter that you can try in your own instruction?

5

Connecting, Consolidating, and Reflecting on Evidence of Student Learning

Eliciting, representing, and discussing multiple solution strategies are essential components of a responsive mathematics lesson, but once those strategies have been explored in depth, what is the next step? How can teachers ensure students understand multiple ways of solving a task and learn the mathematics they need to know? How can teachers help students solidify, extend, and apply their understanding of the central mathematical ideas and concepts that informed the design of the lesson? How can teachers determine whether students need more support, or experience, before moving on to the next lesson or a new task? These are the central questions explored in this chapter, as we think about the teacher's responsibilities in supporting the critical processes during the wrap-up portion of a responsive problem-solving lesson—connecting, consolidating, and reflecting on evidence of student learning.

To better understand what the end of a responsive lesson could look, feel, and sound like, we look back at third-grade teacher Mr. Cooper's lesson using the Sharing Crackers task, first introduced in Chapter 3, to see how he closes out the lesson.

Sharing Crackers

> There are 36 crackers in a box. The crackers are to be shared equally among friends. What are all the different ways friends can share the 36 crackers? How do you know that you found all of the different ways?
>
> (Boaler et al., 2018, p. 78)

DOI: 10.4324/9781003536710-5

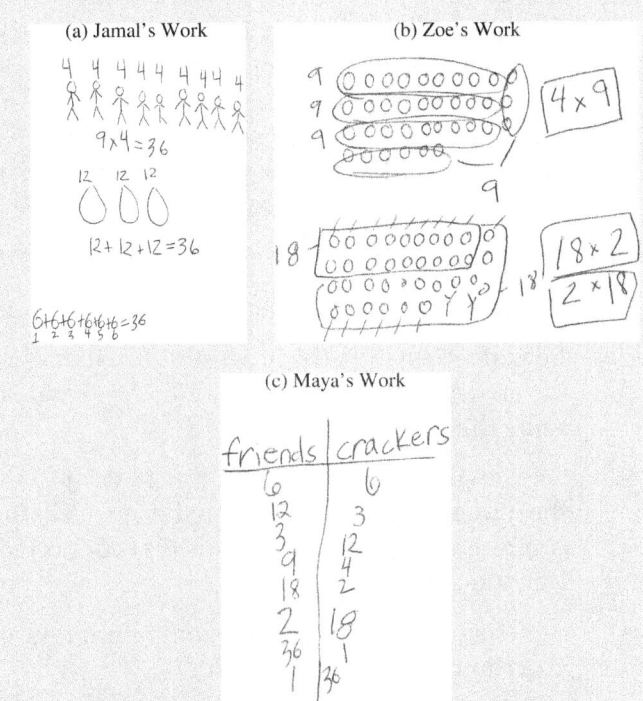

Figure 5.1 Three student solutions to the Sharing Crackers task.

After his students had made progress on finding multiple solutions for this task, Mr. Cooper engages them in a discussion of the three pieces of student work shown in Figure 5.1, surfacing ideas about the relationships between repeated addition, multiplication, and division, and the notion that the commutative property can be used when finding factor pairs. Mr. Cooper wants to help students formalize their emerging understanding of the commutative property by layering on mathematical vocabulary and highlighting where this was evident in the work discussed. Several students made comments during the discussion that Mr. Cooper thinks he can build upon as he wraps up the lesson.

Mr. Cooper: We have looked at three ways to approach this problem. Jamal used addition. Zoe used a drawing to make equal groups, and Maya made a table showing the number of friends and crackers each friend would get. Kai said something a few minutes ago that I want us to think about again. When we looked at Zoe's solution, Kai said, "She did not have to draw another picture because she knew 18 groups would have to have 2 crackers because she already figured out 2 × 18." Kai noticed that if 2 × 18 = 36, we also know 18 × 2 = 36. (He writes the two equations on the board.) This reminds me of something we talked about a few months ago. (He writes 5 + 7 = 12 and 7 + 5 = 12 on the board.) Does anyone remember when we talked about properties of addition and looked at equations like this? (Several students nod. Others look perplexed.) What do you remember?

Aleem: When you add, the numbers can be in any order.

Mr. Cooper: Can anyone build on what Aleem has just told us?

Kyra: Like, if you switch the order around, it does not change the answer. You could do 5 + 7 or 7 + 5 and still get the same thing.

Mr. Cooper: So changing the order of the things we add together, or the addends, does not change the sum. That is called the commutative property. How is that connected to what Kai noticed about 2 and 18?

Aleem: It is basically the same thing, only with multiplication. You can put them in any order.

Mr. Cooper: What does Aleem mean by "put them in any order?"

Ray: The things you are multiplying together, like the addends. You can switch the order of the numbers and get the same answer.

Mr. Cooper: So you are telling me the Commutative Property works with multiplication, too? [Ray looks nervous and shrugs.]

Mr. Cooper: Hmm. Sounds like what we have here is a theory we are not quite sure about. What do others think? Give me a thumbs up if you think the Commutative Property works for multiplication too, a thumbs down if you think that is not true, and a wavy hand if you are unsure.

[A few students show thumbs up, one shows a thumbs down, and there are lots of wavy hands.]

Mr. Cooper asks the class to take another look at the work on the board to find evidence of whether the commutative property works for multiplication. Students point out the 4 groups of 9 and 9 groups of 4 in Jamal's work. Mr. Cooper records $4 \times 9 = 36$ and $9 \times 4 = 36$ on the board. Other students spot examples from Maya's work, and Mr. Cooper records them on the board. He then asks students what other answer Jamal could have come up with if the commutative property worked for multiplication. A student recognizes that since Jamal found 3 groups of 12, he could also use 12 groups of 3. This launches the class into an interesting discussion of whether 1×36 is a solution. Can one person share 36 crackers? The students decide that this would not qualify as sharing. Mr. Cooper notes that this is a good example of considering the meaning of the quantities in a problem, an important thing that good problem solvers always do.

With just a few minutes left in the class period, Mr. Cooper is happy with how the discussion has wrapped up and is encouraged by the group's ability to make the connection to the commutative property that he hoped would emerge from this task. He realizes, however, that he does not yet know the extent to which individual students have made this connection or their ability to apply the property of commutativity. He asks students to take out their mathematics journals and answer two questions, which he also writes on the board:

- How would you explain the commutative property to a friend?
- What are some ways 24 crackers could be shared equally among friends?

Mr. Cooper encourages students to think about the approaches they just discussed and incorporate their classmates' ideas. From the first question, he hopes to understand students' emerging understanding of the commutative property for multiplication. Mr. Cooper plans to compare their responses to the second question to their work on the 36-cracker problem to see if they use any new strategies. Ideally, he wants to see evidence that students recognize that they can use the commutative property to generate pairs of solutions (e.g., if 2×12 works, then 12×2 will also work). He plans to use the evidence from this exit ticket to determine whether his goals for this lesson were met, for which students, and whether he needs to adjust his plans moving forward.

Why is Connecting, Consolidating, and Reflecting Important for Student Learning?

The end of a lesson is an ideal time to take stock of learners' developing understanding, provide additional support to help them solidify, synthesize, or extend that understanding, and make informed decisions about next instructional steps. To ensure that every student has adequate access to mathematics, teachers must continually help students progress from their current and often incomplete understanding of a mathematical concept to a more sophisticated, nuanced understanding. This involves providing opportunities for students to form new or stronger connections to key mathematical concepts, integrate different ideas that have been shared into a coherent whole, and to express their developing understanding of those ideas. Connecting new knowledge to prior knowledge, applying it in new situations, and reflecting on its meaning have all been shown to promote consolidation and deep learning (Sousa, 2022). In addition to strengthening student learning, engaging in these processes provides valuable information for both teachers and students, which can guide future adjustments and refinements to instruction.

Providing students with opportunities to make explicit connections to mathematical concepts is essential for learning mathematics with understanding (Hiebert & Grouws, 2007). However, teachers cannot simply provide those connections for students, or leave it to chance, hoping that students will make the connections on their own. Instead, teachers can help narrow the focus from making sense of many different solution strategies and ideas to zoom in on salient features of the solutions that are related to the mathematical goal. By guiding, scaffolding, and steering the wrap-up discussion, teachers can draw out key points, layering on vocabulary or ways of representing mathematical ideas and asking questions to help bridge between students' nascent ideas to a more sophisticated and coherent conceptual understanding. Meaningful connections and sensemaking can be fostered in ways that build mathematical agency and confidence by prompting students to reflect on the meaning behind procedures, compare different solution strategies, or make connections between concepts, tasks, or activities.

Sometimes teachers may need to take a more direct role in helping students to formalize or generalize their ideas. For example, they may interject a counterexample that will promote further justification or revision, or introduce standard mathematical vocabulary, ways of recording, symbolic notation, or conventions. These are things that learners are unlikely to discover or develop on their own, and when introduced at the right time, can help them move forward productively along the trajectory of learning and understanding. At the same time, responsive teaching involves prioritizing sensemaking by ensuring learners always maintain ownership over their learning. Introducing new ideas should move the discussion in a productive direction without providing a prescription to follow or diminishing student agency.

During a responsive mathematics lesson, students will be exposed to many ideas and strategies, some more fully formed and explored than others. Taking time at the end of the lesson to focus in on a few important mathematical ideas and help learners make those ideas more explicit, organized, and connected can help them solidify and deepen their learning. In the context of mathematical activity, consolidation involves a learner combining several ideas into a more cohesive entity that is stronger than the sum of its parts, which then becomes a foundation from which to solve future problems (Liljedahl, 2020).

Reflection and communication are processes central to learning; learners need to both individually make sense of concepts and relationships and explain or justify those ideas to others (Hiebert, 1997). Engaging in written reflection and discussion helps learners consolidate knowledge and facilitate the transfer of that knowledge to new situations (Sousa, 2022). If we do not prioritize connecting, consolidating, and reflecting at the end of a lesson, we risk creating a mathematical learning community where students feel good about their contributions, but may not get to the deeper understanding that builds their capacity for more advanced mathematics. Learners will need different levels of support to feel successful and reach new levels of understanding. While some will make the connections on their own, many will require intentional support from the teacher to recognize and make sense of the underlying relationships.

By providing opportunities for students to connect, consolidate, and reflect on the mathematical concepts and relationships that emerge during the lesson, teachers will have rich sources of evidence to draw on to determine the extent to which students are making progress toward the goals of a lesson, unit, or grade level. This in turn, helps inform decisions about future instruction.

> The fact that students can do something at the end of today's lesson does not guarantee that they will be able to do it in two weeks' time, but if they cannot do something at the end of today's lesson, it is rather unlikely that they will be able to do it in two weeks' time. Better evidence leads to better decisions which in turn leads to better learning.
> (Wiliam, 2021)

Being intentional about collecting and analyzing the evidence of what students can do at the end of the lesson is, therefore, another important part of responsive mathematics teaching. It provides the connective tissue between lessons, making it a cyclical and continuous improvement process for both learners and teachers. Connecting, consolidating, and reflecting on evidence of student learning serves as both a culmination of the collaborative learning community's work and a time to take stock and consider how to continue to move productively toward grade-level goals.

CONNECTING, CONSOLIDATING, AND REFLECTING ON EVIDENCE OF STUDENT LEARNING	
What It Is	**What It Is Not**
• Helping students synthesize the strategies and ideas surfaced in the discussion • Making connections from student strategies to a more standard procedure • Layering more formal mathematical vocabulary or symbolic notation onto student generated ideas • Providing learners with opportunities to reflect on and communicate their understandings of key mathematical goals or objectives • Assessing evidence of students' developing understanding of the key mathematics to be learned	• Allowing the lesson to end wherever the students' ideas land • Convincing students to use a preferred solution or strategy • Introducing mathematical vocabulary or symbolic notation before it is needed or relevant to learners • Presenting the mathematical goals or objectives of the lesson to learners • Administering a test or quiz to determine if students have mastered the lesson content

Connecting, Consolidating, and Reflecting: The Role of the Teacher

At the end of a responsive mathematics problem-solving lesson, the teacher's role shifts somewhat, from eliciting and building on student thinking to more directly connecting student thinking to the central mathematical ideas, relationships, or concepts that the lesson was designed to address. Learners may also need additional time to try out, practice, and reflect on those ideas or concepts before moving on to the next lesson or task in the curriculum. To determine when it is appropriate to move on, the teacher will need some way to evaluate learners' progress toward the mathematical goals of the lesson and identify areas where more support is needed. Thus, the responsibilities of the responsive mathematics teacher at the end of a lesson are threefold:

1   Help learners make explicit connections from strategies that have been discussed to key mathematical ideas and goals of the lesson

2   Provide opportunities for learners to solidify those connections and consolidate their understanding

3   Collect evidence of student understanding to inform subsequent instruction.

Although we explore these responsibilities separately in the following sections, they often occur simultaneously and in concert with each other.

The First Responsibility: Help Learners Make Explicit Connections to the Mathematical Goals

Helping learners make explicit connections to the mathematical goals of the lesson is in many ways an extension the last responsibility of discussing learning thinking explored in Chapter 4—surfacing the important mathematics behind each strategy that is shared. The main difference is that the focus shifts from unearthing the mathematical ideas in specific examples of learner thinking to more intentionally making connections across the solutions and strategies that have been explored. In this portion of the lesson, the teacher's role is to shine a spotlight on important ideas and build a bridge to essential concepts by restating, summarizing, or naming them. In the vignette, for example, Mr. Cooper focused on an important idea that Kai had noticed about Zoe's solution, drew a connection to a concept students already understood about addition (naming it as the commutative property), and then prompted them to see if the same idea applied to the operation of multiplication.

We have found it helpful to think about the teacher moves for making explicit connections to the mathematical goals in relation to the different purposes a teacher may have, depending on the context of the lesson, where it falls in the curriculum, and how students have responded to the task (Table 5.1). Teachers do not need to use all these types of moves at the end of a lesson; rather, one or more types of moves may be more appropriate depending on the concepts or goals of the lesson. The types of moves the teacher can use to get students to reflect on the work done and articulate their developing understanding may differ depending on the expected knowledge, understanding, or proficiency.

Highlighting moves can help learners focus their attention on the important concepts embedded in or emerging from the discussion of solution strategies. These moves are an important way to help learners synthesize and consolidate new learning and are appropriate for all types of learning goals. They are often the first moves used in a wrap-up discussion to narrow the group's focus from many different strategies and ideas to key features of student work connected to the mathematical goal. This is an opportunity for the teacher to pose directed questions or summarize important ideas that have

Table 5.1 Connecting, Consolidating, and Reflecting Tool, Responsibility #1

Responsibility #1: Help Learners Make Connections to Explicitly Bridge Their Thinking and Strategies to the Mathematical Goals	
Highlighting Moves focus learners on the key mathematical ideas and concepts that emerge	
Invite students to explain a key concept or idea	• Turn and talk to your partner and see if you can explain how 23 times 6 is the same as 20 times 6 plus 3 times 6 • When we find the mean, what is that really telling us about the data? • Thinking about the work we did today, how do you know when two fractions are equivalent?
Summarize a key concept or idea	• Today we saw how making groups of 10 was a helpful way to organize our collections so we can count accurately. • So the rate of change, or how fast it is growing, is the same value as the slope of the line.
Draw explicit connections between concepts or ideas	• Does that remind you of anything we did yesterday? • In both Lara's visual model and Sammi's equation, we can see that we needed to split the original third into fourths, which is how we ended up with twelfths in both strategies.
Elicit remaining uncertainties around key concepts or ideas	• What parts of this strategy are still confusing for you? • Is anyone else not convinced that the volume will remain the same?
Analyzing moves engage learners in understanding and evaluating strategies, approaches, or procedures	
Connect ideas and concepts across student strategies or solutions	• Where do you see the idea of doubling in all these drawings? • How does the graph that Briana drew help us see the way the numbers are changing in Gill's table? • One thing I noticed when I was walking around was that everyone was breaking numbers apart into easier chunks.
Support flexibility by encouraging learners to compare and contrast strategies	• What makes compensation a good strategy to use for the numbers in this problem? • Let's look at all the different ways that people used representations to make sense of this problem. Which representations do you find most helpful? • When would counting back be more efficient than counting up?

(Continued)

Table 5.1 Connecting, Consolidating, and Reflecting Tool, Responsibility #1 *(Continued)*

Generalizing moves support students to engage in mathematical reasoning and justification to develop a useful strategy, mathematical truth or principle	
Ask students to articulate and generalize patterns and relationships	• *Do you see any patterns in our solutions?* • *What do you notice about the relationship between the total number of cubes and the number of groups of ten?* • *Let's look at the table. How could we write an equation to represent that relationship?*
Have students prove or disprove conjectures, arguments, or theories	• *Janine said we can't subtract a larger number from a smaller number. Do you agree or disagree?* • *Can you think of an example where that wouldn't be true?* • *What if we had different numbers? Would this still work?*
Formalizing moves provide learners with standard language, notation, and conventions that they can draw upon	
Introduce mathematical vocabulary to label an idea a learner is using or expressing	• *That number we are dividing by each time-- mathematicians call that a "divisor."* • *Today, we made different objects with cubes and compared them by the amount of space they take up. We call this volume.*
Introduce standard recording methods or representations for learner-generated strategies	• *Now I'm going to show a new way to record those steps.* • *How can we show Jamir's strategy using an area model?* • *When we arrange solutions in tables sometimes we can see patterns we otherwise might not be able to see.*
Introduce symbolic notation	• *Mathematicians use this symbol to show that we are dividing the number into equal shares.* • *So, if we insert parentheses here into Katrina's number sentence, then we will know to do the computation in the order she wants us to.*

emerged through the discussion of learner thinking. Following a highlighting move with a prompt for students to "turn and talk" can be an effective way to ensure broader engagement with the central ideas of a lesson. Mr. Cooper began the wrap-up discussion by summarizing the various approaches students had taken to solve the Sharing Crackers task. He then highlighted a comment made by Kai as student work was being discussed, "She didn't have to draw another picture because she knew 18 groups would have to have 2 crackers because she already figured out that $2 \times 18 = 36$" to focus the students' attention on the commutative relationship. Highlighting this moment in the larger discussion of student work enabled Mr. Cooper to transition the class from talking about lots of ideas to zero in on his mathematical goal.

Analyzing moves engage learners in understanding and evaluating strategies, approaches, or procedures. These moves can be helpful when the learning goal focuses on developing procedural fluency (accuracy, efficiency, and flexibility) or strategic competence (the ability to formulate, represent, and solve problems) (National Research Council (NRC), 2001). Students in Mr. Cooper's class employed various strategies when tackling the Sharing Crackers task. Some used physical models, making groups of beans to represent the crackers being shared. Others drew pictures of equal groups, used repeated addition or skip counting, or made lists of known factor pairs. If Mr. Cooper's goal for the lesson had been build on students' understanding to develop division strategies, he could have used analyzing moves to prompt students to compare these different methods, focusing on how equal groups are represented in each, for example.

Generalizing moves help learners move from making sense of specific solutions to noticing and articulating broader patterns and relationships, including properties of operations. They can support adaptive reasoning, or the ability to use logical thought to prove or disprove conjectures, arguments, or theories (NRC, 2001). Mr. Cooper used generalizing moves to build conceptual understanding of the commutative property. In his wrap-up discussion, he encouraged students to look across the student work shared for examples of commutativity, drawing out a list of equation pairs. He also asked students to build on and extend the students' answers by using the commutative property to suggest other factor pairs not on their initial lists. He could have extended the conversation with additional generalizing moves like, "Will that always work? How do you know?" or by asking students if they thought this property would also hold for division. An overall goal of generalizing moves is to help learners extract ideas from their work on a particular task to generate and own a strategy, truth, or principle that they can draw upon to solve other problems or tasks.

Formalizing moves are used when the teacher inserts or introduces information in the form of vocabulary, representations, or symbolic notation to bridge learners' ideas with the conventions of mathematics as a discipline. Mr. Cooper reintroduced the concept of commutativity in his wrap-up discussion, activating the group's prior learning about the commutative property of addition. Had Mr. Cooper had a different goal for the lesson, formalizing moves could have been used to introduce vocabulary related to division (e.g., quotient, divisor) or symbolic notation for division. These moves can also introduce standard or practical ways of recording the steps in a process or procedure. For example, if students are adding multi-digit numbers by decomposing and recomposing the quantities by place value, the teacher might introduce the partial sums method to record and keep track of the parts that are being added.

To explore these moves in more depth, we turn to a different example from an eighth-grade class where the students had been exploring linear relationships, or situations with a constant rate of change.

The Pizza Task

Ms. Oliver was having her eighth-grade students solve the following task that she found in her curriculum materials:

> A restaurant offers delivery for its pizzas. The total cost is a flat delivery fee added to the price of the pizzas. One customer pays $25 to have 2 pizzas delivered. Another customer pays $58 for 5 pizzas. How many pizzas are delivered to a customer who pays $80?
>
> (Illustrative Math, Grade 8, Lesson 3.5)

Before you read on, taking a few minutes to solve this task for yourself may be helpful.

After giving students a few minutes to grapple with the task individually, Ms. Oliver had her students work in groups of three. Each group worked collaboratively to solve the task and record their final solution on chart paper to share with the class. As she facilitated their productive struggle on the task, she was pleased to see that students were engaged and excited to figure out the problem, and the context seemed to be a relevant and accessible way for them to think about a rate of change. Several groups started by choosing a cost for one pizza and then adjusting the delivery fee to make it sum to the total but then had to readjust when the situation changed for five pizzas. In the end, every group figured out that the pizzas must each cost $11 with a $3 delivery charge to reach the given totals, and therefore, seven pizzas would cost $80 or $(7 \times 11) + 3$.

Knowing that she wanted her students to be able to identify that the $11 was the rate of change and the delivery fee was a constant, as she circulated, Ms. Oliver prompted groups to see if they could write an equation to represent the cost of getting any amount of pizzas delivered. For the last portion of the class, she had the students participate in a gallery walk where they stood up and rotated in groups around the room, studying each solution to make sense of other groups' thinking and writing questions or comments on sticky notes (Figure 5.2).

Although Ms. Oliver was confident that her students understood how to solve the task, had communicated their thinking clearly on the posters, and were making sense of the different ways that other groups had solved the problem, she was not sure that they were all engaging with the key ideas about linear relationships. She decided to wrap up the discussion by calling students over to gather around a poster where, after her prompting, Kyle and Savannah had written the equation $y = 11x + 3$ next to the table they had

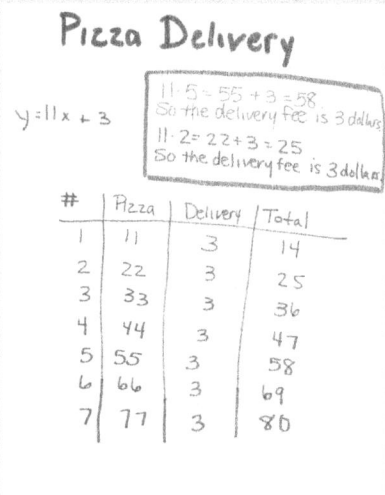

Figure 5.2 Kyle and Savannah's Poster.

constructed. She intentionally chose this work to focus on because Kyle and Savannah were not always confident about sharing their thinking. After hitting some roadblocks, they used a systematic approach to create a table and find a solution. Moreover, their table illustrated how the price changed as the number of pizzas increased.

After asking the other students to make sense of the table Kyle and Savannah had shown on their poster and eliciting the idea that the cost increased by $11 in each row, Ms. Oliver focuses the students on the written equation $y = 11x + 3$.

Ms. Oliver:	What can you tell me about this equation? Take a minute to think about it, and then everyone be ready with one thing to share. (waits) Desiree? What is one thing?
Desiree:	The 11 is the m and the 3 is the b.
Ms. Oliver:	(writes $y = mx + b$ on a sticky note and puts it above $y = 11x + 3$). Okay, so let's unpack that a bit. What does it mean that 11 is the m?
Desiree:	Slope?
Ms. Oliver:	So Desiree is reminding us that the m means the slope. How does that relate to the problem? Where are the pizzas and the people? Tia?
Tia:	Well, the 11 is really the rate of change, like how much it's changing when you go to the next one.
Ms. Oliver:	The next what?
Tia:	I don't know what you mean.
Ms. Oliver:	Let's pause for a sec. Do we agree that the 11 is the rate of change? Give me a thumbs up if you agree, thumbs down if you do not agree, and a shaky hand if you are not sure. (waits) Okay, Tia, it looks like we have some agrees and some are not sure that the 11 is the rate of change. So my question is, what is it that's changing?
Tia:	The price. I mean not the price. Like the total price. How much you pay. Wait, now I am confused.
Ms. Oliver:	Anyone else feeling confused right now? (waits and nods as a few people raise their hands) Can anyone help clear things up? What is that 11?
Tia:	It's the cost of a pizza.

Ms. Oliver:	Okay, so the 11 is the cost of one pizza, and what is the x? Kyle?
Kyle:	We put this on our chart, actually. So, the 11 is the cost per pizza, and the x is how many pizzas you are getting. So two pizzas are 2 times 11, three pizzas are 3 times 11, or whatever. So every time you get another pizza, you add another $11 to the price. Or the total. Like what you pay.
Ms. Oliver:	I think what is tripping us up here is that there is a price for one pizza, and Tia and Kyle both told us that is $11. Then there is how much money you actually hand to the pizza guy—the total that you owe. Can we call that something else, like the total cost? Is that helpful?
Tia:	(nods) Yeah. So the pizza price does not change, but the total cost changes by $11 every time you get another pizza.
Ms. Oliver:	Tia, that's a really nice explanation of how the rate of change is working here. Every additional pizza makes the total cost go up by $11. So the total cost increases by $11 as x gets bigger. So Desiree's point earlier about that 11 being the slope makes sense. Can you picture that line going up by 11 in the y direction as the x values get bigger? (waits, a few students nod) Where does the total cost show up in this equation? Let's take a moment to turn and talk. Talk to your partner about how the equation represents the total cost of the pizza delivery.

In this example, Ms. Oliver used several types of connecting moves. As they were developing their solutions, she primed students for the discussion by using *generalizing* moves as she circulated to talk to groups about their work, prompting them to look for patterns, write an equation, or identify what value was changing. Then, in the whole group discussion she used *analyzing* moves to support student reflection on the meaning of the rate of change in both the context of the problem ($11 per pizza) and the slope-intercept form of an equation ($y = mx + b$), asking "What does it mean that 11 is the m?" and "Desiree's reminding us that the m means the slope. How does that relate to the problem?"

She then employed a series of *highlighting* moves to elicit remaining uncertainty. Even though Tia confidently stated that 11 was the rate of change, her hesitation after being asked what was changing prompted Ms. Oliver to invite students to "give me a shaky hand if you are unsure" and then ask, "anyone else feeling confused right now?" These moves prompted deeper reflection and normalized confusion as an important part of learning while bringing the important concept to the forefront. She then framed it as a collective question ("I think what is tripping us up here is that there is a price for one pizza … then there is how much money you actually hand to the pizza guy"), followed by a *formalizing* move to introduce the term "total cost." This terminology supported Tia's ability to articulate her understanding of what was changing: "So the pizza price does not change, but the total cost changes by $11 every time you get another pizza."

After complimenting Tia's explanation, Ms. Oliver further *highlighted* the big idea. She began by summarizing it in her own words. She then asked students to imagine the slope of the line, drawing explicit connections to their understanding of graphing, and then asking them to identify the total cost in the equation. Finally, she asked all students to articulate their understanding of the big idea by having them turn and talk about "how the equation represents the total cost of the pizza delivery."

Through this combination of analyzing, generalizing, formalizing, and highlighting moves, Ms. Oliver transitioned her students from thinking about the price of the pizza that worked in this context ($11 per pizza) to a more generalized and abstract understanding of rate of change and the meaning of the slope-intercept form of a linear equation ($y = mx + b$). Without this focused wrap-up, the lesson could have been about figuring out how many pizzas could be bought with $80 in a hypothetical situation, rather than understanding key ideas about linear relationships. Ms. Oliver could have been happy that all the groups got the correct answer and ended the lesson there. However, by engaging all students in formalizing and generalizing, she gave them access to some important mathematical ideas central to understanding linear relationships and graphs.

The Second Responsibility: Provide Opportunities for Learners to Solidify Connections and Consolidate Their Understanding

The use of connecting moves at the end of a discussion is an important way to help learners focus on the mathematical ideas that emerge from working on a challenging task. However, they will still need individual reflection and communication time to cement their understanding. In the Japanese approach of teaching through problem solving, the final stage of a lesson is engaging students in *matome*, or "summing up" their learning (Watanabe, 2021). In this phase, the teacher's role is to review, summarize, and support students to reflect on and summarize the key ideas that emerged. The teacher restates and writes a summary on the board, using student voice as much as possible, and prompting students to record their learning in their journals. Sometimes the teacher has students solve additional problems to extend and support increased levels of mathematical sophistication.

Setting time aside for this kind of consolidation and reflection at the end of the lesson does not mean that learning will be finished or neatly wrapped up, or that all students will have made sense of the mathematics similarly. Some may have lingering questions, confusion, or be at early or developing stages of understanding. These are all normal and productive aspects of learning and need to be recognized as such, rather than avoided. Allowing students to express their understanding and confusion enables the teacher to gather evidence to inform instruction. It is also a way for students to develop their awareness of their progress in relation to the learning goal.

In our work with teachers who are implementing responsive problem-solving lessons, we focus on five pathways that can be productive to pursue at the end of a mathematics lesson to help learners consolidate and reflect on their learning, shown in Table 5.2: (1) collaboratively create a record of collective learning; (2) conduct a targeted gallery walk; (3) have students revise their work; (4) engage students in written reflection; or (5) provide a new, but slightly different task or set of tasks to solve. Each of these pathways has different goals and affordances, and various approaches could be taken within each pathway.

Creating Collaborative Charts

Creating a chart that reflects the collective learning of the class helps students consolidate their developing knowledge, enabling them to draw on it in the future. These charts should be designed to intentionally support ongoing learning and growth. To do this, they must be developed collaboratively with students, authentically reflecting and building on their learning. Collaborative charts can be used to record shared definitions or explanations of concepts. For example, a fourth-grade teacher had her students explore equivalent fractions by drawing models on chart paper. After discussing selected posters of their work, she asked them to help her create the chart in Figure 5.3 to represent what they had learned about equivalence. She first asked, "Tell me what you know about equivalent fractions," and then wrote down three definitions they came up with, using their own words to craft something that was both mathematically correct and accessible. Then she asked them to choose some illustrative examples from the drawings they had made. To further push on their thinking, she asked them how she could draw examples that were not equivalent. She then hung this chart in the classroom so they could refer to their understanding of equivalence, visually and in words, while continuing

Table 5.2 Connecting, Consolidating, and Reflecting Tool: Responsibility #2

Responsibility #2: Provide Opportunities for Learners to Solidify Connections, Consolidate, and Reflect	
Collaboratively create a **record of collective learning**	• Develop class definitions of important concepts (e.g., mean, median, and mode) with illustrations. • Record concepts, ideas, or strategies that emerged through the discussion of learners.' • Represent multiple strategies that could be used to solve similar problems or multiple solutions to a task that illustrates an important pattern.
Conduct **a targeted gallery walk**	• Ask students to look for evidence of something in other posters. • Find a solution that is different from yours and compare and contrast. • Post notes on anything that is unclear or that you have questions about.
Have students **re-examine and revise** their work	• Make the work clear and understandable. • Craft a more convincing argument. • Revise mistakes or add to incomplete ideas • Add additional solutions. • Look for patterns or generalize a pattern or rule.
Engage students in **reflection** on content and/or process	• Summarize learning: *What is something you learned today? What do you still have questions about?* • Understanding of specific concepts: *In your own words, what makes a relationship proportional?* • Mindset: *How do you feel about being called on to share your thinking? What's it like to listen to other people's strategies?* • Group process: *How well did your group work together?*
Provide a new task that requires students to apply or extend their understanding	• Pose a similar task situated within a different context (e.g., if students have been solving an add to, result unknown problem, give them a change unknown problem). • Adjust the complexity of the quantities in the task.

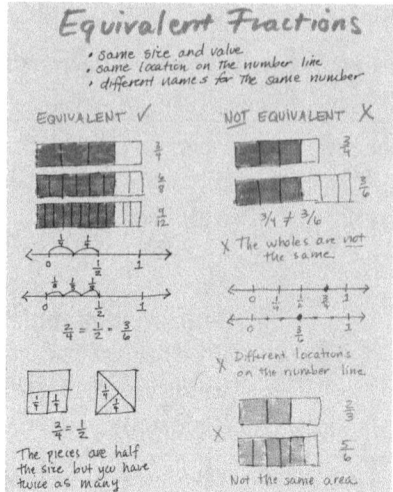

Figure 5.3 A chart to summarize the collective understanding of equivalent fractions.

to work with fractions. In this way, the chart represented their learning and became a tool to support further learning.

Mr. Cooper created the chart in Figure 5.4 after the Sharing Crackers lesson. He captured his students' articulation of the commutative property and the two examples they generated as a visual reminder of how commutativity works. As the class made the chart, Mr. Cooper reviewed the terms "addend" and "sum." He also introduced new terms, "factor" and "product" to help them communicate more effectively, saying, "These are the terms that

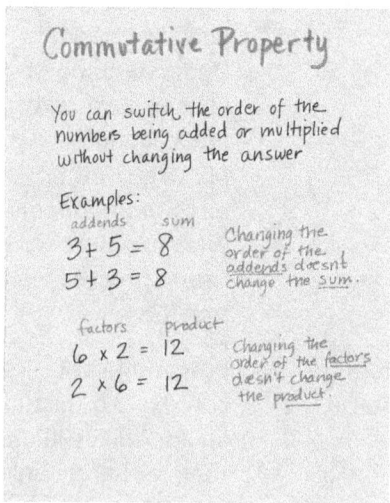

Figure 5.4 Mr. Cooper's chart on the commutative property.

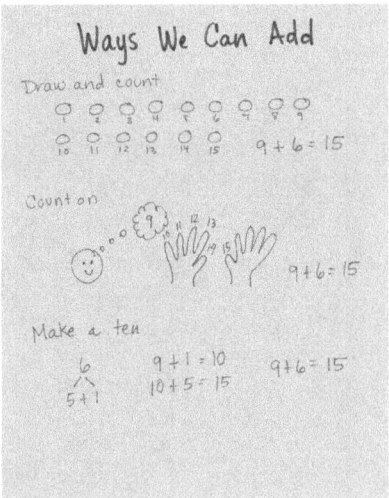

Figure 5.5 A chart of addition strategies.

mathematicians use to talk about these numbers in a multiplication problem" adding the text on the chart and capturing the group's re-articulation of the commutative property using this new vocabulary. Importantly, he did not introduce these terms at the beginning of the lesson or out of context, but rather to express what they were doing when solving the task. The chart then served as a record that learners could reference as they worked on future tasks and concepts.

Collaborative charts can also help represent multiple strategies that students have used to solve a problem, so learners can look to these charts if they need help getting started on a similar problem. For example, after a first-grade class had been solving various types of put-together and part-part-whole problems, and sharing solutions that ranged from counting all, to counting on, to using number combinations and relationships, the teacher decided to create a collaborative chart for "Ways We Can Add" (Figure 5.5). Knowing that some students in her class were still getting comfortable with the counting on strategy, she made sure to include an illustration that showed how students could "put one number in their head" and then count from there and to show the make a ten strategy that some students were starting to use. In this way, the chart showed different strategies and served as a helpful scaffold to support her students' future use of more efficient strategies without dictating the use of one.

Creating a chart to illustrate an innovative or useful method or process that emerged from students' work on the task can also be productive. For example, when Ms. Sanchez used the Sharing Crackers task with her fourth

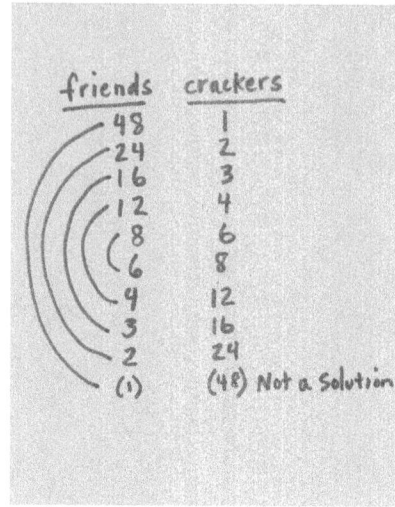

Figure 5.6 A chart to record collective solutions.

graders (using 48 crackers instead of 36), her mathematical goal was that her students would be able to find all factor pairs for 48. In her wrap-up discussion, she gathered all the solutions students found by creating a table on the board showing friends and crackers (Figure 5.6). She then asked the class whether they had found all possible solutions and how they could be sure.

One student suggested that they make sure every solution had a "partner," pointing at each set of partners as he named them. Ms. Sanchez drew lines on the chart to capture the partners, and a student noticed that this made a "sideways rainbow." Recognizing this as a helpful way for students to ensure they have included all possible factors of a given number, Ms. Sanchez captured this idea in a new chart, generalizing from the cracker task to any situation in which you are trying to find factors of a number (Figure 5.7). She also asked the class to consider what happens when they encounter a square number, and the students decided that "double factors," like 4 × 4, pair with themselves to make a small rainbow arc.

On the other hand, when a chart is created to show students the steps of a standard or teacher-taught procedure or is pre-made without any student involvement, it loses its effectiveness in promoting understanding and ownership; instead, it becomes a tool for following a series of steps without critical thinking. Collective charts should support learners while allowing them to take ownership of their ideas and the methods they choose for solving tasks. For this to happen, the chart must be connected to and supportive of their thought processes, rather than merely reflecting external mathematical authority.

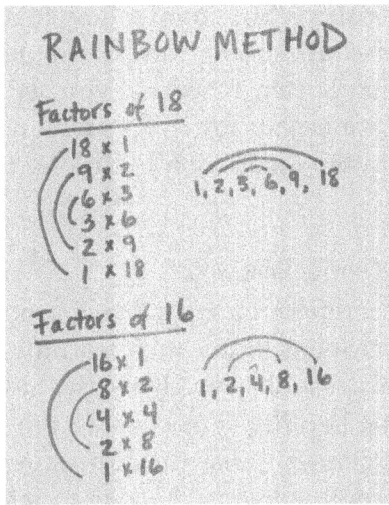

Figure 5.7 A chart to show a procedure that emerged from student solutions.

Many teachers are familiar with the concept of an anchor chart, but in a responsive mathematics lesson, a collaborative chart has some important differences:

- It is developed after students have had the opportunity to explore and discuss a concept or problem.
- It captures the ideas, strategies, or discoveries that emerge, then adds standard mathematical notation or language to those ideas.
- Rather than serving as a recipe for solving problems, its purpose is to help learners consolidate their understanding of essential mathematical concepts.

Conduct a Targeted Gallery Walk

A targeted gallery walk is effective when students work collaboratively in pairs or small groups on a task and then record their solutions on chart paper. In a gallery walk, students make sense of and discuss each other's work, moving through the displays posted around the room. Giving students a targeted focus for their observations can provide authentic opportunities to make connections and consolidate their learning, rather than just giving compliments. A focusing question or task also helps students look beyond correctness in examining their classmates' work to focus on a deeper and more productive analysis.

Ms. Oliver had her students engage in a gallery walk to make sense of each other's solutions to The Pizza Task and post questions or comments with sticky notes. To ensure they had an opportunity to connect their learning to her goals for the lesson, she focused on one solution to lead a discussion of the key ideas in linear relationships. She could follow this up with another gallery walk focused on a targeted question, prompting students to look for specific evidence, such as "in each poster, where do you see the rate of change, that the cost increases by $11 for each pizza?" This would allow students to apply their understanding from the discussion to different representations (tables, graphs, and equations).

Have Students Reexamine and Revise Their Work

Asking students to revise, reflect, or solve a new problem can provide opportunities for every student to consolidate their learning, and this, in turn, makes a mathematics lesson truly responsive. Although students are taught to revise and improve their writing in other subject areas, they rarely get those opportunities in mathematics classes. Jansen (2020) writes about the importance of revision, using the term *rough draft thinking* to refer not only to students' written work but also to their mathematical discourse:

> Mathematics is commonly viewed as black and white, correct or incorrect. Rough draft thinking puts into perspective that, in the math classroom, all learners, including the teacher, are trying to make sense of ideas over time. Students in classrooms that incorporate rough draft thinking experience learning mathematics as a process of constantly extending, connecting, and adjusting thinking.
>
> (p. 10)

Providing opportunities for students to share their rough draft thinking and then revise is another way to engage them in the important processes of communication and reflection, supporting deeper or more refined understanding (Hiebert, 1997). Giving students time to revise and add to their work after sharing strategies is also a way to support the development of productive mathematical practices and dispositions. Making space for revision also helps to humanize mathematics, promoting the notion that the most elegant mathematical solutions and arguments are a product of collaboration, discussion, continual improvement, feedback, refinement, and perseverance, rather than the result of innate ability or talent.

Ms. Oliver's Pizza Task provided multiple opportunities for the sharing and reexamination of rough draft thinking. After Ms. Oliver launched the task, she gave the students time to start working individually. Then she moved them into small groups, while student ideas were still in their early stages. This move was intentional because it gave students space to gather their thoughts and begin jotting down ideas, but not so much time that they had final solutions to share in their groups. The work of putting forth ideas that were not fully fleshed out and revising them occurred in collaboration with peers, and students continued to draft solutions before moving on to putting a more polished version on their chart paper. Even the posters were viewed as rough drafts because Mrs. Oliver pressed groups to add equations and encouraged students to post questions and comments on their peers' work during the gallery walk. After the gallery walk and discussion, Ms. Oliver gave her students additional time to revise or add to their posters.

Engage Students in Written Reflection on Their Learning

The end of a lesson is also an ideal time for students to reflect on the problem-solving process. Metacognition, or thinking about one's thinking, is an important part of any learning process, and students can benefit from learning to monitor and evaluate their understanding, as well as to adapt and adjust their strategies and processes when necessary. In a well-known conceptualization of mathematical problem solving, Polya (1957) described four phases: understanding the problem, making a plan, carrying out the plan, and looking back to reflect on the work. He argued that this last stage (which includes asking oneself questions such as, Am I sure of the answer? Is there a different way to get to the solution? Could this method be used to solve other problems?) is important for being able to consolidate knowledge and further develop problem-solving ability.

Communication is an important part of the K-12 mathematics standards, because writing in mathematics requires students to "reflect on their work and clarify their thoughts" (NCTM, 2000, p. 61). Pugalee (2001, 2005) shows that writing supports mathematical reasoning and problem solving, supports the internalization of effective communication skills, and helps to develop metacognitive skills. He argues that writing requires the learner to consolidate what Vygotsky called "inner speech," or the act of talking to oneself, to make an idea understandable, through the process of making associations between existing and new knowledge. There is also evidence that some students can express their mathematical understanding and reasoning better in writing than orally (Baxter et al., 2005).

In mathematics, journal writing can help students clarify and solidify their learning (Countryman, 1992), connect to their lives outside of school, or reflect on their beliefs and mathematical identities. Examples of prompts that focus on clarifying and solidifying understanding of content include:

- Explain in your own words what *division* means.
- What does it mean for fractions to be *equivalent*? Explain in your own words.
- What properties do squares have?

It can be helpful to have students engage first orally (e.g., talk with a partner) before formulating a written response. Sentence starters can also be helpful prompts, particularly for English Language learners or students who are just getting started with written explanations, e.g., "I know these fractions are equal because_____."

Baxter et al. (2002) illustrate that using a prompt that deliberately highlights a misconception can reveal the depth of student understanding. Responding to the prompt, "Do 0.2 and 0.020 equal the same fraction? Why or why not?" some middle school students wrote "the zeros don't matter," showing a shallow understanding of decimal magnitude. In contrast, others drew visual diagrams to show that 0.2 was much bigger than 0.020.

Prompts, such as the following, that help students make connections between their learning in mathematics class and their lives outside of school, are a way to leverage the cultural resources that diverse students bring to any mathematics classroom:]

- Where do you see the mathematics you did in class today outside of school?
- Can you think of any examples where you see perpendicular lines in your home, school, or neighborhood?
- What are some things that come in equal groups?
- What do you know about measurement? What does measurement help you do?
- What are some ways that you use fractions in real life?

Allowing students to connect to their lived experiences and see themselves as mathematical thinkers is also an important way for responsive teachers to push back against stereotypes about who is and is not mathematically capable and learn about and access the assets or "funds of knowledge" that students bring to the classroom from family and community activities (e.g., playing games, cooking, crafts, sports, storytelling, pop culture.) These contexts can make tasks more culturally and locally relevant (see Chapter 6 for more on selecting and adapting tasks). As students connect to and from their cultural identities, they see how mathematics and mathematical ways of thinking occur everywhere and develop cultural competence in the process (Ladson-Billings, 1995).

The end of a lesson can also be an ideal time to gather evidence of students' affective and emotional responses to the problem-solving experience and understand how their mathematical identities develop and interact with the content they are learning. Students' mathematical identities include beliefs about their ability, the importance of mathematics, what it means to know and do mathematics, motivation, and the intersections with their racial and cultural identities. One way to gather this evidence and learn about how

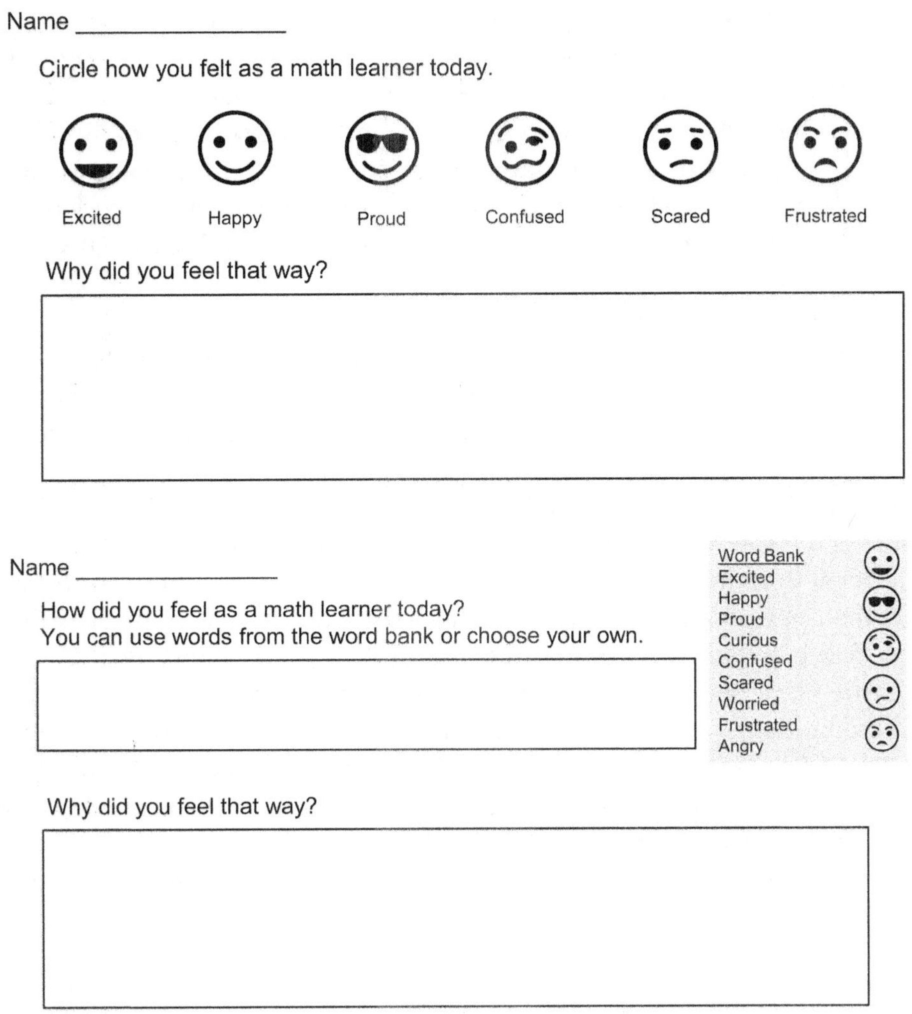

Name _____

Circle how you felt as a math learner today.

😃   🙂   😎   😕   😨   😠

Excited   Happy   Proud   Confused   Scared   Frustrated

Why did you feel that way?

Name _____

How did you feel as a math learner today?
You can use words from the word bank or choose your own.

Word Bank
Excited
Happy
Proud
Curious
Confused
Scared
Worried
Frustrated
Angry

Why did you feel that way?

Figure 5.8 Two versions of a feedback form to collect evidence of student dispositions.

students' mathematical identities may be interacting with their problem-solving experience is to administer a short survey at the end of a lesson. In our work with teachers, we developed two formats, shown in Figure 5.8, to collect information about students' emotional responses.

Younger learners are asked to select an emoji representing their feelings as mathematics learners, while older students are given a word bank. Teachers found that collecting this evidence helped them know when to check in with individual learners (e.g., a student says they feel frustrated or confused) or address something with the whole class. For example, when one student wrote that they were frustrated that another student had "stolen their answer," the teacher discussed how sharing ideas is essential to a learning community. Another teacher decided to anonymously share some of the positive and negative comments so that her students could see that others shared their struggles and that she took their feelings about mathematics seriously. Teachers also found that giving this form out regularly allowed students to see how their emotional responses changed over time. They might feel frustrated one day, but then proud when things started to click and make sense. Finally, and perhaps most importantly, collecting these responses can help teachers avoid culturally biased misperceptions about behavior (e.g., perceiving a student's lack of participation as laziness when the student feels confused or defeated).

Provide a New, and Slightly Different Task to Solve
Giving students another task to solve, one that is not exactly like the one they just worked on, is another way to support consolidation of learning while gathering additional evidence of their developing understanding in relation to the mathematical goal. Repeated opportunities for practice are essential for all types of learning, but solving the same kind of problem repeatedly promotes the rote use of procedural knowledge rather than problem solving and critical thinking. On the other hand, providing tasks where students can apply their new understanding, but in a slightly different context or situation, helps stretch, extend, and ultimately deepen that understanding.

In the vignette at the beginning of the chapter, after making connections from the student work to a more formal understanding of the commutative property, Mr. Cooper wanted to see if his students could apply that understanding to a situation with a different number of crackers. It can also be illuminating to give students a task that has a different problem structure (e.g., a problem where the number of groups or number in each group is known) so that they are not just replicating strategies they have explored in the discussion of learner thinking.

Looking Back to Move Forward: Collecting Evidence of Student Understanding
Providing students with opportunities to consolidate their learning at the end of a lesson can also serve as a way to collect evidence of student understanding for formative assessment purposes. There are many sources of evidence of student understanding of the mathematical goal that can be collected throughout a responsive mathematics problem-solving lesson: emergent theories or misconceptions that surface during the launch, struggles, questions, or breakthroughs that students experience while working on the task, student thinking that comes out during the discussion of solutions, and the written work or explanations that students produce. However, the end of a lesson is an ideal time to be more systematic about eliciting evidence of developing understanding from every student.

Formative assessment, or the process of eliciting and interpreting evidence for use by both students and teachers to adjust teaching and learning,

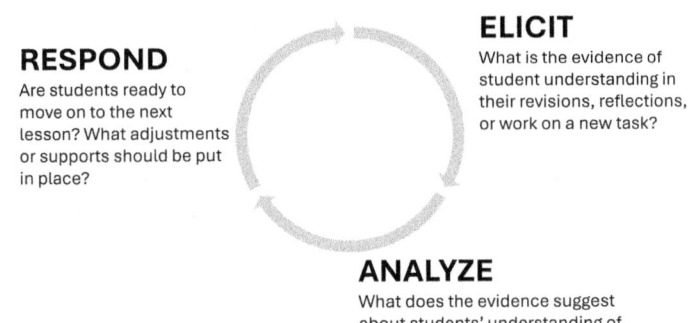

Figure 5.9 The formative assessment cycle during responsive mathematics instruction.

is one of the most powerful ways to improve students' learning (Black &Wiliam, 1998; Hattie, 2011). Figure 5.9 illustrates the cyclical process of eliciting evidence of student thinking during a responsive problem-solving lesson, analyzing that evidence, and then using that analysis to respond or adapt future instruction.

To engage in this cycle, teachers must systematically and intentionally collect evidence of students' developing understanding in every mathematics lesson. Making sense of this evidence involves analyzing students' understanding and continually thinking about how to close the gap between their current understanding and the mathematical goal (Heritage, 2010). Research-based learning progressions, or "descriptions of successively more sophisticated ways of thinking about a topic that can follow one another as children learn about and investigate a topic over a broad span of time" (NRC, 2001, p. 8), can support this analysis. The Ongoing Assessment Project (OGAP), for example, has developed a series of learning progressions in additive, multiplicative, fractional, and proportional reasoning explicitly designed for teachers to use to inform instruction. These progressions can be used to analyze student work in relation to the strategies students use to solve the task, as well as underlying issues and errors, rather than only looking at the correctness of the solution (see Ebby et al., 2021; Hulbert et al., 2024; Petit et al., 2020, 2023).

When analyzing student understanding in relation to the mathematical goal of a responsive problem-solving lesson, it is important to remember that lesson goals are often designed to build on each other sequentially over time, gradually increasing in complexity and sophistication. This means that analyzing the evidence of student understanding should consider both the short-term goal of the lesson and the longer-term goals represented by the trajectory of the unit or mathematical domain of study over the year, and across grade levels. In our experience, many current curriculum materials or guidelines provide this information in helpful ways, but it is not always easy to find. Reading through the unit overview is a good place to start, where there is often information about what concepts come before and after the unit and explanation or examples of how concepts and ideas build throughout the unit, across the year, or over several years.

It is unlikely and unrealistic that all students will come away from a lesson with the same level of understanding of the mathematical concepts or ideas, and so deciding how to respond to the evidence can involve weighing multiple factors: How many students are showing adequate understanding of the mathematical goal? What is the range and variation of the levels of understanding in the class? Where does this lesson fall within the larger trajectory of understanding of the topic? Will the central ideas be revisited in future lessons or units? Is this goal part of a grade-level expectation that will be built upon in the coming years?

The tool shown in Table 5.3 was created as a guideline for teachers to use in responding to the analysis of evidence of student understanding of the mathematical learning goal of a lesson. Given the diverse levels of understanding that may

Table 5.3 Connecting, Consolidating, and Reflecting Tool: Responsibility #3

Responsibility #3: Collect Evidence of Student Understanding to Inform Subsequent Instruction	
Analysis of Evidence of Understanding of the Mathematical Goal	**Potential Response**
Most students show evidence of understanding of the mathematical goal	• Move on to the next lesson(s) while planning supports for students who may need it. • Look at the next few lessons in your plans to see if students are going to have more opportunities to learn the same concepts. Consider inserting more opportunities for practice and consolidation (warm-up, fluency routines, centers).
There are a variety of levels of understanding across the class	• Choose 2–3 examples of student work that represent the different levels of understanding to discuss at the beginning of the next class. Use this discussion to help bridge students' thinking to the learning goal.
A majority of students do not understand or are at beginning levels of understanding	• Look at the next few lessons in your plans to see what students will need to access that content: What supports can you put in place to make sure students will have access? • Adjust the pacing to allow for additional lessons or tasks: Is there a different way you could approach the same concept?

emerge, teachers need to consider how to determine if their learning goals were met at the end of the lesson. This involves planning the final phase of the lesson in a way that both deepens understanding and informs next steps for instruction.

Planning for Connecting, Consolidating, and Reflecting

Planning for the last portion of the lesson involves thinking through how to help learners make concrete connections to the mathematical goal and consolidate the ideas that emerge during their work on and discussion of the task, while also collecting evidence of their developing understanding that can be used to plan for future instruction.

Earlier in this chapter, we had a window into Ms. Oliver's responsive mathematics lesson. She used the Pizza Delivery task to develop her eighth-grade students' understanding of linear relationships. Table 5.4 shows the

Table 5.4 Ms. Oliver's Plan for Connecting, Consolidating, and Reflecting

Planning for Connecting, Consolidating, and Reflecting
Connect Student Strategies to the Mathematical Goal
• Prompt students to write an equation to show the total cost
• Have students unpack the equation $y = 11x + 3$ (from a student poster).
o Identify the rate of change (11) and the constant (3) in the tables and solutions.
o Relate rate of change to the problem and to slope-intercept form
o Make sure students can visualize how rate of change is shown by the slope.
Consolidate Mathematical Understanding
• Give each group 5–10 minutes to revise their posters for clarity and content.
o "Read the feedback from other students. Is there anything that was confusing, that you can make clearer?"
o "Think about our discussion around the equation. How can you make sure that your poster demonstrates your understanding of how this equation works for this problem?"
• Give students a new task to solve (exit slip)
Collect Data about Student Understanding
• Exit slip: Andre starts babysitting and charges $10 for traveling to and from the job, and $15 per hour.
o Write an equation to represent Andre's total earnings.
o Use your equation to figure out how much Andre would earn if he babysat for 3 hours.
o What is the rate of change in your equation? How do you know?

plan she created for connecting, consolidating, and reflecting on their learning from this task.

Plan to Connect Student Strategies to the Mathematical Goal

The first step in planning for this portion of a responsive lesson is to consider how to create a bridge from discussing students' strategies on the task to the mathematical goal. In Ms. Oliver's plan above, she highlighted the equation $y = 11x + 3$, which shows how to find the total cost (y) for any number of pizzas (x) in the Pizza Delivery task, to further solidify students' understanding of linear equations. She planned to use a piece of student work that included this equation to push students to think about the rate of change and the constant and connect it to the slope of the line in graphical form, which they were already familiar with.

Plan to Consolidate Mathematical Understanding

The next step is to think about providing opportunities for students to consolidate their understanding of the ideas and strategies that emerge during the lesson. The four pathways in Table 5.2 provide a solid basis for planning, each with its own considerations. If the plan includes the pathway for creating a record of collective learning, a teacher might think about how the chart could be organized and what important information would be included. If the teacher decides to have students revise their work, they could plan for what instructions they will give and what they are looking for in the revisions. If a new task is going to be given, the teacher will need to select a task, thinking about how it differs from the original task and how students might apply their learning to it. Finally, if students are engaged in a written reflection, the teacher should develop a question that will allow students to express their current understanding.

Ms. Oliver planned to give students time to add to or revise their posters, based on feedback from other students during the gallery walk and the connections made during the discussion of the equation $y = 11x + 3$. By planning how she wants students to revise their work, every group will have work to do to draw on what they have learned to improve the content and clarity of their posters.

Plan to Collect Evidence of Student Understanding for Formative Assessment

The final part of planning for a responsive problem-solving lesson is to go back to where it started, i.e., develop a plan to collect evidence of student understanding that can inform the planning of subsequent lessons. If the plan for consolidating mathematical understanding includes a journal reflection or an alternate task, the student responses can be collected and used for formative assessment. In Ms. Oliver's case, because the student posters were completed in groups, she wanted to ensure she had evidence of each student's understanding of linear equations. She decided to have each student complete a new task as an exit ticket, both to provide a way for each student to consolidate their understanding and to provide evidence that she could use to make instructional decisions. She chose a slightly different task that gave the rate of change and constant, but not the total earnings and asked students to apply their developing understanding in a new situation rather than repeat or replicate what they had already done on the Pizza task.

The End of Every Lesson Is the Beginning of a New One

The three processes described in this chapter—connecting, consolidating, and reflecting—are important ways to ensure that a responsive mathematics problem-solving lesson helps all learners develop understanding of the mathematics that they need to learn to be confident and capable learners of mathematics with positive mathematical mindsets. However, learning mathematics is a trajectory rather than a process that can be neatly divided into discrete or stand-alone lessons. Although the teacher may determine that it is time to move on to a new lesson, the responsive mathematics problem-solving experience should leave behind understandings that can be applied to new situations (Hiebert et al., 1997). We have argued in this chapter that it is the teacher's responsibility to ensure students develop this understanding through connecting and consolidating, and help students recognize and build on this understanding in the future through reflection.

Many approaches to lesson planning focus on a lesson having closure—a marked ending or a wrap-up of any loose ends or partial understandings—and imply that it is the teacher's job to provide this closure for learners. The metaphor of wrapping up implies that the problem-solving experience can be tied up neatly with a bow, put away on a shelf, and perhaps never opened up again. Instead, the model for responsive mathematics teaching (Figure 5.10) uses the image of a continuous cycle with no real beginning or ending. In this cycle, each problem-solving experience is linked to the next by the reflection and planning process that the teacher engages in, either individually or collaboratively with other teachers, focusing on evidence of the mathematical understandings or residue that students are taking away. Through these processes, the responsive mathematics teacher intentionally analyzes what students are learning and continuously builds on their developing understandings. The next chapter, appropriately, begins where this one ends, using the information about students' developing understanding to plan for responsive mathematics instruction.

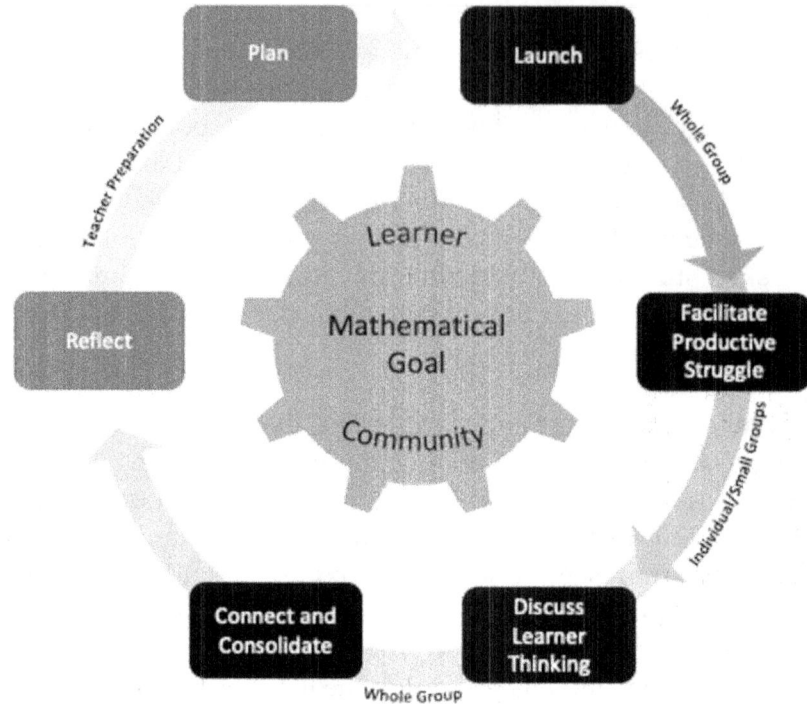

Figure 5.10 The model for responsive mathematics teaching is cyclical.

Reflection Questions

Teacher Responsibilities	Guiding Principles
1 Help learners make explicit connections from strategies that have been discussed to key mathematical ideas and goals of the lesson. 2 Provide opportunities for learners to solidify those connections and consolidate their understanding 3 Collect evidence of student understanding to inform subsequent instruction	1 Prioritize mathematical sensemaking 2 Promote collaborative learning communities 3 Support a positive mathematical identity 4 Ensure all students have access to mathematics

1. How do each of the teacher responsibilities described in this chapter address the guiding principles of responsive teaching?
2. Suppose that Mr. Cooper's goal in using the Crackers Task was to have students understand the relationship between multiplication

and division. After discussing the three pieces of student work in Figure 5.1, what connecting moves could he use? What strategies could he use to help students solidify and consolidate those connections? What strategies could he use to collect evidence of individual student's understanding?

3 As you think about integrating connecting, consolidating, and reflecting into your instructional context:

    a What is already in place that you can build on?
    b What challenges do you foresee?
    c What can you do to try to overcome those challenges?

4 What are you taking away from this chapter that you can try in your instruction?

6
Planning for Responsive Mathematics Teaching

Intentional planning and preparation are critical components of responsive mathematics teaching. This claim might seem paradoxical because responsiveness suggests an in-the-moment, spontaneous reaction to student ideas. However, as identified in Chapter 1, responsive teaching requires both adaptivity and anticipatory practices. Teachers with strong, responsive teaching practices but little preparedness may find themselves quickly overwhelmed as they try to make sense of a variety of student strategies. Alternatively, they may facilitate a discussion that builds on student ideas but does little to help students progress toward the mathematical learning goals. Planning enables teachers to consider multiple potential student ideas in advance, map out how they want the discussion to unfold, and anticipate bumps in the road that may arise. This preparation helps teachers more effectively connect students' existing understandings to meaningful new learning or core mathematical concepts. Teachers who are both well-prepared and can improvise in relation to lesson goals are well-equipped to be responsive teachers.

In the previous chapters, we focused on responsive teaching practices, addressing strategies and moves teachers use during instruction. This chapter focuses on anticipatory practices that support responsive mathematics teaching. We present vignettes and artifacts from a collaborative teacher planning session to spotlight the essential preliminary work that prepares teachers to effectively respond to students' thinking as it emerges and build understanding toward the mathematical goals.

Dwight D. Eisenhower famously said, "Plans are worthless, but planning is everything." To a large extent, this statement is true for responsive mathematics instruction. The *Responsive Math Lesson Planning Template* presented in this chapter is designed to assist teachers in anticipating and preparing for the various responsive moves that are used during a responsive mathematics problem-solving lesson. Each part of the tool will be explored in detail throughout the chapter. The completed plan and a blank template are available online: www.routledge.com/9781032882222.

Lesson plans are not meant to be a script to follow rigidly, nor is it possible to anticipate every student's strategy, every way they might get stuck, and every twist and turn that may occur during the launch or the discussion of learner thinking. The purpose of the detailed planning highlighted in this chapter and illustrated by the vignettes is to do as much thinking in advance as possible to cut down on the cognitive demand during the inevitable improvisation that will arise during the lesson. The planning process also allows teachers to deepen their content knowledge, refine their ability to identify multiple solution pathways, and understand the connections between them.

Selecting and Adapting a Task

The first step of planning a responsive mathematics problem-solving lesson is choosing an appropriate task, one that is open to multiple strategies or solutions and has the potential to elicit student thinking around the mathematical goal of the lesson or unit. Tasks suitable for responsive mathematics lessons can be found in various places, including existing curriculum resources. Still, it is the teacher's responsibility to select, adapt, or create tasks that meet both the needs of their students and the mathematical goals. Good tasks for responsive teaching provide opportunities for students to engage in (1) rigorous problem solving and productive struggle—to genuinely grapple with essential mathematics concepts in ways that have not been prescribed in advance, and (2) rich discussion of valuable mathematical ideas when looking across different solutions or different solution methods. There are several characteristics of tasks that have the potential to provide these learning opportunities.

One way to assess the potential for tasks to provide these learning opportunities is to use the metaphor of a building to ensure they have a *low floor, high ceiling,* and *wide walls* (Boaler, 2015; Resnick, 2017). A low floor or threshold means that the task allows all students to have an entry point to begin solving, regardless of background knowledge and prior experience, making it accessible. A high ceiling means the task has the potential to engage students in deeper learning by extending their thinking. The concept of wide walls refers to the idea that the task can be approached from multiple directions, leading to either multiple solutions or multiple solution strategies. Taken together, the low floor, high ceiling, and wide walls criteria ensure that the task can be given to a classroom of students who bring very different understandings, skill sets, and needs, and engage them in the work of productively struggling toward a solution, developing new understandings along the way. Moreover, their work on the task will generate diverse solutions that can be the basis of a productive mathematical discussion.

Another important criterion is that the task is suitably challenging or has a *high level of cognitive demand* without being out of reach for most students. As Hiebert et al. (1997) explain, a worthwhile mathematical task should be a genuine problem for students, meaning it does not have an immediately apparent solution or solution method, and they are motivated to figure it out. Tasks should also require significant cognitive effort on the part of the student. In other words, the student should do the work of coming up with a strategy and determining if it will lead to the solution, rather than simply applying a method that has been previously taught or suggested by someone else. Tasks with a high level of cognitive demand involve mathematical reasoning, conceptual connections, and multiple representations (Stein et al., 1996). On the other hand, tasks with low levels of cognitive demand involve recall, the application of procedures, or the reproduction of previously learned facts, formulas, or definitions. Determining the appropriate level of cognitive demand depends on the age and prior experiences of the learners. For example, the task described in Chapter 3, "River has 8

Characteristics of a Good Task for Responsive Mathematics Teaching

Low Floor
- Has an accessible entry point for all students (Low floor)

Wide Walls
- Is approachable via multiple pathways, strategies, methods, or representations OR
- Has multiple solutions that range in complexity

High Ceiling
- Offers opportunities for extending or deepening understanding

High Level of Cognitive Demand
- Does not have an immediately apparent solution or solution method
- Provides an opportunity for productive struggle
- Involves conceptual understanding and reasoning

Relevant
- Connects to or is related to students' lives or interests
- Relates to mathematical learning goals

boxes of crayons. Each box holds 10 crayons. How many crayons does River have?" was challenging and a genuine problem for second-grade students who had not yet developed base-10 understanding or multiplicative strategies. However, this task might require little thinking or reasoning for older students.

The task should also be relevant to students so they will engage deeply and meaningfully in the quest to find a solution. Responsive mathematics teaching involves recognizing students' cultures as valuable assets by drawing on their lived experiences and knowledge to inform and enrich learning (Bartell et al., 2017). This can mean finding or adapting tasks to have local relevance, or connections to students' home culture, interests, and communities (Remillard et al., 2014). For example, a sterile task about driving distances becomes much more engaging for students by rewriting it to include nearby locations, local maps, or landmarks in the community. Real-life contexts and phenomena like traveling, hobbies, or environmental issues can help students see the practical relevance and meaning of mathematics in their lives. For younger children, sharing things fairly, setting the table, and gathering enough ingredients to make recipes (or materials for crafts) are examples of familiar situations involving important mathematics.

Tasks can also be relevant when they are puzzles or challenges that spark students' natural curiosity or imagination, even if they are not situated in real-life contexts. An example is the Four 4's task, where students are challenged to make all the numbers from 1 to 20 (or higher) using four 4's and any operation. The task can be even more engaging if given on May 4, which many students know as Star Wars Day, and renamed "May the Fours be With You." Tasks can also be made more relevant by providing background and helping students see how something unfamiliar connects to things they know and understand. Adding an image or showing a video clip during the launch of a task, followed by some discussion, is an effective way to encourage students to make connections to their prior knowledge.

Finally, tasks should address the content students need to learn and cause them to reflect on important mathematical ideas. This means the productive struggle students engage in should be around the mathematics, not the context, language, or other features of the problem (Hiebert et al., 1997). The task should be interesting and engaging, but that is not enough. Solving the problem needs to generate relevant mathematical concepts, processes, and relationships that will lead to deeper and more connected learning.

There are many places where teachers can find tasks that meet these criteria for students of all ages, and we have listed a few of our favorite sources here. Tasks with these characteristics can also be found in many curriculum resources, but often teachers will need to adjust those tasks to include more of the features described above or to meet specific needs and assets of their students.

For example, Figure 6.1 illustrates how a group of fourth-grade teachers adapted a task from their curriculum materials to allow for multiple solutions. The original task was a situation where the total (1 cup) and one part ($\frac{1}{4}$ cup) is known. Although it is open to multiple solution paths, there is one correct answer ($\frac{3}{4}$ cup brown sugar). The teachers, who had been focusing on unit fraction reasoning, recognized that many students would quickly know $\frac{3}{4} + \frac{1}{4} = \frac{4}{4}$, and therefore, this task would not be truly problematic. It would not require much cognitive effort given that students already had a strong conceptual understanding of fractions. They decided to adapt the task by asking students to find as many combinations as they could to equal $1\frac{1}{2}$ cups, to prove their answers with mathematics, and to look for patterns and relationships in their solutions. They also recognized that students might bring up interesting ideas around measurement based on their real-life experiences with cooking and measuring cups: could you use measurements less than $\frac{1}{4}$ cup?

> **Where to Find Good Tasks for Responsive Mathematics Teaching**
>
> - You Cubed from Stanford University: https://www.youcubed.org/
> - NRICH from the University of Cambridge: https://nrich.maths.org/
> - Illustrative Mathematics Tasks: https://tasks.illustrativemathematics.org/
> - Shell Center: http://map.mathshell.org/materials/index.php
> - Dan Meyer's 3 Act Tasks: http://blog.mrmeyer.com/
> - Graham Fletchy's 3-Act Tasks for Elementary School
> - Fawn Nguyen's Visual Patterns; grades K-12: http://www.visualpatterns.org
> - Mathalicious: http://www.mathalicious.com/
> - EQSTEMM Sharing, Making, and Community-Based Modeling Tasks: https://eqstemm.org/tasks
> - Math for Love https://mathforlove.com/lessons/rich-tasks/

The revised task provides a low floor, or entry point, since students can find more accessible solutions, such as 1 cup of one type, and $\frac{1}{2}$ cup of the other and then build from there. It also creates a higher ceiling, inviting students to move beyond working with familiar fractions to more complex solutions, such as $\frac{7}{8}$ cup and $\frac{5}{8}$ cup. Finally, the opened-up version also incorporates an important mathematical practice—mathematical argumentation—by requiring students to craft an argument to prove that their combinations equal $1\frac{1}{2}$ cups of sugar.

> **1 Cup of Sugar**—Textbook Version
>
> Elena is baking cookies, and the recipe calls for 1 cup of sugar. She has brown and white sugar and wants to use a combination of the two. If she uses $\frac{1}{4}$ cup of white sugar, how much brown sugar should she use?
>
> **Sugar Combinations**—"Opened Up" Version
>
> Elena is baking cookies, and the recipe calls for a total of $1\frac{1}{2}$ cups of sugar. She has brown and white sugar and wants to use a combination of the two. What are possible combinations of white and brown sugar that she could use? *Use mathematics to prove that each combination you come up with equals $1\frac{1}{2}$ cup of sugar. What patterns and relationships do you notice?*

Figure 6.1 Revising a standard textbook task for multiple solutions.

Tasks can often be opened up by modifying the way they are presented to students. Figure 6.2 shows how some third-grade teachers adapted a task from their curriculum materials to be both locally relevant and allow for multiple strategies. Students were immediately intrigued by the inclusion of one of their classmates' names (Malik) and by the familiarity of the locations mentioned in the problem. Removing the stipulations to use a specific representation and to write an equation allowed for multiple solution methods to emerge that could then be explored to help students develop a deeper understanding of subtraction as distance and make meaningful connections to the equation.

The characteristics of good tasks for responsive mathematics teaching can be used to evaluate the potential of tasks as written and guide the adaptations needed to support rigorous problem solving and rich discussion. While some

> **Driving Distances**—Textbook Version
>
> Andrew and his mother took a trip to visit his grandmother, who lives 126 miles away. On the way, they stopped at a roadside stand to buy some peaches. The stand was 38 miles from Andrew's house. Use a tape diagram and write an equation to show how much further Andrew and his mother have to drive to get to his grandmother's house.
>
> **Driving Distances**—Opened-Up Version
>
> Malik took a trip with his family to Wildwood for the weekend. Wildwood is 126 miles away. On the way to the shore, they stopped at Wawa to pick up hoagies for lunch. The Wawa was 38 miles from Malik's house. How much further did Malik's family have to drive to get to Wildwood?

Figure 6.2 Revising a standard textbook task for multiple strategies and local relevance.

will satisfy all these characteristics, a task can still be high quality if it only addresses a few. It is also important to remember to focus on quality over quantity. A single lesson might include dozens of practice problems in many published curriculum resources. Finding a high-quality task and spending more time digging into it can maximize student learning through problem solving and discussion rather than repetition.

Constructing a Responsive Lesson Plan

Once a task has been selected and adapted, it is time to create a plan to support responsive mathematics instruction. Planning is the intellectual preparation for teaching the lesson. Solving the task and exploring multiple solution paths is a critical first step, followed by articulating the mathematical goals, in terms of mathematical content and practices. Next, the main components of a responsive mathematics lesson are planned: launching the task, facilitating productive struggle, discussing learner thinking, and connecting, consolidating, and collecting evidence of student learning. In the following sections, we look at these six planning components in depth, following a group of three sixth-grade teachers as they collaboratively discussed and planned a lesson on proportional reasoning.

The sixth-grade teachers were midway through a unit introducing proportional relationships, and the evidence from recent formative assessment showed that many students needed additional opportunities to make connections between their understanding of fractions and proportional situations. They chose the Fair Shares task because it provides an opportunity to explore a proportional relationship in a familiar context, through the idea of fairness. Since there are multiple entry points and possible solutions, students would have the opportunity to consider different ways of creating equal ratios, or a fair relationship, between the number of chocolates and the price paid by each person. Taking some time to explore this problem and find some solutions before reading on will help you make sense of the vignette.

Fair Shares

Five friends contributed money to buy 60 chocolate candies. The total cost of the candies was $15. Not all of the friends gave the same amount of money, but they all want to split up the chocolates fairly, based on what they each paid.

What are some of the ways that they could have paid for and fairly split the chocolates? How do you know the shares are fair?

Planning for Responsive Mathematics Teaching ◆ 147

Exploring Multiple Strategies and Approaches

The teachers came to the planning session having already solved the task independently. Ms. Fulton, an experienced teacher, had recently been introduced to the concept of responsive teaching and was actively working on making more space for student voice and collaboration. Mr. Kane, on the other hand, had been working on teaching mathematics responsively for several years. Ms. Johnson was a new teacher, enthusiastic and open to trying new ideas, but also sometimes overwhelmed. They started the meeting by sharing their solutions.

Ms. Fulton Starts by Sharing Her Solution with the Group (Figure 6.3) The other teachers take a moment to look over her work and try to make sense of how she approached the task. "Oh, you found the unit rate," Ms. Johnson notices. "I like this strategy because it makes figuring out the cost of any amount of candies pretty easy. Each one costs a quarter." Mr. Kane agrees that the unit rate does make finding the cost of multiple candies straightforward, but he wonders how many students will take this approach. "I think the initial math of dividing 15 by 60 is challenging. My students still get intimidated when dealing with fractions and decimals. They might avoid doing this for that reason." Ms. Fulton agrees that this is also true of her students. "I immediately gravitated to this approach because it is very efficient, and I knew that dividing the cost by the total candies would give me the unit price per candy. But my students probably wouldn't start there. I wonder if we should make getting to the unit rate a goal for the whole group discussion?" Ms. Johnson and Mr. Kane agree that this would be a good strategy to unpack later in the discussion after students make sense of the problem. Mr. Kane cautions that he wants to make sure his students really understand this strategy and are not just trying to apply a procedure. The group then turns their attention to Mr. Kane's solution, shown in Figure 6.4.

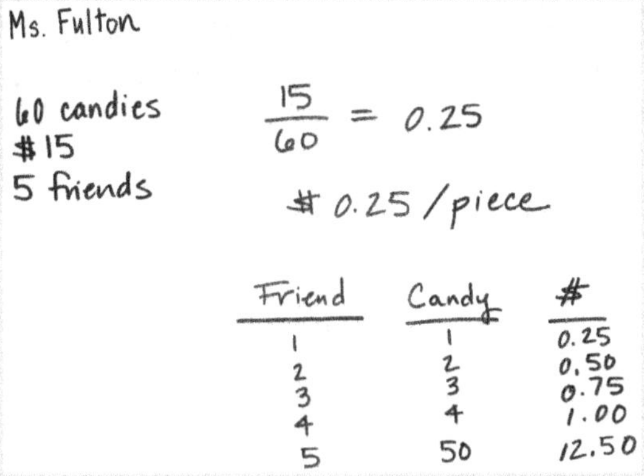

Ms. Fulton

60 candies
$15
5 friends

$\frac{15}{60} = 0.25$

$0.25/piece

Friend	Candy	#
1	1	0.25
2	2	0.50
3	3	0.75
4	4	1.00
5	50	12.50

Figure 6.3 Ms. Fulton's solution to Fair Shares.

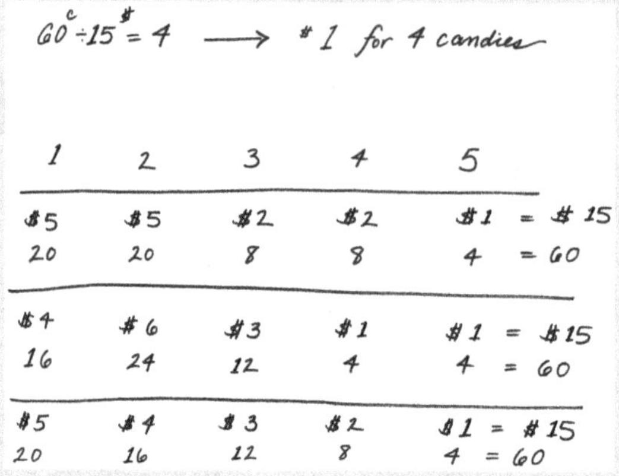

$$60 \div 15 = 4 \longrightarrow \$1 \text{ for } 4 \text{ candies}$$

1	2	3	4	5	
$5 20	$5 20	$2 8	$2 8	$1 4	= $15 = 60
$4 16	$6 24	$3 12	$1 4	$1 4	= $15 = 60
$5 20	$4 16	$3 12	$2 8	$1 4	= $15 = 60

Figure 6.4 Mr. Kane's solution to Fair Shares.

Ms. Fulton immediately notices a connection to her strategy. "Instead of dividing the money by the candies, you flipped it around!" Mr. Kane replies, "Yeah, the math is easier, dividing 60 by 15, and I think some students will approach it this way."

"But do you think they will understand that the 4 means four candies per dollar?" wonders Ms. Johnson. "That's definitely something we should think about when we're planning for facilitating productive struggle. They might make mistakes there or just get stuck," agrees Mr. Kane. "I also noticed as I was doing this that thinking about four candies per dollar only works if the number of candies is a multiple of four. See how all my solutions are divisible by four?"

The teachers talk more about this and anticipate that some students will be able to jump from 4 candies per dollar to 25 cents per candy without support. For other students, they might need to encourage them to think about a number of candies that is not a multiple of four for this connection to occur. Finally, they look at Ms. Johnson's solution (Figure 6.5).

After looking at the work for a minute, Mr. Kane asks, "Did you start by finding a way to split the cost up between friends? That seems like a really

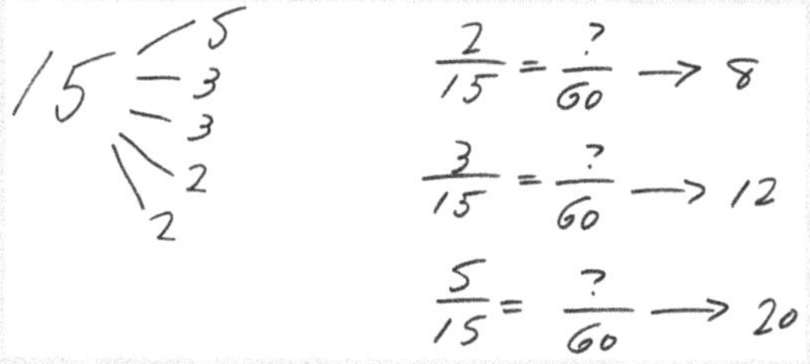

$$15 \begin{cases} 5 \\ 3 \\ 3 \\ 2 \\ 2 \end{cases} \qquad \frac{2}{15} = \frac{?}{60} \longrightarrow 8$$

$$\frac{3}{15} = \frac{?}{60} \longrightarrow 12$$

$$\frac{5}{15} = \frac{?}{60} \longrightarrow 20$$

Figure 6.5 Ms. Johnson's solution to Fair Shares.

different approach than the other work we've looked at." Ms. Johnson confirms, "Yes, I was trying to think like a sixth grader. I thought that might be where they started, working to find a way to split up the money so that they didn't all give the same amount, like the problem says. That's a pretty accessible place to start before thinking about the fairness aspect."

"I really like that you did it like this", Ms. Fulton comments, "because it helps me to think about how my students will likely start and how I'll be able to support them. Before, I would have just taught them how to find the unit rate, but this is really based more on understanding the task than learning a procedure." Mr. Kane notes that students have experience setting up equivalent fractions like Ms. Johnson has done in her solution, and he thinks many will be able to work through a solution using that method.

"I feel like I have a much better understanding of the different ways of thinking about this now that we've looked at each other's work," Ms. Fulton says. "Me too," agrees Ms. Johnson. "What if we just take a few minutes and work through one solution in each of these three ways to be sure we can support a student using any one of them?"

Mr. Kane points out that some students will start with amounts of money and then figure out how much candy each person will get, while others will start with candy amounts and then figure out how much each candy amount will cost. The group agrees and decides that they will use each strategy to figure out how much a friend would pay if they took 12 chocolates and how many candies a friend would get if they paid $4. They each take a moment to work through this task on their own.

After digging into the mathematics and identifying possible confusions, connections, and extensions, the teachers were ready to start planning the lesson.

Before beginning to create a responsive problem-solving lesson plan, it is critical that teachers engage with the mathematics as learners and solve the task using a strategy that makes sense to them. The next step is to generate and work through different strategies students might use to solve the task. Understanding ways of thinking beyond one's own way of approaching the task is essential to creating a thorough plan.

In the vignette, Ms. Fulton used a procedure to find the unit rate to solve the task. Unpacking less straightforward ways of thinking about the task, which are strategies that students will likely try, helped Ms. Fulton to recognize that she should resist the urge to teach her students to find the unit rate, as she might have been inclined to do in the past. Instead, discussing her colleagues' approaches prepared her to support multiple ways of thinking, rather than approaching the lesson from her own preferred method. Having multiple ideas on the table allowed the group to attend to the important mathematics in the task and consider their students' developing understanding. When collaborative planning is not possible, it can be helpful to ask a few other people to solve the task (family members, friends, co-workers, or neighbors), draw on work produced by students in previous years or classes, or use knowledge from research on the strategies students use to solve different types of problems. Collecting and saving examples of student responses over time can be a helpful resource for anticipating student solutions.

> One of the most significant benefits of collaborative planning is the opportunity to learn from multiple voices, perspectives, and experiences. Teachers will bring a range of experiences and levels of fluency with the content into the planning session. They are likely to solve tasks in different ways, and having an opportunity to talk through different strategies prepares all group members for the variety of ways of thinking they will encounter from their students during the lesson. If a teacher feels less secure with the content of a particular lesson, the group gives them access to that knowledge in a non-threatening and non-evaluative context.

Clarifying the Mathematical Goals

The sixth-grade teachers selected the *Fair Shares* task to give their students an additional opportunity to apply proportional reasoning in a real-world context because they noticed that students struggled to see connections between their understanding of fraction concepts and problems involving proportions. They were also looking for ways to integrate some of the *Standards for Mathematical Practice* (National Governors Association Center for Best Practices & Council of Chief State School Officers, 2010) into their instruction more regularly. The following conversation occurred as the group moved from discussing their solutions to the task to mapping out a plan to enact the task with their students.

> Mr. Kane, who suggested the task, opens the conversation by asking whether the task actually does what they want it to do. Ms. Johnson responds, "Well, the biggest thing I was looking for in this task was that my kids would get a chance to work with proportions in a relatable, real-world context. I want them to see that this stuff is relevant and useful." Ms. Fulton adds, "I think the fact that they ultimately have to come up with ways to split up the candy and the cost fairly is a nice feature of this task because it brings in some of the

argumentation skills I've been trying to build in my class. I like that it moves students beyond thinking about a right answer to thinking about an answer they can defend and how they'll convince other people that their solution is actually fair. I'm envisioning a discussion where different students come up with different ways to share the candies, like we just talked about, but where they also have to convince each other that a particular split is *fair*. That's where the proportional reasoning really comes in, so it's like a double whammy – they can work on thinking proportionally and also on putting together a decent argument."

Mr. Kane begins typing in the group's shared planning document. "So, it sounds like the practice standard we're hitting this time is the third one, it's about critiquing reasoning and making arguments." He copies and pastes this standard into the planning template.

Ms. Fulton looks at the curriculum scope and sequence documents from her school and also has the state standards open on her desktop. "We're definitely hitting the real-world applications of ratio and rate reasoning standard with this one. That was your point, Ms. Johnson."

Mr. Kane then presses the group to further articulate a mathematics goal. "So, what do we want to come out of this? Where are we headed with this one in the discussion?" The group brainstorms ideas and ultimately lands on a goal that captures both of the standards they identified: "Students will use proportional thinking to make an argument about fairness." Ms. Johnson adds this to the group's plan, shown in Table 6.1.

Table 6.1 The Mathematical Goals Section of the Sixth-Grade Planning Document

Mathematical Goals
Connection to Standards
• PRACTICE: (SMP3) Construct viable arguments and critique the reasoning of others. • CONTENT: (6.RP.3) Use ratio and rate reasoning to solve real-world and mathematical problems, e.g., by reasoning about tables of equivalent ratios, tape diagrams, double number line diagrams, or equations.
Mathematical Goal
Students will use proportional thinking to make an argument about fairness.

In discussing this section of the plan (Table 6.1), the teachers went beyond simply identifying content and practice standards, drawing on their experiences solving and exploring different strategies to think about the goal for student understanding that they were working toward and articulating this goal in their own words. This step is critical to move beyond thinking about the task as a performance (something that students will do) to thinking about it as a learning opportunity.

Grade-level standards are a good anchor for responsive problem-solving lessons. However, they are usually too broad to provide enough guidance about what specific understanding students need or should develop, and the range and variation of understandings that are likely to emerge from any group of students. Grade-level standards describe what students should know and be able to do by the end of the year, but it is important for teachers to think about and articulate how the task will help students advance from their current understandings toward that standard (Daro et al., 2011). In addition to digging deeper into standards and lesson objectives to focus on goals for student thinking and understanding, teachers also need to consider how these goals are situated within what has come before this lesson and what will come after, or the trajectory of learning within a unit or set of lessons. The goal may also be to gather evidence about what students already know about a concept, particularly at the beginning of new unit or content strand.

Planning the Launch

The launch, as detailed in Chapter 2, involves supporting learners in making sense of the task by building connections to their prior experiences and developing a common understanding that guides their problem solving. Planning for the launch entails considering the three responsibilities of the teacher: (1) establishing an individual understanding of the task, (2) establishing a collective understanding of the task, and (3) building a bridge to solving the task. The *planning template* includes prompts to help teachers think about how to enact each of these responsibilities, as well as space to draft a *launch board vision*. Constructing the launch board vision involves mapping out the key information that needs to be elicited and displayed during the launch discussion.

Before unpacking each of these components of planning the launch in more detail, we return to the sixth-grade planning group as they continue their planning to focus on the launch. In this discussion, the teachers alternated between considering how to build individual and collective understanding of the task and filling out the sections of the launch board vision.

> Ms. Johnson begins this part of the conversation by reflecting on the *launch board vision* that the group had developed in their planning of a previous task: "Having a map of what I wanted to draw out in the conversation was a huge help for me last time. I think my launch was better because I had that

vision in mind and I even found myself using what was on the board when I was talking with students and facilitating their productive struggle. It gave us something to refer back to, like what a solution was supposed to include and what we had agreed we already knew from the problem. Can we start with that? With what we're planning to put on the board for this problem?"

The group begins mapping out a vision of what their board will look like one quadrant at a time, first mapping out the key information in the problem in the *What We Know* section and then moving on to discussing the vocabulary that will need to be clarified (see Table 6.2).

Ms. Fulton comments, "Something that will definitely come up in my class is what we mean by 'fair.' I can see some of my students arguing that fair means everyone gets the same amount of candy no matter what they paid. What can we ask to get them to see that fairness here means everyone gets what they paid for, without just telling them that?" Ms. Johnson suggests starting by asking what "fair" means. The group jots this down in the *Making Sense of the Task* section of the lesson plan. After thinking a bit more, Ms. Johnson adds, "Maybe we could say, 'What does fair mean in this problem?' just to help them see that we're not talking about what does fair mean to you personally when you're splitting up candy with your brothers and sisters but what does it actually mean in the context of this problem." Mr. Kane comments that he likes the idea of making that distinction and suggests that they ask students to justify how they're defining fair with words from the problem itself. "Hopefully, they'll point to "Based on what they each paid." If they don't, we could point to that part of the problem and ask them to explain what that means.

The group continues planning out the launch, jotting notes both in the launch board vision and in the "Making Sense of the Task" section, as they come up with specific questions to ask to elicit the ideas in the board vision.

Launch Board Vision

Crafting a launch board vision involves considering the key points that will be addressed and potentially written on the board during the launch. By thinking through what falls into the four categories outlined in Table 6.3, teachers can set clear goals for the outcome of the launch. The launch board vision allows a teacher to identify the critical information that needs to come out and anticipate questions, misconceptions, or emergent theories that students might generate.

This process supports responsive mathematics teaching in two ways. First, it helps to ensure that the teacher elicits and clarifies all the important and potentially confusing parts of the task to make it more accessible for all learners. Additionally, it guides the teacher in organizing this information clearly so that learners can refer to it while working. Constructing a vision of what this might look like ahead of time makes responding to and representing learners' ideas easier in the moment.

Table 6.2 The Launch Section of the Sixth-Grade Planning Document

Launching the Task	
Launch Board Vision	

What We Know
• There are 5 friends
• The total cost is $15
• There are 60 candies total
• Not all friends pay the same amount
• The share must be fair
• Can't split up the candy (only whole pieces, no halves, etc.).
	Vocabulary/Language
	• What does fair mean?
	  ○ "Fair" here is not everyone getting the same amount of candy
	  ○ Everyone gets what they have paid for
	• "Based on what they paid"
	  ○ There is a connection between the amount of chocolates someone gets and the amount of money they paid

Goal • A solution should include how much each friend paid and how much chocolate each friend received ○ Think about ways to organize your solution so others can understand it • "Some of the ways"—there will be more than one possible solution; if you have found one, try to find another	**Theories and Questions from Learners** • Can we use coins? (Give it a try and see if it works; we can discuss afterwards.) • Can more than one person pay the same? (Yes—some people can pay the same amount as long as not all the friends do.)

Make Sense of the Task (Individually and Collectively)

- Ask students to put on the brakes and refrain from starting to solve, but they may annotate their paper in any way that makes sense to them
- Multiple reads of the question in different voices
- *Can you tell me what is happening in this problem in your own words?*
- *What does "fair" mean?*
  ○ Move from what "fair" means to them to what "fair" means in the context of this problem.
  ○ Ask them to defend this definition of fair with evidence from the problem
  ○ If they don't notice the "based on what they each paid," ask them to explain what this means
- *What are we trying to figure out?*
  ○ *The question says, "What are some of the ways that they could have paid for, and fairly split the chocolates?" What does that tell us about solving this task? Can this problem have more than one solution?*

(Continued)

Table 6.2 The Launch Section of the Sixth-Grade Planning Document *(Continued)*

Build a Bridge to Solving
• *"Remember, a solution will show how much each of the five friends spent and how many pieces of candy each friend received."* • *"You will have five minutes to start working independently, and after that, I may ask you to share your ideas with a partner and keep working on the solution together."* • Keep an eye out for students who don't look ready to get started.

As the plan in Table 6.2 shows, in crafting the launch board vision the sixth-grade teachers not only decided to discuss fairness and what it meant for the amount to be based on what each friend paid but also that the solution needed to show both how much chocolate each person got and how much they paid, and that there might be multiple solutions. They also decided that if a student asked about more than one person paying the same amount or receiving the same number of chocolates, they would clarify that this is ok as long as everyone is not paying or getting the same amount. They anticipated that students might ask about using coins. They noted that if this idea surfaced, they would encourage students to try that out but would delay any discussion of whether it would result in a working solution for later, after students had time to work on the task. Anticipating theories and questions from learners allows the teacher to consider whether to respond to a question with a concrete answer or a decision, open it up to the class to make a collective decision, or decide to hold off on the discussion until learners have had some time to grapple with a solution.

Table 6.3 The Content of each Section of the Launch Board Vision

Section of Launch Board Vision	What Goes in It
What We Know	• Facts, constraints, and contextual information from the task that might be important for solving
Language/Vocabulary	• Terms, words, or phrases that may need to be clarified with age-appropriate working definitions that reflect learners' prior knowledge and experiences
Goal	• What the learner is responsible for producing, in what format, and how they will know when they are finished
Theories and Questions from Learners	• A landing spot for learners' questions or theories that the teacher thinks might emerge

The launch board vision captured in the planning document is merely a guide for the teacher to map out what they intend to draw out in the launch; the actual board may look different depending on the language, questions, and theories elicited from the learners. It is also important to note that the launch board vision is not something the teacher presents to the learners but rather something that the teacher and the class construct together, with the teacher jotting notes on the board as the students generate ideas.

Making Sense of the Task

The sixth-grade teachers considered how to give students time to think through and make sense of the task individually. They decided they would have students jot down their ideas on paper as they listened to multiple reads of the task and discussed the key ideas. They planned to support collective sensemaking by prompting students to retell the situation in their own words and generating potential questions to elicit and deepen their understanding of some of the key ideas listed in the launch board vision (e.g., understanding fairness and the phrase "based on what they paid" in the context of the problem). Finally, they planned to highlight the idea that there is more than one possible solution to the problem by asking students to reflect on the wording of the question in the task (see Table 6.2).

Key considerations in planning for making individual sense of the task include: How will the task be displayed? Who will read the task? What kind of visuals could be used? What materials should students have? Should students be listening and writing, or just listening? For collective sensemaking, after students have had a chance to retell the task in their own words, how will questions be phrased to elicit the important considerations and ideas mapped out in the launch board vision? Writing out those questions ahead of time, considering specific language and phrasing, helps ensure that the focus is on students making sense rather than the teacher making sense for them.

Building a Bridge to Solving

The last section of the plan for the launch focuses on how to help transition learners from making sense of the task to productively working independently, in pairs, or in small groups as they work toward a solution. If students are unsure about what they are supposed to do, the teacher will spend more time answering questions or prompting students to go back and revise their work than on facilitating their productive struggle. This section of the plan might include a reminder to students about their goals and responsibilities during the work time. It should also prepare students for the structure of their work time. Will they be working alone or with a partner? Can they move around the room, or do they need to work at their desks? Are there any tools or materials besides paper and pencil available to them? How much time will they have to work? In the sixth-grade plan, the teachers decided to give students five minutes to work on the task independently (Figure 6.2) and then start to match students who were using similar strategies to work together. This would allow learners to follow their own line of thinking while receiving support from another learner who was thinking similarly.

Planning to Facilitate Productive Struggle

The next component of the plan focuses on thinking through how to support learners as they are working on the task. As described in Chapter 3, this involves two primary responsibilities: understanding learners' emerging ideas and points of struggle and helping them move forward with those ideas. This component of planning requires thinking about the mathematics of the task in consideration of who the learners are and where they are in their understanding.

As the sixth-grade teachers continued planning for the Fair Shares task, grounding the discussion in their own work helped them think through the roadblocks that their students might encounter when working on the task.

> Ms. Johnson begins this conversation by talking about her discomfort when she solved the problem. "I'm not gonna lie. It took me a minute to figure out how to start this problem. There definitely wasn't a clear-cut path." Ms. Fulton looks back through the solutions and asks, "So focusing just on finding one way that the money could be split up was your way in?" Ms. Johnson confirms that when she could not figure out how to get started, she just focused on splitting up the money but notes that she could also have zeroed in on the candies and figured out one way to split those up first. "That seems like something our students might run into. They might fully understand the problem but still be sitting with a blank paper because they can't figure out where to start. If that happens, maybe our move is to say something like, 'You just told me they have to split up the money and the candies, so why don't you think about one of those things and how five friends could split it up. Then you can think about where to go from there.'"
>
> Mr. Kane jots this down on the planning doc and reminds the group of a concern Ms. Johnson mentioned when they looked at each other's solutions. "What about students who divide 60 by 15 and then can't figure out what to do from there because they don't know what the 4 means?" Ms. Fulton suggests that they ask questions that will prompt the student to think about the labels (60 what? 15 what?). Ms. Johnson adds that reminding them that the 4 is really 4/1 might help because they can think of it as a ratio of 4 candies to 1 dollar.

The sixth-grade teachers completed this portion of the plan, shown in Table 6.4, with the potential strategies and struggles they identified in mind.

Table 6.4 The Facilitating Productive Struggle Section of the Sixth-Grade Planning Document

Facilitating Productive Struggle

Students Who Can't Get Started
 	
- *Can you tell me what's happening in the problem in your own words?*
- *What do you know?*
  - *What do you need to figure out?*
  - *You have these candies, this much money, and these friends ... Now what?*
  - *Would drawing a picture or using some manipulatives help?*
    - Have a manipulative that students can split up
      - Cubes to represent candy
      - Fake money (dollars, quarters especially) or encourage them to sketch the money
- If a student knows they have to figure out how much money each paid and how much candy they should get but doesn't know where to start, encourage them to pick one (money OR candy) and figure out one way it could be split up.
  - Check back in and say, "So if this is how much each paid, how much candy should each get" (or vice versa)
 	
Students Who Get Stuck
 	
- Student divides 60 by 15 but doesn't know what the answer represents
  - Ask questions to help students think about labels/what they are dividing (60 *candies* by 15 *dollars*): *What is this 60? What is the 15? Why did you divide?*
  - Encourage them to think about the 4 as 4/1 and to think about what the 4 and the 1 represent
  - Once they know that 4 candies cost $1, have them think of one possible amount each friend could have paid and how many candies they would get, based on this rate.
- Students who find the unit cost (25 cents/candy) but can't figure out how to use this information
  - Refer to launch board: *What will an answer look like (how much each spent and how much candy they get)?*
  - Encourage them to come up with one solution and then expand to other way
- Student splits the candies and the money evenly
  - Point to the launch board "What we know" section: *Does your answer work? Look at each criterion—Does it include 5 friends? Have you accounted for a total cost of $15 and for 60 candies? Do you have an answer where not all friends pay the same amount?*
    - *How can you build an answer that would work using what you have here?*
    - *What adjustments could you make?*

(Continued)

Table 6.4 The Facilitating Productive Struggle Section of the Sixth-Grade Planning Document *(Continued)*

> **Students Who Think They Are Finished**
>
> - For students who only found one solution: *Is there only one way? Can you come up with a way to pay different amounts?*
> - For students who are only finding whole dollar solutions: *Can you come up with more ways—maybe using coins?*
> - For students who have found multiple solutions: *Can you organize your solutions so that you can compare them? Do you notice any patterns?*

The template includes three types of struggle to plan for: getting started, getting stuck, and finishing early, but more can be added if necessary. In each category, the teachers articulated potential questions they could ask learners to elicit, clarify, ignite, sustain, support, press, and consolidate learners' thinking. (These moves are described in more detail in Chapter 3.)

Students Who Can't Get Started

Planning to support learners who struggle to find an entry point into the problem involves considering moves that will help them review or return to the important information that emerged during the launch. Asking learners to retell the problem in their own words is a way to do this and a way to elicit potential misunderstandings or confusion. Other common ways to help get a learner started are engaging them in a simpler version of the task, suggesting a first step (but not a specific strategy), or introducing something to make the task more concrete, such as a visual model, manipulative, or graphic organizer. The sixth-grade teachers thought about several of these options, including narrowing the task temporarily to find only one way and then building from there (e.g., splitting up the chocolate candy between five people and then considering how to distribute the cost fairly).

Students Who Get Stuck

It is also important to anticipate places where learners might get stuck and develop questions or prompts to help get them unstuck. The sixth-grade teachers anticipated that students might approach the problem by dividing 60 by 15 but then be unable to figure out what the answer meant or know where to go from there. They decided they would address this issue by asking questions about what the 60 and 15 represent. They also included a next step to suggest for a student who figured out that 4 candies cost $1 but does not know what to do with that information. Another thing to consider is what to do when a student ignores or forgets about a problem constraint or parameter, such as the fact that the friends had to pay different amounts.

This forethought is crucial because it cuts down the cognitive demand placed on teachers as they circulate and attempt to support a room full of students with myriad struggles and stuck points. Of course, it is unlikely that any plan will include every way that students could get stuck, but having several mapped out in advance enables teachers to address those anticipated struggles quickly and allows them to devote more time and energy to unanticipated struggles that arise.

Students Who Think They Are Finished

Sometimes, students will think they are finished when there is more mathematics to explore. In this case, the goal of planning is to think of ways to re-engage students. That might mean challenging them to defend or justify a solution or find additional solutions. The sixth-grade teachers prepared for learners who had one complete solution and for learners who had multiple working solutions but had not yet tried splitting up dollars. In both cases, there is more mathematics to get out of the task from finding more and different types of solutions. In other cases, a teacher might encounter learners who have completed all parts of the task. With low-floor, high-ceiling tasks, this can be an opportunity to deepen understanding by posing an extension question or an alternate version of the task that introduces new complexity. In Fair Shares, a teacher might introduce an additional friend or change the total number of candies or money to less friendly numbers than the original version of the task. The teachers planned to ask students to organize their solutions to make it easier to compare them (e.g., a chart or an organized list) and then look for patterns. When a task has multiple solutions, finding ways to organize the data and look for patterns can lead learners to see important mathematical relationships.

Planning to Discuss Learner Thinking

The next section of the responsive mathematics lesson plan involves thinking about which strategies could be shared during the discussion and in what order, a process Smith and Stein (2018) call *selecting and sequencing*. Although this will have to be done in the moment based on what students do, the teacher can use the anticipated strategies to map out a pathway toward the mathematical goal. Next, they can think through how they will structure the discussion to help students make sense of each strategy and surface important mathematics (see Chapter 4 for more on discussing learner thinking).

The sixth-grade teachers continued their planning session by making decisions about how to sequence the strategies they thought might emerge in their students' work. They decided to incorporate incorrect and correct answers to focus on the need to keep the problem parameters in mind when tackling this task.

> As the group wraps up their discussion of facilitating productive struggle, they realize that one potential error their students might make is splitting both the candies and the cost evenly so that each person pays $3 and gets 12 candies. While this an incorrect solution, it could still help students realize that each candy is worth 25 cents (or that each dollar buys 4 candies).
>
> Mr. Kane suggests, "What if we start off our discussion with that 'split everything evenly' approach? I think some of my students will go that route and it would be great to show that when you realize you've made a mistake or forgotten a problem parameter, there still might be useful information in your work that you can build upon. We could put it up and ask them if it's a viable solution, then get them to talk about whether it's mathematically sound and what they can use from it."
>
> Ms. Fulton begins typing in the planning document, narrating as she does so. "So, first we'll ask them to figure out how this student approached the problem. Like walk us through their solution method. Then we can ask whether this solution meets the problem constraints. That's actually great practice for them in always looking back at the problem constraints to see whether their answer follows the rules, so to speak."
>
> Mr. Kane continues, "Exactly. And what I really like about this one is that there's still valuable information here. This approach can get you to the 4 candies for $1 or a quarter per candy. We should draw that out."
>
> Ms. Fulton types silently: This solution shows that if someone pays $3 they will get 12 pieces of candy. If you know that information, what else could you figure out. "Does this work? Is this what you mean? I think this would be a really productive conversation and I like that it shows that you don't throw out the baby with the bathwater and crumple up your paper when you have a solution that doesn't quite work. You look at it, see what you can learn from it, and adjust from there. Awesome. I actually hope a student makes this mistake so we can use it!"

As the teachers continued planning, they specified what approaches to the problem they would look for in student work, as shown in Table 6.5. They thought through how they would display the student work, and what questions they could ask to help students make sense of each solution path.

Selecting and Sequencing Student Work

This section of the plan involves choosing several strategies that students will likely use and arranging them in an intentional order. Although the discussion will occur after students have time to grapple with the task, the teacher needs to start looking for these strategies while students work. Keeping both priorities in mind—facilitating learners' struggle while looking for student work to share—is a lot to do at once, so anticipating student thinking and planning

Table 6.5 The Discussing Learning Thinking Section of the Sixth-Grade Planning Document

Discussing Learner Thinking

Student Work to Look for While Students Are Problem Solving
• *Even split*: Someone who split the money and candy evenly (this might be an early step, take a picture if you see it)
• *Equivalent fractions*: Someone who figured out a way to split up the money and then used equivalent fractions to figure out how many candies each person should get
• *Candies per $1*: Someone who figured out that you get 4 candies for $1
• *Price per candy*: Someone who figured out that each candy costs 25 cents
Help Students Make Sense of Work Shared
• How will I ensure my entire class has access to the student work we discuss?
   ○ Display work on the board using a document camera
   ○ Make sure to have students who did not use the strategy in the work displayed do the work of making sense of it
• Even Split
   ○ *How did this learner approach the problem?*
   ○ *Does this solution meet the constraints of the problem?* (No, because everyone has the same amount of candy.)
   ○ *This solution shows that if someone pays $3, they will get 12 pieces of candy. If you know that information, what else could you figure out?* (Ex: For $6, someone could get 24 candies.)
• Equivalent fractions
   ○ *What does this first fraction, $4/$15 represent? Why is there a $15 in the denominator?*
   ○ *Why did this learner put a ? in the numerator and a 60 in the denominator of this second fraction?*
   ○ *Why are the fractions equal if one is talking about money and the other is talking about candy?*
• Candies per dollar
   ○ *What important information did this person figure out?*
   ○ *How does knowing that 4 candies cost $1 help us to find a solution to the problem?*
   ○ Annotate/label work to help show why dividing 60 *candies* by 15 *dollars* would result in *candies per dollar*
• Price per candy
   ○ *Can someone explain how this person was able to figure out how much each piece of candy would cost?*
   ○ *Why does dividing 15 by 60 give us the price per candy?*
   ○ *How does knowing the price per candy help us find more solutions than knowing that 4 candies cost $1?*

teacher responses is crucial. Categorizing and naming the strategies in broad categories can help teachers quickly find student work that meets the needs of the discussion while students are engaged in problem solving. In Table 6.5, the sixth-grade teachers named four categories of potential student work to look for: even split, equivalent fractions, candies per dollar, and price per candy.

Making Sense of the Work

The first step to making sense of the work is ensuring that all the learners can see the work. The sixth-grade teachers decided to project the student work using a document camera, an apt choice for written work. A learner strategy could also be made public to the class by having them record it on the board, gathering learners to look at the solution at the student's desk, or projecting a photograph on an electronic display. The choice of how to share the work will depend on the strategy, room configuration, and available technology.

The next step is to think about how to help other learners engage with each strategy and surface the mathematics behind the strategy. This often includes planning questions to ask the class and annotations to make aspects of it visible to all students. In the sixth-grade teachers' plan, they mapped out questions for each category they identified. Their questions for "Price per candy" solutions include asking another student to explain the work being displayed and then zeroing in on how knowing the price per candy helps generate solutions (see Table 6.5).

Planning to Connect and Consolidate Student Learning

The final section of responsive mathematics lesson planning involves thinking through three considerations to help learners solidify their understanding of the mathematical concepts underlying their work in the lesson. First, teachers consider how to connect to the mathematical goal, bridging between the student strategies discussed in the previous section and the essential mathematical ideas. Next, they consider how to provide opportunities for learners to consolidate their mathematical understanding. Finally, they consider how they will collect evidence of student understanding that can be used to plan future lessons.

> Mrs. Fulton starts the conversation by talking about how her thinking about what she wants students to get out of the task has evolved over the course of the planning session. "When I was doing the problem last night and even when we started talking today, my priority was making sure my students could find the unit cost because that's how I've always done it and what I've always drilled into my kids. I'm wondering now, though, if what we really

want to capture at the end of the discussion is the different ways you can go about solving a problem like this and how they're related."

Ms. Johnson nods. "I love that idea. I've been pushing myself to make collaborative charts to capture stuff like this. And my kids are actually using them. I can see them looking at them when they're working, and I think it's good that they can kind of refresh their memories and think back to something they did before. What if we did that? Like get the group to summarize the different ways."

Mr. Kane asks, "So, what are the ways we want to focus on? Unit cost and items per dollar. Then maybe using equivalent fractions? Does that capture it?" Mrs. Fulton agrees and says that she wants to get the students to summarize how each approach works. "So, what I'm hoping they'll be able to do is summarize how you could do this problem with each of the approaches, then kind of generalize it. Like this." She types into the planning document

Using Unit Cost:

$$\frac{\$15}{60 \text{ candies}} = \frac{\$0.25}{1 \text{ item}} \qquad \frac{\text{Total cost}}{\text{\# of items}} = \frac{\text{Unit cost}}{1 \text{ item}}$$

Divide the total cost by how many items you bought. That gives you the cost for each item (unit cost)

Ms. Johnson asks, "When your kids summarize the process, do you write exactly what they say or do you make it clearer? I'm always torn. Because sometimes they say it in a kind of convoluted way and I'm afraid it won't make sense when they reread it. But I also want it to be their words and their ideas on the chart."

Mr. Kane suggests, "That happens in my class too. Sometimes I'll put the "first draft" on the board instead of the chart paper and see if we can tighten it up. How can we say this more clearly or keep it short and sweet? Something like that."

The group moves on to thinking about what the chart might include for the second approach and Mrs. Fulton adds their ideas to the planning doc:

Items per Dollar

$$\frac{60 \text{ candies}}{\$15} = \frac{4 \text{ candies}}{\$1} \qquad \frac{\text{total items}}{\text{total cost}} = \frac{\text{\# of items}}{\$1}$$

Divide the number of items by how much you paid. That tells you how many you got per dollar.

Ms. Johnson adds, "One of the things I want them to notice is that 4 for a dollar means the same thing as 25 cents each. Do you know what I mean? That 4:1 ratio is there either way."

Mr. Kane nods and says, "I'm thinking that the final part of this discussion could be to get them to look across all the work and find examples that show that relationship. What's cool is that it shows up in the equivalent fraction approach, too. They might just have to look a little harder to see it. And that approach really drives home the point that even though we're using words like ratios and proportions, what's really going on here is still those same equivalent fractions we've talked about before."

Equivalent Fractions

$$\frac{\$2}{\$15} = \frac{8 \text{ candies}}{60 \text{ candies}}$$

Set up equivalent fractions with the amount they paid and the amount of candy they got in the numerator and the total amount of money and total amount of candy in the denominator.

"We've been calling these equivalent fractions but they're also proportions," Mr. Kane notices. "We should point that out. This is actually a good time to introduce the idea of proportionality that cuts across all of these approaches"

As the group finishes up the planning session, they agree that they want the wrap up discussion to highlight the 4:1 ratio that occurs across all "fair" solutions, regardless of what solution path was taken. Mrs. Fulton is excited to see whether her students will be able to see the 4:1 ratio even in the equivalent fraction approach, since that approach doesn't include calculating a per candy cost. They discuss having students go back to their own solutions and evaluate whether they are, in fact, "fair" as a way to assess what students have learned.

In addition to the collaborative chart that Mrs. Fulton sketched out, the sixth-grade teachers also thought about specific questions they might ask to connect and consolidate student understanding. They incorporated an opportunity for students to revisit and reflect on their original solution and thought about how they could get students to reflect even if they could not come up with a solution before the discussion, as shown in Table 6.6.

Plan to Connect Student Strategies to the Mathematical Goal

This part of the planning process is about creating a bridge to link students' work on the task to the underlying mathematics they need to learn (e.g., concept, generalized strategy, symbolic notation, or pattern or relationship). In the plan for Fair Shares, the teachers' goal was for students to "use proportional thinking to make an argument about fairness." They decided to have the students look across the solutions generated in the discussion in the hopes that they would notice that the fairness represented in the solutions involves a relationship between the amount of money a person pays and the amount of candy they receive.

Table 6.6 The Connecting, Consolidating, and Collecting Evidence Section of the Sixth-Grade Planning Document

Connecting, Consolidating, and Collecting Evidence
Connect Student Strategies to the Mathematical Goal   • Have students look across the solutions that were discussed. *What makes these solutions all fair? What do they have in common?*   • Look for students who can articulate that there is a relationship between the amount of money someone paid and the amount of candy they receive.   **Consolidate Mathematical Understanding**   • Create an anchor chart capturing how to use the unit cost, items per dollar, and equivalent fractions approaches (Example from this task, then general summary)   • Have students look across all the different approaches on the anchor chart to find the same 4:1 ratio.   • Introduce the idea of proportionality as a term that explains the relationship the students found in the Fair Shares task.   • Student written reflection: *Does your solution show a proportional relationship between the amount of money and the amount of candies for each person? How do you know? (If you didn't find a solution, how would you look at someone else's solution and determine whether it was proportional?)*   **Collect Data about Student Understanding**   • Look across written reflections to see where students are in their developing understanding of proportionality.

Plan to Consolidate Mathematical Understanding

This section of the plan involves designing more intentional opportunities for learners to deepen or formalize their understanding of the mathematical goals or concepts. In the case of the Fair Shares lesson, this is the point where the teachers decided to build on the student thinking that was shared to introduce the term proportionality or proportional relationship. To help further consolidate and capture their learning, they planned to create a collaborative chart by having students look across all approaches for the 4 to 1 relationship. The teachers also opted to have students complete a written reflection, prompting them to re-evaluate their original solution and articulate their understanding of proportionality.

Plan to Collect Data About Student Understanding

The final part of the lesson plan focuses on intentionally collecting evidence of student understanding so that it can be used to evaluate the current lesson and inform future lessons. Note that the individual student work from the consolidation portion of the lesson can be collected and used to provide evidence of student understanding. The sixth-grade teachers planned to use students' written reflections to help them gain insight into their students' developing understanding of proportionality as they moved forward with the unit. When they convened again, they could discuss what they learned from this data and use that information to help plan the next lesson.

The Best Laid Plans

As stated at the beginning of the chapter, responsiveness entails preparation and improvisation. After reading this chapter, it might seem possible to script out every part of a mathematics lesson—from the opening launch, through facilitating productive struggle, to the end of the discussion, anticipating every student idea and corresponding teacher response. This is neither practical nor desirable.

Instead, planning in advance scaffolds responsive teaching by carefully thinking through what to say and do when different scenarios arise. This slowing down of decision-making is particularly important for teachers new to responsive teaching because it provides a longer runway for learning the complex facilitation of the launch, productive struggle, discussions of learner thinking, and consolidation of the mathematical goals.

While too little planning can lead to the conclusion that responsive mathematics teaching does not work, teachers new to this way of teaching can feel equally frustrated when the best-laid plans do not come to fruition exactly as expected, when unanticipated student ideas emerge, when a discussion veers off in a different direction than intended, or when pre-planned supports for helping a struggling student do not have the intended impact. Keeping in mind that no amount of planning will fully alleviate the need for improvisation can help teachers set realistic goals for themselves and their lessons as they learn to teach responsively. Some teachers do this by focusing on improving one part of the lesson at a time—working first on launching tasks well, then adding in responsive facilitation of students' productive struggle, and then focusing on their discussion facilitation skills. In our experience, teachers who continue to work toward responsive teaching often become better improvisers and better planners simultaneously, equipping themselves with a strong set of questions to have at the ready and making better and better judgment calls about when and how to deploy them over time. Mapping out a list of questions to draw from, like the ones shown in the planning documents in this chapter, can help teachers resist the urge to provide students with a solution path to move things along more quickly.

The planning process described in this chapter may seem daunting and more involved than typical lesson planning practices. The value of this preparation time, however, cannot be overstated. Planning for responsive teaching will get progressively easier as teachers draw from their experiences to better anticipate student thinking and understand the priorities of each part of the lesson.

This work does not have to be done alone. Collaborative lesson planning encourages teachers to take risks and support each other as they try new strategies or approaches. Many teachers will need to break away from the more direct instructional approach they have been using to allow more space for student discovery and discussion. It can be challenging to take up new practices if teachers are not given time to plan, try out, and continue to refine their practice (Stigler & Hiebert, 1999). It can feel less risky to do this in the company of others who can provide support for the challenges that arise and a sense that "we are all in this together." As the vignettes in this chapter illustrate, workshopping a new idea with a planning group before trying it out allows teachers to think through thorny issues or uncertainties while encouraging and supporting each other. These ideas are discussed in more detail in Chapter 8.

| PLANNING FOR RESPONSIVE MATHEMATICS TEACHING ||
What It Is:	What It Is Not:
<ul><li>Identifying multiple solution strategies and pathways for a given task</li><li>Thinking through the key ideas and constraints that need to be clarified to help students develop individual and collective understanding of the task</li><li>Generating questions and prompts that might help students who get stuck or need their thinking extended</li><li>Mapping out a sequence of potential strategies to share to surface the important mathematics</li><li>Planning opportunities for students to consolidate their understanding of the mathematical goals</li></ul>	<ul><li>Identifying the best solution or desired strategy to solve a given task</li><li>Planning how to model a solution strategy or similar task so students will know what to do</li><li>Creating a script to follow verbatim or read from during the lesson</li><li>Planning a "show and tell" of good solutions</li><li>Allowing a lesson to go in whatever direction it ends up going, depending on students' responses</li><li>Providing closure at the end of a lesson by restating the objectives or telling students what they learned</li></ul>

Responsive Mathematics Teaching Is a Cyclical Process

Responsive problem-solving lessons are not meant to be stand-alone, one-off, or "fun Friday" activities that occur outside of the regular, day-to-day curriculum. In fact, a critical first step in planning a responsive problem-solving lesson is considering evidence of student learning from past lessons and using this to guide the construction of the learning goals for the current lesson. In this way, responsive mathematics teaching is a cyclical process, where each lesson builds on what has come before and is designed to gather evidence to inform what comes next. As shown in Figure 6.6 below, these two critical components of teacher preparation—reflecting and planning—comprise the bridge that links lessons together to support the trajectory of student learning over time.

Curricular materials such as daily lesson plans, scope and sequence, and pacing guides are important and helpful for planning, but teachers need to continually assess how the students in front of them are making sense of mathematical concepts and progressing toward grade-level standards and then adjust instruction as necessary. Marching through a curriculum to "keep pace" without attending to student understanding is not only unproductive and frustrating for students and teachers but also runs the risk of widening

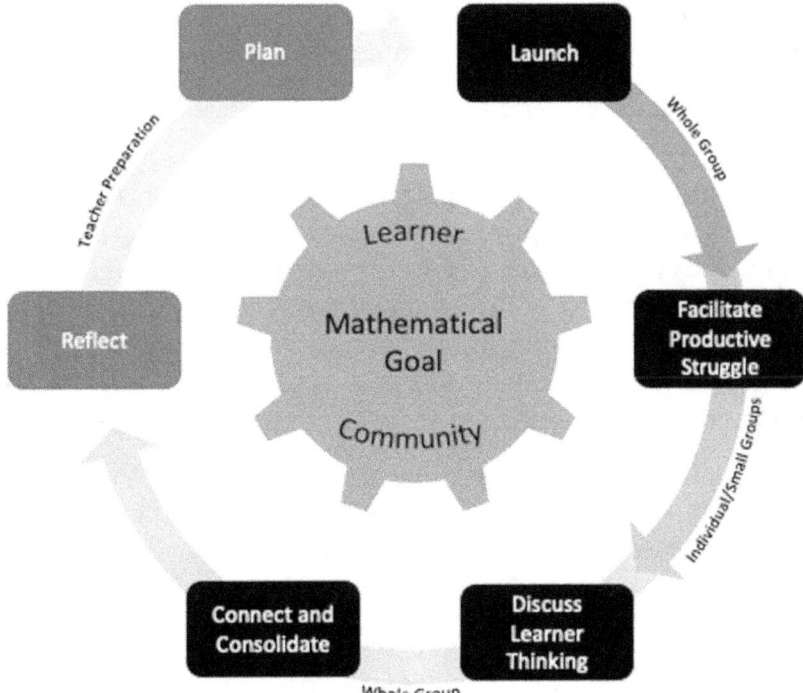

Figure 6.6 Model for responsive mathematics teaching.

the gap between students' current ideas about mathematics and grade-level mathematical goals.

Evidence of student thinking elicited and collected from problem-solving lessons can help teachers better understand where students are within a learning progression and what next steps are necessary. If the evidence shows that many students are not ready for the next lesson or set of tasks in the curricular materials, a responsive problem-solving lesson can be planned to allow students to revisit those ideas. If teachers are unsure what prior experience and initial understandings students might have about a new topic, a responsive problem-solving lesson could be designed to elicit students' current understanding and background knowledge. Careful consideration of what has come before and will come after is critical to the planning process. This intentional focus on where students are and attention to what students need is the essence of responsiveness.

Reflection Questions

Guiding Principles
1 Prioritize mathematical sensemaking
2 Promote collaborative learning communities
3 Support a positive mathematical identity
4 Ensure all students have access to mathematics

1 How does the approach to planning described in this chapter address the guiding principles of responsive teaching?
2 How does your current lesson planning look different from the planning described in this chapter? What can you adopt and implement into your current planning routine?
3 As you think about integrating collaborative planning into your instructional context:

    a What is already in place that you can build on?
    b What challenges do you foresee?
    c What can you do to try to overcome those challenges?

7

Building a Responsive Mathematics Community

The guiding principles for creating an inclusive and responsive mathematics classroom include making space for sensemaking, ensuring access, promoting active collaboration, and building positive mathematical identities, as outlined in Chapter 1. Chapters 2–5 detail the main components of responsive mathematics teaching—launching tasks, facilitating productive struggle, discussing learner thinking, and helping learners connect, consolidate, and reflect on their growing understanding. However, it is essential to recognize that these principles and components do not occur in a vacuum. The vignettes in the previous chapters take place in classrooms where students develop positive mathematical identities, actively collaborate with their peers, freely share their mathematical ideas, and participate in whole-group discussions in which mistakes are leveraged as access points to deeper understanding. How does a teacher create that kind of classroom culture? What are the conditions under which responsive mathematics teaching can flourish?

This chapter explores two vital processes at the center of responsive mathematics teaching: *attending to the learner's experience* and *cultivating the classroom community*. As shown in Figure 7.1, these elements, together with ongoing connections to mathematical goals, can be viewed as the gears that power the essential components of the model for responsive mathematics teaching. Teachers new to responsive teaching might think, "This won't work in my classroom" or "This won't work with my students." It is important to recognize that shifting to the type of community described in the previous chapters does not happen overnight, especially in classrooms where students have not had the opportunity to engage actively and collaboratively as mathematical

DOI: 10.4324/9781003536710-7

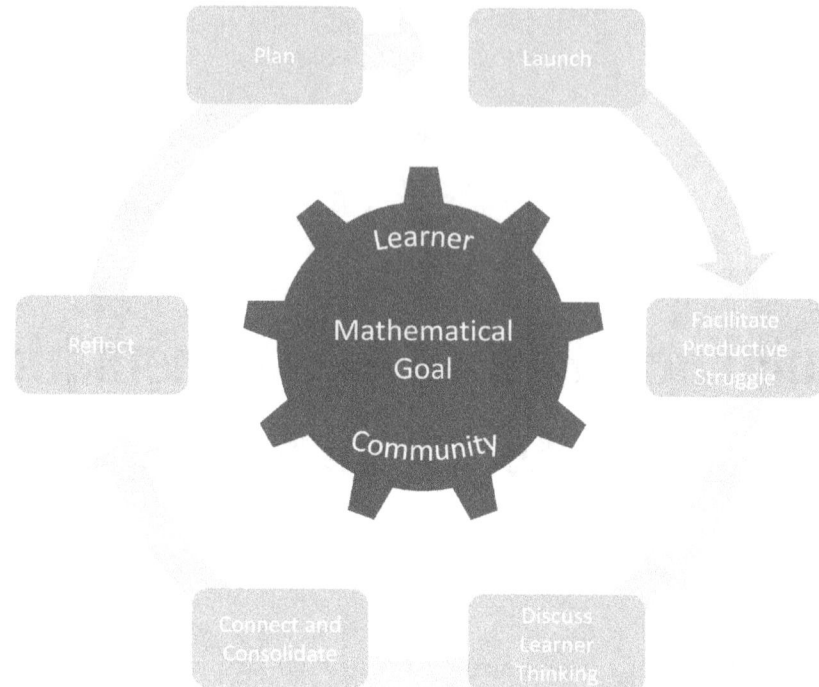

Figure 7.1 The learner's experience and community building are central to the model for responsive mathematics teaching.

learners. To support this transition, we provide some practical tools that can be used to "prime the pump," assisting students in developing the necessary mindsets, communication habits, and trust that are foundational to a responsive mathematics community.

We begin with a vignette in which Mr. Charles, an eighth-grade teacher, decides to try responsive mathematics teaching in his classroom by facilitating a number talk. A number talk is a routine where students solve a computational problem mentally, without using paper or pencil. After arriving at their solutions, they share out the different strategies that they used to figure out the solution. The teacher facilitates this discussion by recording various strategies and guiding the discussion to highlight mathematical connections (Humphries & Parker, 2015).

> Mr. Charles was introduced to number talks in a course he was taking. He noticed that in the videos they watched, the students engaged in mathematical sensemaking and discussions of each other's ideas in a way that his students rarely did. He wanted to try a number talk to see if he could replicate that enthusiastic engagement around mathematics in his own classroom.

At the start of the class period, Mr. Charles tells the students that they will be doing something different for the first part of class and lays out some rules for the number talk. He tells students they should attempt the problems using only mental math (no paper and pencil) and instructs them to put a thumb on their chest when they have an answer instead of raising their hands, so everyone has enough time to think.

He then writes the problem 25 × 8 on the board and gives his students time to think. When he sees some thumbs up, he pushes himself to give more wait time than he typically does, but eventually, no new thumbs are turning up. He asks, "OK, what did you get as your answer?"

Four of the students who typically participate raise their hands. Mr. Charles calls on one of those students, who answers "200." He asks if anyone got a different answer, hoping there might be a variety of answers to explore, but no one raises a hand. He tries calling on Eric, who rarely participates, asking what answer he got. "Yeah, I got 200, too," Eric says without making eye contact. Eager to draw Eric into the conversation, Mr. Charles asks, "Can you share your strategy with us, Eric?" to which Eric responds, "What do you mean?" Pressed to explain how he got his answer, Eric shrugs, slouches in his chair, and says, "I don't know. I just knew."

Mr. Charles calls on Kayla, who is eagerly waving her hand in the air. Kayla explains, "I multiplied 5 × 8, put down the 0, and carried the 4, and then 2 × 8 is 16 plus 4, and that's 20." As Kayla explains, Mr. Charles notices that others in the class seem disengaged. He asks if anyone used a different strategy, but gets no volunteers. He calls on Amelia, who says, "I was thinking of quarters, so I counted 25, 50, 75, a dollar, 25, 50, 75, 2 dollars." As she talks, Amelia uses her fingers to show how she counted. "Brilliant," exclaims Mr. Charles. He asks if anyone in the class understood Amelia's strategy and could restate it. Andre comments on how she was counting on her fingers like a baby, and several students laugh. Amelia turns red, and Mr. Charles reprimands Andre, reminding him to be respectful. No one else volunteers.

Mr. Charles tries a second problem, 25 × 9, but the discussion proceeds in much the same manner—with the same few students willing to share an answer or a procedure but little engagement from the rest of the class. To draw in some other voices, he tries calling on Tyler, who is at least looking interested, but Tyler slouches in his chair and shrugs.

Frustrated, Mr. Charles skips the rest of his planned number talk and teaches the rest of the lesson as usual. He wonders why his number talk looked so different from the videos he had watched, where students eagerly explained different ways to break apart numbers and make sense of the problems.

Mr. Charles' experience exemplifies what can happen when students have not had the opportunity to develop the mindset and communication skills crucial to building a productive mathematical community. Only a few students in his classroom seem to feel comfortable sharing their thoughts, likely because of underlying beliefs about who in the room is "good at math" and has worthwhile ideas to share. Mr. Charles' experience also illustrates how students pick up messages about the types of strategies that are acceptable (and unacceptable) in a mathematics community. Individual beliefs, relationships among students, and classroom community values can be deeply entrenched and take time and effort to reshape. Building a strong foundation for a responsive mathematics community requires attending to these dimensions and, in many cases, doing some explicit work to help students reenvision themselves as learners, reshape the ways in which they interact with each other, and reconsider what it means to do mathematics. After exploring these three shifts in more detail, we present concrete actions teachers can take to establish norms, shift the classroom culture, and build students' capacity for engaging in mathematics collaboratively and productively.

Shifting Perceptions and Practices in the Mathematics Classroom

Robust, healthy, mathematical learning communities are collaborative and inclusive. They are spaces where individual members perceive themselves and others as having valuable ideas to share. In these spaces, risk-taking is encouraged, valued, and used to move the understanding of the entire group forward. Implicit values of respect and academic humility are visible in the way that members respond to the ideas of others and in the way they present their own. Questions are seen as opportunities for investigation, and productive struggle often gives way to joy. Budding mathematicians feel empowered to be brave because they know they are in a safe space. Most importantly, healthy mathematical learning communities result from active and intentional cultivation; the fruit of seeds that have been planted, fed, watered, and lovingly nurtured over time. Cultivating this type of learning community requires supporting shifts in three key areas: (1) learners' perceptions of mathematics and what it means to engage in the discipline, (2) learners' perceptions of themselves in relation to mathematics, and (3) learners' participation in the mathematical community. The cultivation tools we present in the second half of this chapter are designed to support shifts and nurture growth in these three areas.

Shifting Perceptions of Mathematics

Mathematics is the art of explanation. If you deny students the opportunity to engage in this activity—to pose their own problems, to make their own conjectures and discoveries, to be wrong, to be creatively frustrated, to have an inspiration, and to cobble together their own explanations and proofs—you deny them mathematics itself.

(Lockhart, 2009, p. 29)

Lockhart and several other mathematicians describe mathematics as a creative and dynamic field where problems are approached from multiple perspectives, through exploration and the use of different methods. Risk-taking and making mistakes are essential components of the process, as they contribute to refinement, revision, and deeper understanding (Cheng, 2022; Devlin, 2009; Hardy, 1992; Su, 2020). These writer humanize mathematics, revealing that it is not just a static collection of numbers, computations, procedures, and rules to be learned but a human endeavor that is accessible to all. However, mathematical work in many school settings continues to be reduced to the replication of procedures and answer-getting, presenting a bleak and woefully incomplete picture of what it truly means to do mathematics (NCTM, 2000; Stigler & Hiebert, 1999).

Learners need to see and experience mathematics as a process of exploration and invention that includes both struggle and joy. In a responsive mathematics classroom, students build on each other's ideas, articulate arguments to explain their thinking, and refine incomplete understandings or interpretations. Much as students learn to use the scientific method or literary analysis, using the tools of professionals in those fields, they learn to use the disciplinary tools of mathematics. Doing mathematics involves actively engaging in sensemaking, exploration, and collaboration, posing questions, testing ideas, embracing and learning from mistakes, and building understanding through dialogue with others. Since learners will almost certainly enter the classroom with pre-existing, often narrow, ideas about mathematics, a new vision of mathematics must be established, one that reinforces the notion that doing mathematics is exploratory, dialogic, and social.

Shifting Perceptions of Self in Relation to Mathematics

The belief that everyone can do mathematics and engage in the disciplinary practices mentioned above is a powerful idea, but rarely embraced. Regardless of age, many learners do not feel that mathematics as a discipline is accessible to them. When they think of mathematicians, they do not see themselves or individuals like them (Martin, 2009). Fostering inclusive mathematics learning communities involves broadening the understanding of mathematics and creating intentional opportunities for learners to embrace the idea that they can be successful in that space.

Key to helping students make this shift is increasing access by using activities that meet them where they are and provide every learner with an entry point. Accessible activities offer opportunities to take risks in a controlled environment and to experience the rewards of positive feedback from teachers and peers. These experiences accumulate, laying essential bricks in the foundation of students' self-concept and enhancing their willingness to take greater risks. It is important to note that accessible does not mean easy, nor does it always imply arriving at the correct answer. Learners must become comfortable with the idea that both struggle and mistakes are integral to what it means to engage in mathematics and contribute to valuable, knowledge-building experiences.

Shifting Perceptions about Mathematical Participation

Some learners already embrace the idea that they are mathematical thinkers with ideas to share. However, they may not believe that everyone in the learning community has valuable insights and ideas. Recognizing that we are all mathematical requires a shift in how students perceive themselves and how they view others. Classroom culture—the blend of perspectives and attitudes about mathematics and who is seen as mathematical—can be communicated implicitly or explicitly, sending signals to other learners about what counts as doing mathematics and who holds mathematical authority in the classroom. Classroom culture affects how individuals behave in this space. Consequently, developing a community or classroom culture that supports responsive teaching practices requires deliberately addressing the beliefs and mindsets that learners hold, not only about themselves but also about one another.

Learning is inherently social (Vygotsky, 1978). The relationships students form with one another—and the classroom culture that shapes how they listen, speak, and respond to each other—profoundly impact their comfort in participating, making mistakes, and exploring ideas aloud and in collaboration with others. Collaboration can feel jarring for students who are used to working on mathematics independently. For those accustomed to receiving positive feedback for correct answers, sharing ideas—especially incomplete or uncertain ones—can feel overwhelming. By its nature, collaboration is a skill that needs to be nurtured and developed over time.

A foundation for true collaboration is establishing trust among the group. Students are more willing to take intellectual risks when they feel safe sharing ideas (Aguirre et al., 2013). Learners need to know that their contributions to group discussions will not be judged, dismissed, or ridiculed. When students are encouraged to share their reasoning and make sense of their peers' contributions, they begin to see that mathematical understanding is not fixed or solitary. Just as professional mathematicians listen to and evaluate ideas, disagree respectfully, and revise thinking in response to conversations with their peers, so, too, should student mathematicians in a K-12 setting.

Focusing on relationships in a mathematics classroom goes beyond simply creating a friendly atmosphere; it involves intentionally centering community, collaboration, and mutual respect as essential components of the learning process. Establishing an environment where community members interact as mathematicians also requires broadening the concept of who holds mathematical authority—that is, where knowledge originates and how it is validated in the classroom. Many students believe that mathematical authority is determined by the teacher and the textbook; in a responsive mathematics classroom, it is critical to challenge that belief. Students need to learn to embrace the idea that mathematical insights can come from their peers and be validated by their peers, not just the teacher. They should be encouraged to look to one another as sources of mathematical knowledge. This decentralization of authority empowers students as active contributors and acknowledges diverse strategies, approaches, and experiences.

Cultivating a Mathematical Learning Community

Trust and mutual respect in a mathematics classroom cannot be established by decree, nor achieved in a single lesson. Developing a space that supports responsive mathematics teaching practices requires that teachers communicate what is expected and valued by establishing explicit norms or agreed-upon guidelines for productive student engagement and participation. This is most effective when students themselves are involved in co-constructing the norms. When students help to define the expectations, they are more likely to understand, value, and uphold them. The responsive mathematics teacher's responsibility in cultivating a learning community involves working with students to establish and maintain norms for a supportive learning environment, norms for participation, and norms for doing mathematics.

Co-constructing a Vision for a Supportive Learning Environment

A generative way to begin this process is to use some class time to co-construct a vision for what the ideal mathematical learning environment looks, feels, and sounds like—by asking students to consider what conditions make them feel joyful, successful, and supported in mathematics, and conversely, what factors make them anxious, disappointed, and isolated. This conversation often brings to light students' prior experiences and ways they may have felt welcomed or excluded in mathematics class. A brainstorming session where students' thoughts are captured on chart paper can effectively initiate this process of building a vision. Figure 7.2, for example,

> **Room 103's Math Class Vision**
>
> - Teacher doesn't get mad when you don't understand
> - Students are kind to each other and don't laugh or make fun when you get things wrong
> - You can ask someone for help if you need it but you should try it yourself first
> - It's okay if everyone does a problem a little differently
> - Students are doing what they are supposed to be doing and not fooling around
> - You can use things to help you, like counters and hundreds charts
> - You can't just give up and have to try even if it seems hard
> - Sometimes you get to work with other people and not just alone
> - The teacher can't just call on you without any warning and make you look dumb

Figure 7.2 Mrs. Carter's class vision of a supportive learning environment.

shows how Mrs. Carter captured her fourth graders' ideas in their own words.

Note that these norms are written in student language because they were generated through discussion. Offering opportunities to share ideas about this vision in private or anonymously (e.g., in writing rather than speaking in a group) can also be helpful because some students may have had painful experiences with mathematics in the past. Once a preliminary class vision has been developed, norm setting becomes a way to put some guardrails in place to ensure the vision is achieved.

Establishing Norms for Participation

Setting norms for specific activities helps the students learn to work together as a mathematical community in small and large group settings. Their roles and how they engage with each other may differ depending on whether they are participating in a whole group discussion or working collaboratively with a partner or small group.

Mr. Michaels started his school year by asking his fifth graders to reflect on and then talk about their previous experiences learning mathematics. He learned that while a few of the students in his class liked mathematics better than other subjects, a large portion of the class said that they either did not like the subject or thought they were not "good at it." Mr. Michaels pressed them to describe what they liked and did not like and what conditions made them feel comfortable or uncomfortable in mathematics class. During these conversations, Mr. Michaels jotted notes on the board, recording the students' ideas about what constitutes a positive and supportive mathematics environment. Then, he asked the group to consider two common activity structures in his mathematics class: discussions and group work. Drawing from

Math Discussion Norms	Group Work Norms
• Listen when other people tell how they did a problem and try to make sense of their idea • You can participate by sharing your own idea or adding on to someone else's idea • Ask questions when you don't get it • Share the mic	• We all work with everyone respectfully (friends or not) • Focus on the task at hand and don't get too distracted • Let everyone have a chance to talk and try out different ideas • All group members contribute

Figure 7.3 Discussion and group work norms generated by Mr. Michael's students.

his notes and their experience in other classes, the group developed the list of norms shown in Figure 7.3.

A slightly different approach to norm setting is talking about roles and responsibilities for both students and the teacher, asking for student input and seeking consensus about what responsibilities the teacher agrees to uphold (the Teacher's Job) and what responsibilities the students agree to uphold as productive contributors in mathematics class (the Students' Job). Figure 7.4 shows the responsibilities that Mrs. Carter's class came up with for the teacher and the students to execute their vision of an ideal learning community

After delineating the jobs shown in Figure 7.4 on a piece of chart paper posted in the room, Mrs. Carter added her signature under her job description. Each student signed the student side, indicating they agreed to those roles in Mrs. Carter's classroom. The class continued to add to this initial list of jobs over the school year. One of the key additions on the student side

Mrs. Carter's Job	Room 103 Students' Job
• Be nice when someone asks a question • Give good directions so students know what they're supposed to be doing • Give students tools when they need them • Let students work together sometimes • Warn people before you call on them and give them time to think	• If someone gets a problem wrong, help them understand and don't make them feel bad • Do what you're supposed to be doing and don't fool around • You have to try even when you feel frustrated. • When you get frustrated, ask for help instead of just quitting

Figure 7.4 Teacher and student responsibilities generated by students in Mrs. Carter's fourth-grade classroom.

was this one: "Everyone should take a turn to share their answers because even if you are wrong, people learn from what you said." Revisiting norms periodically and allowing students to suggest new ones or revise old ones can provide a necessary reminder, give students a chance to assess whether the norms are working to realize their vision, and allow for new needs to be addressed.

Reinforcing Norms for Doing Mathematics

Setting mutually agreed-upon norms is important for establishing a collaborative and productive mathematics classroom. However, it is also important to help students understand what those norms look and sound like in the context of doing mathematics. This means proactively noticing, acknowledging, affirming, and reinforcing the practices that are valued in the mathematics classroom, as they are happening.

The *Standards for Mathematical Practices* (NGO/CCSSO, 2010) describe the habits of mind and expertise that should be developed at all levels of mathematical learning in school, such as "make sense of problems and persevere in solving them" and "look for and make use of structure." Although most state standards and curriculum materials reference these practices, it can be difficult for students and their teachers to understand what the practices mean in the context of day-to-day mathematics instruction, particularly at the elementary levels. A contrasting approach, illustrated by the following vignette, is to engage students in co-constructing norms for doing mathematics in the context of their work on rich problem-solving tasks and activities.

> After Mr. Charles had trouble getting his students to engage with each other's ideas during his number talk, he thought about the role of mathematical norms in his classroom. At the beginning of the school year, he purchased a set of posters for his classroom that named and illustrated the eight *Standards for Mathematical Practices* with colorful images and icons. "Make Sense of Problems and Persevere to Solve Them" showed a cartoon image of a student bent over her work at a desk with gears in her brain, while "Attend to Precision" showed a large colorful bullseye. Although the posters help to make his classroom vibrant and welcoming, he rarely remembered to reference them, and he realized that the practices were not always evident in the ways his students interacted with each other.
>
> One day, he walks across the hall to visit his teammate, Ms. Harper. He sees that she has two large bulletin boards in the back of her room with the heading "What Mathematicians Do." Scattered on the boards are phrases

written on sentence strips, such as "Look for Patterns," "Take time to make sense of problems," and "Be precise and check our work." Mr. Charles notices that these reflect many of the same practices he has posted in his classroom, but are written in student-friendly language. Sprinkled across the board are photos of students and their work that exemplify those practices. For example, under the phrase, "Share our work and build on the work of others," is a photo of Mia and Alex holding up their work on the Sharing Crackers task described in Chapter 3. In that lesson, Mia had built on Alex's use of a table to find all the different ways that 36 crackers could be shared. Mr. Charles reflects that rather than being a one-and-done static feature in her room, Ms. Harper's bulletin board served as a living and ever-evolving testament to the mathematical work students were doing and truly illustrated what it meant to engage in mathematical thinking and reasoning. Later, he returns to her classroom to ask her how she developed these bulletin boards.

Ms. Harper explains that in September, her bulletin board is largely blank and features just a few phrases she chose to begin with. Whenever one of the practices is being demonstrated, like the "persevere and keep trying," she capitalizes on the teachable moment by calling out what she sees occurring and snapping a picture of students in action—like a picture of a group of four students triumphantly displaying their construction of a square pyramid after much trial and error. When a new practice not yet featured on the board arises, she leverages the teachable moment to call it out. To her students, new practices and additions to the board seem to occur organically throughout the year. While some additions occur spontaneously, behind the scenes, Ms. Harper has a list of the kinds of practices she wants to highlight over the year. The wording varies from year to year based on how her students articulate and demonstrate the practices, but by the end of the year, Ms. Harper's bulletin board typically includes most of the ideas on her list.

Mrs. Harper's list of mathematical practices

- Look for patterns
- Take time to make sense of problems
- Be precise and check our work
- Share and build on each other's work
- Disagree respectfully
- Look for "the good" in someone's work
- Give each other credit for ideas
- Feel "fuzzy" or confused before something "clicks"
- Ask questions to help themselves understand
- Try different ways to solve a problem
- Use what we already know
- See mistakes as opportunities to learn
- Take risks and share "rough draft" ideas

This vignette highlights the contrast between naming or posting pre-established norms for doing mathematics and co-constructing those norms with students in the context of their ongoing mathematical work in the classroom. Ms. Harper created a living display that was designed to continuously highlight authentic mathematical contributions from her students. By doing so, she created a culture where students can see themselves and others as capable mathematicians.

Developing Skills and Practices for a Responsive Mathematics Community

For a mathematics community to function in a way that honors the norms established by the students and teacher, specific skills must be built, reinforced, and strengthened over time. By intentionally incorporating opportunities to practice these skills, teachers can help learners maintain positive relationships with mathematics and each other. Doing mathematics often requires vulnerability, perseverance through mistakes, and being open to new and different ideas, all of which can be challenging for learners of any age to navigate. In this section, we focus on the responsibility of the teacher in cultivating healthy mathematical communities through the development of learners' (1) listening and sensemaking skills, (2) discussion participation skills, and (3) collaboration skills. We offer practical tools to support teachers in building these three important skill sets.

Listening and Sensemaking Skills

Depending on their previous experiences, students may enter the mathematics classroom with little practice explaining their mathematical thinking or listening to others' explanations. Even those who have been in classrooms where student work was shared may have experienced this as a more passive activity. The listening necessary in a responsive mathematics classroom is intertwined with active sensemaking, and students may need support in developing those skills.

Explicitly talking about what it means to listen actively and to try to make sense of someone else's thinking is a good first step. Following this discussion with opportunities to practice and using *orienting* moves can help students understand what it looks and feels like to try to understand another person's ideas. As shown in Table 7.1, teachers can use orienting moves to help focus students on listening and sensemaking, prime them to listen for

Table 7.1 Building a Responsive Mathematics Community Tool, Responsibility #1

Responsibility #1: Build Listening and Sensemaking Skills	
Orienting Moves help students understand what it looks and feels like to try to understand another person's ideas	
Focus students on a particular aspect of the explanation and task them with making sense of that piece	• As Macy explains, I want you all to watch what she is doing with her fingers and see if you can figure out how her strategy works.
Prime students to listen with purpose	• Listen carefully as Zaire explains his process because when he is finished, I will ask you to turn to a partner and put his idea into your own words.
Model sensemaking	• As Mika is talking, I am trying to picture what she is describing in my head. That helps me make sense of what she is saying.
Highlight positive examples of active listening and sensemaking	• When Kiley showed us her open number line and told us about what she did, I noticed that Tasha was using her finger and making hops in the air. Tasha, can you tell us how that helped you make sense of Kiley's idea?

understanding, model what it looks or sounds like to do so, and highlight positive examples when it happens.

A number talk, like the one Mr. Charles was attempting to facilitate in the opening vignette, can serve as fertile ground to practice listening and sensemaking in tandem, especially when moves like the ones in Table 7.1 are used to help students engage with the speaker. These moves set a clear expectation that students should listen actively as others share. They also remove some of the cognitive load by focusing students directly on what they should be paying attention to or doing.

Providing opportunities to work on sensemaking without the listening component can also reduce cognitive load. Student explanations can be meandering and challenging to follow, but having students make sense of written work that is not their own can be a way to practice that skill without the added burden of language processing. Chapter 4 offers additional moves that teachers can make to help learners engage with sensemaking around each other's work in the whole group discussion portion of a responsive problem-solving lesson.

Having students analyze errors in incorrect or incomplete work is also an effective way to help students build sensemaking skills and has the added

$$\frac{1}{2} \times \frac{4}{5} = \frac{5}{10} \times \frac{8}{10} = \frac{40}{10} = 4$$

Figure 7.5 Incorrect student work to analyze.

benefit of normalizing mistakes as a springboard for learning. Analyzing the student work shown in Figure 7.5, which shows a common error that students make when relying on procedures for fraction operations, could begin by asking students what they "notice and wonder" (Fetter, 2016), and encouraging them to try to follow the logic in this student's approach. Asking guiding questions like the ones that follow supports students in the sensemaking process:

- Does the student's answer make sense? Why or why not?
- What has this student done correctly?
- Where have they made an error?
- Why do you think they made this error?
- What did looking at this error help us understand about multiplying fractions?

Initially, teachers may need to provide these prompts to support students in the process. Using similar prompts every time work is analyzed can help students internalize the sensemaking process. As time goes on, teachers can begin to remove this scaffolding, placing more of the cognitive load on the students by asking, "What questions are you asking yourself as you look at this work?"

While listening and sensemaking are individual skills, they are vital to the mathematics community because they shape the nature of the classroom interactions. When students begin listening to each other and trying to make sense of each other's ideas, the classroom becomes a place where students learn from and with each other. Moving from executing these skills individually to executing them communally, in discussions with peers, may require developing additional skills.

Discussion Participation Skills

What passes for discussion in many mathematics classrooms is often more of a question-and-answer session, where the teacher poses a question, and students elect or are selected to respond with an answer, idea, or explanation. This type of discourse offers little opportunity for students to engage with each other's ideas, since most communication occurs between teacher and student. Picture a teacher passing a ball to one student, who catches it and returns it to the teacher. The teacher then passes the ball to a different student, who catches and returns it to the teacher while the rest of the class observes or tunes out. This image represents the communication flow in many well-intended mathematical discussions.

In a responsive mathematics classroom, the flow of communication is different. Questions come not only from the teacher but also from students, so students are passing the ball to each other as they build on one another's mathematics ideas or ask questions about each other's thinking. Again, however, this kind of environment does not create itself, and given the previous experiences students may have had in mathematics classrooms, preliminary skill-building may be necessary. Specifically, students may need to learn:

- What kinds of comments they can make about each other's work
- What kinds of questions they can ask about each other's work
- How to disagree with another person's idea respectfully
- How to monitor their participation in a discussion

The student work analysis described in the previous section is an excellent starting point for students to develop a repertoire of questions to ask when making sense of written solutions. However, there is a difference between analyzing an anonymous, simulated piece of student work found in a textbook or devised by a teacher and analyzing a living, breathing classmate's work in front of and with peers. Handling errors with tact and understanding is a skill necessary when discussing real students' work that will not necessarily come into play when analyzing static, fictional work.

Sharing partially formed ideas or thinking that might contain an error can be daunting for learners of any age. In addition to the facilitation moves described in Chapter 4, teachers can also use *protecting* moves to help create a safe space for sharing and building ideas in a mathematical community (see Table 7.2). Having a conversation about how it feels to take risks in mathematics class and put your work out there, especially with older students who have a heightened sense of vulnerability, can be an essential and worthwhile use of class time. Introducing specific practices around how students will speak to each other and about each other's work can also lay some pivotal groundwork.

The teacher can use these protecting moves to slow things down, make a safe space for students to share their thinking, invite revision, and validate their contributions, even when their ideas are not fully developed. Calling for a *pause* models the importance of sensemaking and allows for processing

Table 7.2 Building a Responsive Mathematics Community Tool, Responsibility #2

Responsibility #2: Build Discussion Participation Skills	
Protecting Moves actively make a safe space for the sharing and building of ideas	
Pause and give time for processing	• Let's take our time and look at Matt's strategy first.
Offer opportunities to **try ideas out with a partner** first	• Turn and talk with your partner about whether you think Matthew's claim is true or false.
Treat **mistakes as an opportunity for learning** for everyone	• I'm so glad you made that mistake because it helped us all to understand how this works better!
Invite students to **revise their thinking**	• Now that we've had this discussion, is there something about your idea you want to revise? • What are you thinking now?
Attribute ideas to students	• Rakeem's idea to check that his answer is reasonable is really important for us to think about.
Validate struggle	• Trying to make sense of other people's thinking is hard work. It's normal for it to feel a little confusing at first. Let's work together to get through that feeling.

time. Allowing students to turn-and-talk or *try ideas out with a partner* can help them solidify their thinking before they share in a whole group setting. Inviting students to *revise their thinking* highlights an essential part of mathematical thinking that is often overlooked. We often encourage students to revise their writing to improve it over time but fail to support that process in mathematics.

As is true in the community of professional mathematicians, giving credit where credit is due is often the key to helping students feel more comfortable sharing and borrowing mathematical ideas with and from one another. In a discussion setting, this could mean using the protecting move *attribute ideas to students* by naming them explicitly, as in "Building on Jason's idea …" or "I used Maddie's strategy of finding factor pairs." Having a conversation about how to use and build on others' ideas and creating norms around doing so, modeling these practices, reinforcing students who demonstrate them ("I noticed you gave Maddie a shoutout in your explanation. That helps us see how your strategy grew out of hers!"), Moreover, reminding students when necessary ("It looks like you used the idea that Stephan shared earlier and tried it with this second task!") can help establish a community in which ideas become the property of the group and in which students become more willing to share with and borrow from others. Finally, teachers can *validate struggle* as essential and necessary by intentionally calling it out and highlighting it as an integral part of learning.

In addition to these moves, explicit practice in how to *treat mistakes as an opportunity for learning* and responding tactfully to errors or disagreements can also be beneficial. This might entail taking a fictional piece of student work with a mistake and asking students to respond to it as if the person were in the room. Teachers can play the role of the student, answering questions about the piece of work and responding to feedback on how to address the error and make improvements. Better yet, students can take turns playing the role of the author of a piece of work containing an error, hearing, and responding to feedback from their peers. Using simulated pieces of work for these activities can reduce the personal stakes involved while still building empathy and providing practice in tactful disagreement and giving constructive feedback to peers.

Providing sentence stems, such as those shown in Figure 7.6, and generating lists of appropriate questions or comments together can be a helpful support for students, particularly for English Language Learners or those developing academic language. It is important to note that the stems provide the linguistic structure, but not the content. This allows students to think critically while providing a structure and model for respectful discourse.

As trust develops, discussions in responsive mathematics classrooms become spaces where students build on each other's ideas, whether they are fully developed approaches to a problem or murkier ideas that are not yet fully formed. One of the primary purposes of this sharing is to give all students access to different ways of thinking about a problem to expand their repertoire of strategies. However, sharing mathematical ideas and using each other's methods may not come naturally to students who have previously

---

- I like how you did _____ in your work because _____.
- What made you decide to do _____?
- One of the things you did well was _____ because _____.
- Something you should take another look at is _____ because _____.
- I think there's an error in this part of your work _____ because _____.
- Have you thought about adding _____ because _____.

Figure 7.6 Sentence stems to help students respond to each other's work.

been told to work independently, or "cover your paper" so that others cannot copy answers. Students sometimes come into mathematics class believing that ideas are proprietary, that mathematics is a solitary endeavor, and that using others' ideas is wrong. Acknowledging and directly addressing students' feelings about sharing their mathematical ideas with others is essential to creating healthy community dynamics.

In addition to developing tact, empathy, and a repertoire of appropriate feedback to give to classmates, self-monitoring is another vital skill for productive mathematical discussions. Helping students be aware of their own level of participation and assess whether they are taking up too much (or not enough) of the air space can go a long way toward making mathematics discussions more inclusive. Teachers can enforce this monitoring externally ("I am looking for someone I have not called on yet to explain"), but cultivating self-awareness puts the onus on the students to monitor their participation. Teachers can pause a discussion for a quick self-assessment: "Think about how this math discussion is going. Are you contributing too little? Too much? Just right? How can you adjust? Remember, our best math discussions happen when everyone contributes."

Collaboration Skills

During the productive struggle phase of a responsive mathematics lesson, described in more detail in Chapter 3, students are often called upon to collaborate with peers—sometimes to work with a student who is using a similar strategy and sometimes to pool their resources and combine their different ideas into a cohesive whole. Simply putting students next to each other does not mean they will have the requisite skill set to work together productively. Much like the sharing of student work discussed in the previous section, collaborative work involves trust, strong communication, and interpersonal skills like tact and empathy.

Once again, intentional skill development plays a key role. The third responsibility of the teacher in building a responsive mathematics community is to build collaboration skills, as shown in Table 7.3. It can be tempting to allow students to pick their partners, which typically ends with them working with their friends, or for the teacher to choose people they think will work together without conflict. ***Varying partners*** or making it the norm that students will work with anyone in the room in a way that involves focusing on the task at hand and equitable contributions from both partners, however, requires repeated opportunities to practice. Constantly changing partners gives students opportunities to work with different peers. This can be random, using an online generator, or popsicle sticks with students' names to choose pairs quickly. However, other times, a teacher may want to group students intentionally. In these cases, it is important to be explicit with students about the reasoning ("Get started

Table 7.3 Building a Responsive Mathematics Community Tool, Responsibility #3

Responsibility #3: Build Collaboration Skills	
Vary partners/groups for each activity	• Use a random generator to choose groups. • Intentionally pair students based on strategy rather than personality or perceived ability.
Assign roles	• *Peanut butter partner, you are going to share first. Jelly partner, your job is to listen and understand what your partner is saying. I'm going to ask you to share their ideas when we come back together.*
Scaffold participation	• *Everyone pause where you are. You have five minutes left to work in your groups. I want you to make sure that everyone has had a chance to share. If there is someone who hasn't had a turn yet, give them a chance to share their thinking.* • *Anna didn't count the first five marbles; she just started at six and counted up. Josh, does that make sense to you? Why can she do that?*

working on the task individually for a few minutes. I will come around and pair you up with someone who is thinking similarly to you.")

Assigning roles can also support students' collaboration skills. To help her students learn how to take turns when working together, first-grade teacher Ms. Wright assigned each student in a pair a role: peanut butter or jelly. This arrangement allowed her to give instructions to specific individuals. For example, she might tell them that the peanut butter partner would first share their idea while the jelly partner listened and asked questions to help them understand. Then the jelly partners would be asked to share what they learned by listening to their partner before reversing the roles. This practice helped her students learn how to collaborate with a partner, in both the sharing and listening roles.

Groups of three are ideal for students to share multiple ideas while ensuring every student has the space to participate fully. To further promote participation, students may be assigned roles within the group. A wide variety of potential roles can be assigned depending on the activity. Some common ones are a timekeeper, who makes sure that the group is completing their work in the time allotted; a notetaker, who is responsible for recording the group's ideas in writing; and a reporter, who shares the group's thinking orally with the class. When using group roles, it is critical that each role is well-defined and understood by the students and that roles rotate so that students can practice each responsibility (Cohen, 1994).

While groups are at work, teachers can *scaffold participation* to support student collaboration. Sometimes, a teacher might address the whole class by calling a timeout during their work time. They can then ask the groups to take stock of their focus, the equity of the group members' participation, or their progress on the task. This pause can help to reorient students who have stopped actively participating or have gotten off task. Teachers can also step in and scaffold participation in a select group. When doing this, teachers might ask students to engage with each other's ideas or ask a less-actively involved student to explain the group's ideas.

Getting Started

When seeking out ways to build students' belief in their capacity as mathematicians and willingness to contribute their ideas in class discussions, an important consideration is the guiding principle of ensuring that all students have access. Do all students have the access they need to offer a worthwhile contribution? Instructional routines like *Notice and Wonder* (Fetter, 2016), *Which One Doesn't Belong?* (Danielson, n.d.), dot talks, or number talks based on real-world images, invite a wide array of acceptable answers and strategies. For example, projecting the image shown in Figure 7.7 and asking students to determine how many muffins there are allows students to share strategies based on counting, skip counting, doubling, addition, subtraction, or multiplication. Importantly, these routines lend themselves to sensemaking rather than the use of algorithms or procedures. They provide access by allowing students with various skills in their repertoire to find a viable and mathematically sound solution. They also help students realize that mathematics conversations are not just for a few prized students who are quickest or most efficient.

Starting the year or each mathematics class with a variety of accessible number sense routines can bolster students' sense of their own value as mathematicians. It can increase their willingness to take risks by sharing alternative strategies and partially formed, rough draft ideas that the rest of the group can build upon.

Imagine if Mr. Charles spent a week or two using image-based number talks to acclimate his students to the experience of sharing different ideas and having their ideas welcomed in mathematics class. Using the image in Figure 7.7, he might have elicited counting strategies, or skip counting by 2's, 3's, or 4's, perhaps with some addition or subtraction to account for stray muffins or empty spaces. His students might also have discovered a multiplicative approach, using multiplication and an understanding of arrays or area to find the number of muffins in a whole container and then subtracting 2 for

Building a Responsive Mathematics Community ◆ 191

Figure 7.7 An image talk: How many muffins? How do you know?

the empty spots. This experience might have convinced some of his students that mathematics problems can be approached in many equally valid ways and are worth thinking and talking about. With that pivotal groundwork laid beforehand, Mr. Charles' first foray into number talks might have gone more smoothly and yielded more diverse answers, participation from more students, and better receptivity to divergent thinking like Amelia's approach of counting by 25s.

During these routines and other activities that provide opportunities for small-scale risk-taking and gradual gains in confidence, specific teacher moves can help ensure that the activity has the desired effect. As Mr. Charles' experience demonstrates, simply posing a worthwhile task is not enough. Building students' sense of themselves as competent mathematicians and increasing their willingness to contribute to mathematics discussions requires careful effort on the part of the teacher in the form of protecting and discussion skill-building moves.

Let us now rewind and imagine, for example, that instead of scolding Andre for being disrespectful and then moving on to a different problem, Mr. Charles had used some of these moves to focus on building Amelia's sense of mathematical capacity and willingness to contribute to the community.

> Mr. Charles calls on Amelia, and she says, "I was thinking of quarters and like counting by 25s. So I did 25, 50, 75, a dollar, 25, 50, 75, 2 dollars." As she talks, Amelia uses her fingers to show how she counted.
>
> Mr. Charles asks Amelia to pause and turns to the class. "Amelia just highlighted an important relationship between multiplication and

> repeated addition, and she came up with a strategy that uses money to make it easier. How cool! I want you all to listen to her idea one more time and I want you to figure out why her strategy works. After she explains again, I'll ask each of you to show me a thumbs up if you understand her strategy or a wavy hand if you don't quite understand it or are not sure if its works. Then I'm going to ask someone to explain her approach in their own words."

In this reimagined vignette, Mr. Charles uses protecting moves to pause, giving the students time to listen individually before being asked to evaluate her strategy. He then attributes a mathematically valuable idea to Amelia, signaling to the class that her contribution is not only worthy of respect but also mathematically sound, and by pointing out the relationship between multiplication and repeated addition, he calls out its importance. These protecting moves bolster students' sense of mathematical capacity and increase the likelihood that they will continue to participate in class discussions and perhaps take greater risks—sharing ideas that are not fully formed or ideas they are not sure are correct—in the future. Protecting moves impact the student whose idea is being shared and send important messages about what it means to participate in a mathematical learning community.

There are other powerful ways to help learners broaden their vision of what it means to do mathematics and participate in a mathematical community: engaging them in solving logic puzzles, playing games, working collaboratively on "groupworthy" or team-building tasks (Cohen & Lotan, 1997), analyzing visual patterns, or activities that blend teamwork and healthy competition. These break the mold tasks, different from what students typically encounter in school, can help students move away from their habits or the usual modes that they adopt in mathematics class and broaden their perspective on what it means to do mathematics.

> **A Selection of "Break the Mold" Activities:**
>
> - Building Shapes: https://www.youcubed.org/wim/building-shapes-3-5/
> - Visual patterns: https://www.visualpatterns.org/
> - Solve-Me mobiles: https://solveme.edc.org/mobiles/
> - Four 4's: https://www.youcubed.org/tasks/the-four-4s/
> - Year Math Game: https://www.nctm.org/Classroom-Resources/Year-Game/The-Year-Game/
> - Julia Robinson Foundation Math Puzzles: https://jrmf.org/puzzle/

Potential Challenges to Building a Responsive Community

> *In the past few years, I became interested in using different strategies for teaching math in the classroom, ones which would deemphasize my role as the guide, and strengthen student voice and engagement. My students are good at receiving direct instruction. They know how to raise their hands, listen, take notes, and view the board in the front of the classroom. However, I wanted to step off to the side and let my students work through problems in small groups rather than always modeling their solutions the way I told them to. There is so much that goes into getting this right! Would my students get along and be able to engage in respectful, ordered discourse? Would they have the supplies they need? Could they reach a successful conclusion as a group even if it is incorrect and could they show and articulate that conclusion as a group? Could they listen within their group and to other groups? How could I create activities and tasks which support this type of learning so that all students are engaged in standards-based activities?*
>
> — Eighth-Grade Teacher

Throughout this chapter, we have argued that developing a responsive mathematics classroom community represents a significant cultural shift for students and educators alike. Most students arrive in a mathematics classroom with pre-existing ideas about what it means to do mathematics. Shifting toward a mathematics community that values collaboration, risk-taking, and sensemaking may feel unfamiliar, or even uncomfortable, for students who have equated success in mathematics with speed and accuracy. Just as students must learn new mathematics content, they must also learn how to engage productively in a learning community. It is therefore important to explicitly name this shift and patiently guide students in learning new ways of participation. Establishing norms and regular routines can help students develop and practice the skills needed to participate in a responsive learning environment. Establishing these routines early, especially during the first month or two of the school year, will go a long way in setting the foundation for this kind of classroom culture.

This shift can also be challenging for veteran educators working to unlearn long-held understandings about what it means to be "good at math" or how mathematics should be taught. Years of experience can come with ingrained ideas about which students are likely to succeed, what mathematical success looks like, and what effective instruction entails. Responsive mathematics teaching asks educators to pause and reflect on these assumptions and consider how instructional choices may unintentionally reinforce exclusionary definitions of mathematical ability. Disrupting these patterns requires awareness, intentional reflection, and a willingness to try new approaches—even when those approaches feel unfamiliar. It means reimagining who is seen as mathematically capable and creating space for every student to contribute and thrive.

This kind of classroom culture does not develop overnight; students and educators need ongoing support to embrace and internalize the norms of a collaborative learning community. Early in the year, teachers can expect to devote time to teaching mathematics content and teaching students how they will learn mathematics together. This entails modeling what it looks like to ask thoughtful questions, highlighting respectful interactions, and revisiting classroom expectations regularly. It also means acknowledging and working through resistance, whether from students or teachers, as everyone works to unlearn familiar patterns.

Adding to these challenges is the reality that many teachers face significant pressure to keep up to speed with curricula, standardized assessments, and school-wide pacing expectations. With so much content to cover and limited instructional time, it can feel challenging to slow down and devote time to community building. However, investing in the building of classroom community pays dividends over time. Rather than being a detour from instruction, building this kind of classroom culture lays the groundwork for deeper, more sustained learning.

While building a responsive mathematics community within a single classroom can be transformative, this work can also be powerful when it takes root across different classrooms, grade levels, or schools. Sustaining and scaling responsive teaching can be made richer with teams of educators collectively building an instructional vision, sharing responsive teaching experiences, and forming structures that support ongoing collaboration and reflection. In the next chapter, we shift our focus from the individual classroom to these broader educational structures, exploring how educators, coaches, and administrators can collaborate to expand responsive teaching practices across grade levels, school-wide professional learning communities, or even cross-school networks.

> *So many more children are talking about math. It's really joyful to hear students be brave and share their thinking, even not knowing if their thinking is completely correct. Learning about responsive math teaching has provided me with a framework to get as many people talking about math as possible. It has had a huge impact on my math instruction.*
>
> — Sixth-Grade Teacher

Reflection Questions

Teacher Responsibilities	Guiding Principles
1 Build listening and sensemaking skills 2 Build discussion participation skills 3 Build collaboration skills	1 Prioritize mathematical sensemaking 2 Promote collaborative learning communities 3 Support a positive mathematical identity 4 Ensure all students have access to mathematics

1. How do each of the teacher responsibilities of building a responsive mathematics community address the guiding principles of responsive mathematics teaching?
2. What ideas are you taking away from this chapter that you want to try?
3. When you think about your current mathematics community:
   a. What is already in place that you can build on?
   b. What challenges do you foresee?
   c. What can you do to try to overcome those challenges?

8

Supporting Responsive Mathematics Teaching

If you have read the previous chapters of this book, you likely have gained a deeper understanding of both the power and the complexity of responsive teaching practices, as well as specific ways that teachers can change their mathematics instruction (and let go of some old practices) to be more responsive to students and their thinking. In this chapter, we shift the focus to those working to support teachers in becoming more responsive, including school-based teacher leaders, professional developers, and teacher educators.

Throughout the book, we have argued that in the mathematics classroom, making sense of a problem, discovering a problem-solving strategy, and following that strategy toward a solution are responsibilities that lie with the student, not the teacher. Likewise, when it comes to supporting teachers as learners, making sense of responsive teaching, figuring out what works in the classroom, and refining instructional decisions are responsibilities that lie with teachers, not leaders. Nevertheless, just as responsive teachers can guide and support students on their mathematical journey, instructional leaders play a vital role in supporting teachers as they develop responsive teaching practices. While teachers need time and space to engage in experimentation and reflection, instructional leaders can offer the guidance, structure, and encouragement to help that learning take root.

We start with a vignette that illustrates and contrasts the experiences of two teachers who spent part of their summer break attending professional development sessions to improve their instructional skills. Ms. Lloyd and Ms. Price are both fifth-grade mathematics teachers from different schools who, with the encouragement of their school administrators, attended the same set of professional development workshops focused on learning to facilitate

DOI: 10.4324/9781003536710-8

discussions in the mathematics classroom. Both teachers learned how important it is for students to engage in discussion, and both gained a better understanding of what discussions could look and sound like in an elementary classroom. They took away some key strategies for posing questions and facilitating discussions, and at the end of the week, they left feeling excited and motivated to try out the new ideas they learned in their classrooms.

What Happens After the Workshop?

Ms. Lloyd: The Challenges of Changing Practice

Ms. Lloyd returned to her classroom in the fall, enthusiastic about implementing the ideas she learned in the summer workshops. She set aside time in her mathematics lessons for students to engage in whole-group discussions about their problem-solving strategies. Immediately, she ran into some challenges. Her students had not been asked to engage in these types of mathematical discussions in previous years, so they were hesitant to share and struggled to make sense of each other's ideas. It was clear that they did not understand the purpose of the discussions she was trying to facilitate. She felt unsure about what to do because the discussions in her classroom did not look or sound like the ones she had seen and experienced over the summer. She remembered watching some video recordings of teachers facilitating rich discussions. However, her students were not engaging in the same way that the students in those videos did, and she did not know how to help them. Because she was the only teacher from her school to attend the summer workshops, she did not have other people in the building to reach out to for support.

A few weeks into the school year, Ms. Lloyd was discouraged because she did not see the time she was spending to facilitate student discussions contributing to her students' learning. To increase the level of mathematical discourse, she found herself telling the students the ideas she hoped would emerge through the discussion. She decided that if they could not formulate the key ideas for themselves, at least they would still be exposed to the essential concepts. She continued to ask students for their input, but when she did not hear the answers she was looking for, she took the reins and told them what she wanted them to know.

Ms. Price: The Power of Ongoing Support

Ms. Price, several other teachers, and the mathematics specialist from her school attended the summer training together. They started the school year eager to implement ideas about facilitating discussion strategies and formats they learned. As the first month of school got underway, Ms. Price planned her mathematics lessons to allow regular time for discussion of students' work and strategies. She quickly realized how challenging discussion facilitation is, as her students were unfamiliar with talking about their own and their peers' mathematical ideas.

The principal at Ms. Price's school recognized that learning new skills takes time for teachers, and she wanted to provide continued support because increasing student discourse was a focus area for the school that year. During professional development days, the mathematics specialist had teachers watch and discuss more videos of mathematical discussions and continue to develop their skills. Ms. Price took the mathematics specialist up on her offer to plan and co-teach a lesson together, where they could practice implementing the instructional moves they had focused on in professional development. Through these learning opportunities, Ms. Price continued to discover and refine new discussion techniques in the context of her classroom with her students.

Ms. Price and her grade partners also had weekly meetings built into their schedule that the mathematics specialist facilitated. In these meetings, the teachers debriefed their most recent lessons and talked about how their discussions were going, troubleshooting difficulties, and sharing successful strategies. They also spent time planning for upcoming mathematical discussions, anticipating ways that they could elicit and build on student thinking. These meetings helped Ms. Price feel less alone and motivated her to continue improving her discussion facilitation skills.

Ms. Price worked on developing the mathematical discussions in her classroom throughout the school year. It was not easy, and change did not happen quickly. Many discussions did not go according to plan. However, she brought these challenges to her grade group and professional development sessions to get support. Over time, she noticed that her students were improving at sharing their thinking and making sense of their classmates' ideas. The level of discourse in her classroom rose, and with her guidance, her students could engage in rich discussions around new mathematical concepts.

In these stories, both teachers left the professional development experience enthusiastic and eager to implement their new learning. They also encountered early challenges, which is to be expected as changing and improving instructional practice is complex and challenging. However, from that point, their experiences began to diverge. Once the school year started, Ms. Lloyd implemented these new practices independently. Her school administration supported her participation in professional development but did not provide additional support. When she struggled and had no one to turn to for guidance or collaboration, she reverted to her more familiar modes of teaching, away from being responsive to student thinking and toward more traditional, teacher-centered instruction. If an administrator came to observe her class, they might even think that the professional development was ineffective because they would not see many changes in her instruction. When professional learning is provided through short-term or isolated training sessions, without sustained follow-up support and opportunities to practice, teacher learning is likely to be superficial and short-lived (Darling-Hammond et al., 2017; Loucks-Horsley et al., 2010). Exposure to new ideas in a setting outside of the classroom is not enough to effect real and lasting change.

Ms. Price had a very different experience. Her school provided sustained, structured support, dedicating time and resources to ensure that a team of teachers could engage in an ongoing cycle of professional growth: learning something new, trying it out in their classrooms, and receiving feedback and support from peers and instructional leaders. Multiple teachers and the school's mathematics specialist attended the same professional development, allowing them to reconvene and work through challenges together throughout the school year. This approach leveraged the collaborative aspect of learning and helped Ms. Price feel supported, even when she encountered bumps in the road, maintaining her motivation to continue improving her practice. If an administrator visited her classroom, they would likely observe her actively applying and refining her discussion facilitation skills and see gradual but meaningful changes in her teaching and students' engagement. Because she was a part of a broader learning community, similar shifts likely occurred in her colleagues' classrooms, building momentum for schoolwide instructional change.

In this chapter, we describe strategies for fostering the kinds of support Ms. Price experienced, ensuring that teachers working to transform their practice have a professional community to depend on for guidance, feedback, and collaboration.

Supporting Teacher Learning and Transforming Practice

All learners benefit from instruction that prioritizes sensemaking and builds on their current understanding, including teachers learning a new way of teaching mathematics. Students thrive in classrooms that honor their thinking, and teachers need to be engaged and supported as learners in the same way. Responsive teachers seek to understand their students' current thinking in relation to mathematical goals and then strategically design and orchestrate learning experiences to bridge the gap between the two. They make space and time for productive struggle and practice, prioritizing sensemaking over rote acceptance of novel ideas. They recognize that grappling with new ideas and processes takes time. They create opportunities for students to learn with and from each other. Those supporting teacher learning can embrace these same principles, while recognizing the additional challenge that teachers are being asked to teach in a way that differs not only from how they have previously taught but often from how they learned it themselves.

Whether you are a teacher leader, instructional coach, school principal, teacher educator, or professional development provider, supporting responsive instruction involves a shift in responsibility from telling or showing others how to teach more effectively to facilitating and supporting change. The responsive mathematics leader designs and orchestrates a process through which teachers can build the expertise they need to become more responsive in their classroom instruction.

In this chapter, we outline and describe three essential components of professional learning to support the development of responsive mathematics instruction: (1) establishing a common vision of responsive mathematics instruction; (2) providing opportunities for practice-based professional development; and (3) creating and sustaining regular collaborative learning communities. Establishing a common vision is an important first step, while interweaving practice-based professional development with regular collaborative learning communities focused on planning, enacting, and reflecting on responsive mathematics instruction is a particularly effective way to help teachers put the vision into practice (see Figure 8.1).

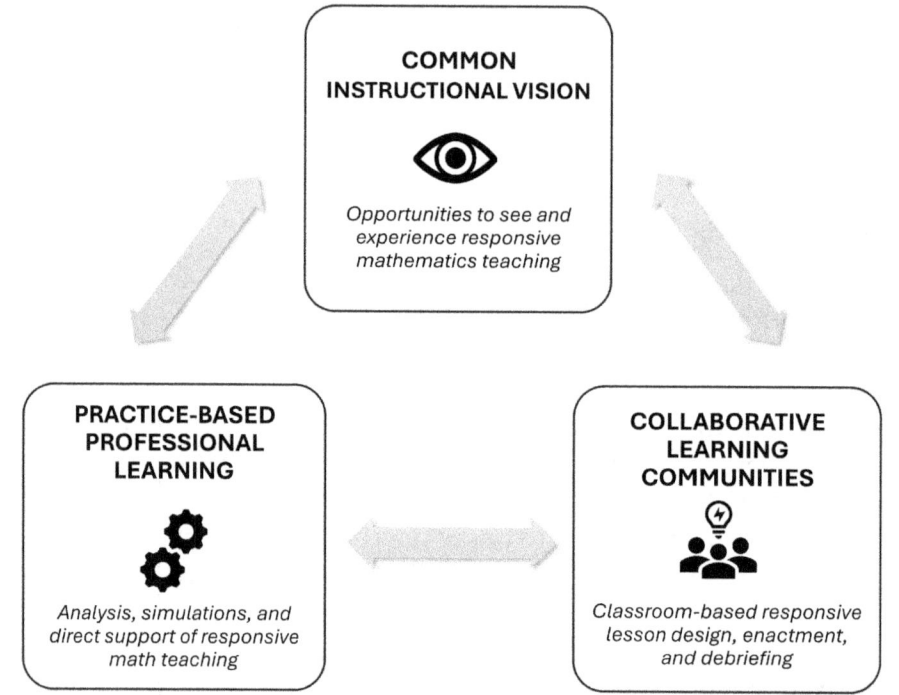

Figure 8.1 Essential components of professional learning for responsive mathematics teaching.

At the heart of this model for professional learning is the recognition that teachers are learners, and, like students, they deserve intentional support, space to grow, and opportunities to make sense of new ideas through practice and reflection. While the means of application will vary depending on role and context, the components are relevant to anyone who supports preservice or in-service teacher development, including classroom teachers, instructional leaders, district administrators, or university faculty.

Establish a Common Vision of Responsive Mathematics Instruction

To support the instructional shifts described in Chapters 2–6, an important first step is to help teachers develop a vision of responsive mathematics teaching. Watching video recordings of responsive instruction can help teachers to see what it looks and sounds like in practice. However, experiencing responsive mathematics teaching as learners themselves allows teachers to understand what it feels like to engage with mathematics in a responsive, learner-centered environment. To create these opportunities, teachers need dedicated time to engage in problem solving, productive struggle, and collaborative discussion. In other words, they need to experience the role of a student, within a community of peers, guided by a skilled facilitator who models the core components of responsive mathematics teaching: launching the task, facilitating productive struggle, discussing learner thinking, and connecting, consolidating, and reflecting on understanding of the mathematical goals.

Tasks suitable for upper elementary and middle school levels are often appropriate for teachers to work through together. In our work, we have frequently used tasks presented in the vignettes throughout the book (e.g., Sharing Crackers, Fair Shares, Pizza Task). These tasks work well because they are open-ended, allowing for multiple strategies and solutions, and can be approached using both intuitive reasoning and more formal mathematical methods. As teachers engage with these tasks individually, in partners or groups, and then through facilitated discussion of various solution strategies, they gain insight into the

> *What it feels like not to understand something or to be confused about something is always an important position to put yourself in as a teacher, because there are always going to be kids who are in that position in your class. You need to remind yourself of what that feels like, what was helpful for you when you were feeling that, and what was not helpful for you when you were feeling that.*
>
> —Kindergarten Teacher

> **Facilitation Moves**
> - Giving a real problem to solve
> - Multiple entry points
> - Not solving right away
> - Reading aloud
> - Clarifying questions
> - Identifying key points and vocabulary
> - Making it visual (leaving the visual up while solving)
> - Not constraining our solving time
> - Strategic partnering
> - Showing actual learner work
> - Strategic sharing of work in a trajectory
> - Productive struggle
> - Probing questions
> - Encouragement

Figure 8.2 Facilitation moves identified by teachers after experiencing responsive mathematics teaching as learners.

process of doing mathematics from the learner's perspective. They experience what it feels like to genuinely make sense of a task before jumping into solving it—to struggle to get started, feel confused or stuck, encounter roadblocks, and reach the moment when a concept finally clicks. They also experience the power of making sense of someone else's thinking and the affirmation that comes from having their own reasoning heard and validated by peers.

Teachers report that these experiences affect them both emotionally and cognitively. Engaging as learners helps them develop confidence in their ability to make sense of challenging mathematics as they forge new connections and deepen their understanding of content that they have encountered differently in the past. Moreover, reflecting on the facilitation practices that propelled their learning allows teachers to recognize and appreciate the characteristics of responsive mathematics teaching. Figure 8.2 shows what one group of teachers noticed about the facilitation of their collaborative problem-solving experience and their insights into the moves that made their learning productive.

By identifying and naming the instructional moves they experience and unpacking the pedagogical reasoning behind those moves, teachers can begin to articulate a new vision for mathematics instruction. This can also lead to a shift in expectations around the teacher's role (e.g., the teacher's job is not to ... but rather to ...). Having

> *Once you get that feeling of, 'Oh, this is how it is supposed to feel, this is how it is supposed to look,' then when you bring it back into your classroom, you can kind of tell. Is that how it looks in here? What am I striving for? How am I going to get my classroom to look like what we're doing at the training?*
>
> —Grade 1 Teacher

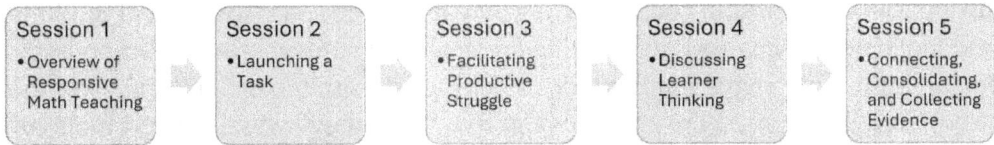

Figure 8.3 A sequence of collaborative problem-solving sessions focusing on different components of responsive mathematics teaching.

a well-articulated instructional vision to aspire to is an important factor in teachers' learning to change their practice (Munter & Correnti, 2017; Wilhelm, 2014). As with learning anything new, change is more achievable and sustainable when there is a clear goal to work toward.

Providing teachers with multiple, repeated opportunities to engage in collaborative problem solving and reflect on those experiences gives them space to explore, refine, and deepen their instructional vision over time. Starting with a single component of responsive teaching and then gradually adding more can make this more manageable. For example, the facilitator might focus on the launch of the task in one session, using the model for responsive mathematics teaching to anchor discussion around specific facilitation moves made during the launch—what was said, how the task was launched, and how those choices influenced teachers' learning, sensemaking, and participation in the session. Each time teachers come together for facilitated problem solving, the focus can shift to a new component, gradually filling out their visions to encompass the entire cycle (see Figure 8.3).

Grounding this process in the separate components of the model for responsive mathematics teaching gives teachers time to develop and use a common language when planning and reflecting on their instruction. Taking time with each component ensures that teachers have the chance to dig deeper and gain a more thorough understanding of the practices through experience. When coaches and school-based leaders participate in these sessions alongside teachers, a common language and school-wide vision can be cultivated.

Our experience engaging teachers in a series of collaborative problem-solving sessions throughout the year led to several important outcomes. Teachers developed more confidence and competence in their problem-solving abilities and began to develop more student-centered and inclusive visions of mathematics instruction. They gained a deeper appreciation for the planning and preparation required by responsive teaching and recognized the need to shift their instructional practices. Although they were not explicitly asked to change their instructional practice, many teachers began incorporating elements from the sessions into their classrooms. They became more intentional about launching tasks, started using rich and challenging tasks, embraced productive struggle as a meaningful part of learning, created more space for student thinking, and facilitated discussions that uplifted a variety of strategies and solution paths. Engaging in responsive mathematics teaching as learners and reflecting on that experience illuminated the gap between the vision they aspired to and their current practices. It motivated them to make changes. At the same time, teachers recognized the complexity of this kind of teaching and understood that they needed more knowledge and support to carry these changes off in their classrooms.

Practice-Based Approaches to Professional Learning

While developing an instructional vision for responsive mathematics teaching is a critical foundation, it is only the first stage of the journey toward more responsive practices. Once teachers formulate new ideas for how they want to shift their instruction, they need repeated opportunities to try out those ideas and hone their developing skills in a supportive environment. This includes learning about new instructional practices, but more importantly, it involves learning how to make the necessary shifts to implement these practices with real students in the context of their own classrooms. A practice-based approach to professional development embraces the need for teachers to learn both *the what* and "the how" through repeated opportunities to break down, try out, and reflect on complex instructional practices (Grossman, 2018). The underlying principle, as illustrated by the opening vignette, is that teachers' learning occurs not only in the professional development context but is also embedded in the ongoing work they do in the classroom. In other words, teachers learn in and from their own practice (Ball & Cohen, 1999; Lampert, 2010).

Our approach to supporting teacher learning draws on a framework that includes three components of practice-based professional learning identified by Grossman et al. (2009). First, *representations* are used to make the work of responsive mathematics teaching visible to teacher learners, through case studies, vignettes, modeling, observations, videos, or artifacts like student work or lesson plans, providing further illustrations of practice to support and develop their instructional visions. *Decomposition* involves breaking complex responsive practice into digestible parts for professional learning and includes naming different instructional moves, analyzing the relationships between them, and the pedagogical reasoning behind each move. The tools presented in Chapters 2–5 are decompositions of responsive mathematics teaching, as each part of our model is broken down further into teacher responsibilities, and each responsibility is then illustrated through specific teaching moves. The third component of a practice-based approach, *approximation*, involves opportunities to try out responsive practices in a supportive environment, where some, but not all, of the complexity is reduced. Just as a musician rehearses sections of a complex composition before performing in a concert hall, approximations of practice give teachers the opportunity to rehearse new pedagogical moves in a low-stakes setting. Structured spaces for practice allow educators to try out new teaching moves, get feedback, and refine them before implementing them in the classroom environment. In the following sections, we describe examples of how we provided opportunities for teachers to engage with representations, decompositions, and approximations of responsive mathematics teaching practice in professional development sessions, as well as through more direct support of classroom enactment.

Analyzing Artifacts of Practice

In addition to the tools presented in Chapters 2–5, video recordings and transcripts of excerpts of responsive teaching can be used to help teachers identify specific responsive moves and understand how those moves support student learning in real classroom contexts. These videos need not be polished exemplars of practice to be effective tools. In fact, it can be more meaningful for teachers who are just learning about new approaches to examine authentic, in-progress examples. Seeing the real work of responsive teaching, including moments of imperfection, can reduce the pressure to replicate an idealized version of practice immediately.

Video recordings of responsive practice are valuable tools for capturing the verbal and non-verbal elements of responsive teaching. They allow viewers to observe not only what a teacher says or does (e.g., gestures) but also what they do not do (e.g., not interrupting the student), and how students respond. These subtle choices are often just as important as more visible actions, and video can help teachers start to identify the range of ways that responsive mathematics teaching can look and sound like in real classrooms.

A Structure for Decomposing Video for Responsive Teaching Moves

1 *Introduction to context.* Provide relevant context about the teacher, students, and classroom setting to help viewers better understand the video.
2 *First viewing—general.* Have teachers watch the video in its entirety, allowing them to develop a general understanding of what is happening.
3 *Second viewing—focused.* Prime teachers to watch the video, focusing on a specific goal or component of responsive mathematics teaching, and record the instructional moves they observe (specific words, questions, or body language).

> 4 *Turn and talk.* Allow teachers to share their ideas with a partner or group, flesh them out, and add to their notes.
> 5 *Full group discussion.* Invite teachers to share the instructional moves they observed, prompting them to describe each move in detail, unpack its purpose, and name it in relation to responsive teaching goals.
> 6 *Record ideas.* Record the group's discussion using categories of responsive teaching moves to help teachers identify the different aspects of the teacher responsibilities and the kinds of decisions involved in each category.
> 7 *Replay as needed.* If necessary, have teachers watch the video again to ground their observations in specific evidence—this can be useful when confusion arises or an important part of the practice has not been addressed.

Before having teachers watch videos of practice, it is important to frame the context of what they will be seeing and the focus of what they should be paying attention to, and to provide a structure for taking notes. It can also be helpful to show the video multiple times. The first viewing should focus on a more general understanding of what is happening, allowing teachers to share general observations and ask questions. The second viewing should be structured with more specific prompts that prime teachers to look for specific instructional moves and their purpose in the larger practice. Specific moments can be reviewed as necessary to look for details or help teachers focus on something they have not yet noticed.

After teachers have had a chance to share their initial observations with a partner or small group, they can engage in a whole group discussion, during which the facilitator should elicit observed teaching moves, prompting for specificity when necessary, and record observations in a way that helps teachers group the moves and see connections to the pedagogical reasoning. For example, if a teacher says, "The teacher asked a lot of good questions," a follow-up prompt might be, "Yes, she asked many good questions. Did anyone notice a specific question or phrase that she said that you thought was effective?" Figure 8.4 shows how one facilitator organized the ideas that emerged from watching a short clip of a teacher facilitating a student's productive struggle. The goal was to help teachers understand that facilitating productive struggle involves: (1) understanding a learner's ideas and points of struggle and (2) helping the learner move forward with their ideas (see Chapter 3 for the Facilitating Productive Struggle Tool).

Providing a written transcript of the video can also be helpful as it allows teachers to see how responsive teaching practices play out in the classroom

Drawing out student ideas and points of struggle		
Type of Move	**What it looks like/ sounds like**	**Purpose of Move**
• Eliciting	"Show me what you were doing with the blocks"	Figuring out what approach the student is using
• Clarifying	Watching the student work without interrupting, but closely following what they are doing	Understanding the logic they are using and seeing where they are making an error
Helping students move forward with their ideas		
• Pressing	"Are those groups even? What should you do?"	Drawing the student's attention to key math idea (even groups) Asking them to notice error and think about how to solve it
• Sustaining	"I see what you did there . . . . Would that same process work for different sized-groups?"	Helps student extend productive work they've already done and see how it might help them solve the problem

Figure 8.4 A record of teacher observations from a video of responsive mathematics teaching.

setting and zoom in on specific words and phrases that the teacher and students are using. Providing a transcript allows teachers to go back and review what happened without having to rewatch the video and supports the process of looking for different responsive teaching moves and reflecting on their purpose.

Using a transcript alone (without watching a video) can also be a productive format for decomposing teacher practice, particularly when focusing on the teacher's use of questions or prompts. A transcript slows down the practice and provides word-for-word examples teachers can try in their classrooms. A transcript can also remove potentially distracting elements like classroom setup, behavior, or perceived tone, allowing teachers to more clearly identify the types of moves used and how those moves support students in connecting key mathematical ideas.

In all these approaches to analyzing artifacts of practice, the common thread is to have teachers notice, describe, and name specific teaching moves according to the pedagogical goal or teacher responsibility they serve. Through both teacher-identified moves and those highlighted by the facilitator, the group can collectively build a deeper understanding of what the practice entails and what it looks and sounds like to execute it in the classroom.

Engaging in Simulations of Practice

Once teachers have had the opportunity to decompose responsive mathematics teaching practices, they are well-positioned to engage in approximations, or opportunities for supported enactment. Learning to execute complex practices such as facilitating productive struggle can sometimes feel overwhelming for teachers. However, well-crafted hypothetical experiences can offer a protected context in which to practice generating possible teaching moves, engage in decision-making, and execute teaching moves in response to cues from learners. These simulations of teaching can relieve the pressure of learning new practices because they offer teachers chances to rewind and try again. They also provide opportunities for teachers to receive feedback and/support from their peers and an experienced facilitator.

One simulation structure is the *fishbowl*, where one participant acts as the teacher and a subset of participants acts as students. The rest of the participants observe the interactions from outside the fishbowl. This structure can be helpful in creating simulations of whole group practices like launching a task or discussing learner thinking, where the teacher must engage and respond to multiple students. For fishbowl simulations, it can be helpful to give participants acting as students specific strategies, mistakes, or incomplete understandings to offer when called upon. Pausing the action at key decision points allows the observers to weigh in by suggesting discussion moves, reflecting on the reasoning behind those moves, and considering the affordances or drawbacks of different responses. Once the group has discussed possible moves, the participant acting as teacher picks one and tries it out with the group of students. Together, the group can reflect on what went well and what was challenging.

A slightly different structure is a *hivemind simulation*, where one participant takes on the role of the teacher while the facilitator acts as the student. The rest of the participants serve as the collective "brain" behind that teacher's voice, collaborating with each other and the teacher during key decision-making moments in the simulation. Participants in any role (facilitator, teacher, members of the brain) are encouraged to "pause" at any time during the simulation to pose a question or make a suggestion or to "rewind and replay" to try something again in a slightly different way.

In the following vignette, four teachers are meeting online to learn to facilitate productive struggle using the task shown in Figure 8.5. The task involves using the information in the photos to figure out how many tennis balls would be in a whole box. The facilitator, Mariella, is playing the role of the "stuck" student. With the support of the other teachers (the hive), teacher Don takes the lead in supporting Mariella's productive struggle. Before the simulation, all the teachers spent time solving the task, anticipating ways learners might approach it, sharing different ways learners might get stuck, and identifying possible teacher responses.

Supporting Responsive Mathematics Teaching ◆ 209

Some of the cans of tennis balls from this box of balls have already been used. How many balls would be in the box if it were full?

Figure 8.5 The tennis ball task.

Student Mariella:	Teacher Don, I'm confused. I thought I understood this problem, but I don't.
Teacher Don:	Okay, Mariella, can you tell me where you are stuck?
Student Mariella:	I don't know. I just can't figure out how many cans are in a full box.
Teacher Don:	Okay, I can see you have drawn some lines on the image. Can you tell me more about them?
Student Mariella:	I was trying to figure out how many cans are missing, so I drew lines to make rows. I thought drawing lines on the rows might help me see it better.
Teacher Don:	And how many rows did you find? Can you show me?
Student Mariella:	Well, I think there are three rows.

Mariella slowly drags her finger down a column of three tennis balls on the right side of the box (as shown by the vertical). Don expected Mariella to point to a horizontal row and realizes he does not have a clear understanding of what Mariella is seeing. He pauses the simulation to ask the hive for help on how to proceed.

Teacher Don:	I need a pause. I thought Mariella was seeing three horizontal rows of cans. She is using the word rows but pointing to a column. Maybe I could tell her that she is on the right track and that what she has identified is a column. Then I could show her what a row looks like.

> Two members of the hive share that they also expected Mariella to draw a horizontal line. Another suggests Mariella may have drawn the line down to show that each one of the containers in that line is part of a row, so she is demonstrating that there must be three rows. The hive quickly decides that Don needs to get a better sense of Mariella's thinking to support her productive struggle and recommends he engage in more clarifying moves using the following questions. "Mariella, can you point to each container or space in the row you have identified?", followed by, "How many of those rows do you see in the box?" The simulation resumes with Don posing the clarifying moves identified by the group.

In the hivemind simulation, Don paused to seek input from his peers when he felt unsure about how to proceed. Together, the group processed and decided on the best next step; then Don had a chance to practice different instructional moves while the other teachers had the chance to see those moves enacted. It is important to note that, if needed, Mariella (the facilitator) could have stepped out of her role as the stuck student to move the conversation forward. In this case, it was unnecessary as the group suggested questions Don could ask to get Mariella unstuck.

When the teacher has gotten the student unstuck or the facilitator thinks it is a good place to stop, the group comes together to reflect on the simulation. This reflection allows the facilitator to surface important take-away messages from the activity by asking participants to articulate which kinds of moves worked, in which situations, and why. This reflection is crucial to help all participants, no matter their role, formalize important responsive teaching moves and the pedagogical reasoning behind using them.

It is possible to complete one of these hivemind simulations with a group of teachers in about ten minutes. In a class or professional development session, three or four of these simulations can be done in a row, rotating who plays the role of the teacher and varying both the problem-solving strategies and the types of challenges the students face. This variation increases teachers' capacity to adapt their responses to diverse student thinking.

A third type of simulation is to have teachers **plan and rehearse** a component of responsive teaching with the rest of the participants engaging as learners. This works particularly well when planning a launch or a discussion of learner thinking. Participants can be divided into small groups; each group is given a different rich task and asked to work collaboratively to plan out the launch of that task. The groups are then mixed up into new groups, jigsaw-style, so that every member of the new group has planned a different task. Each participant then takes a turn rehearsing the launch, with the other participants (who have not seen the task) acting as learners. This provides a simulation where teachers can practice the moves they planned in a realistic setting where the learners, unfamiliar with the task, can respond genuinely.

A plan-and-rehearse simulation is also a good choice for practicing selecting and sequencing student work to lead a discussion of learner thinking, as described in Chapter 4. Figure 8.6 shows a set of five sample responses to the Tennis Ball task (Figure 8.5). Teachers are asked to make sense of these

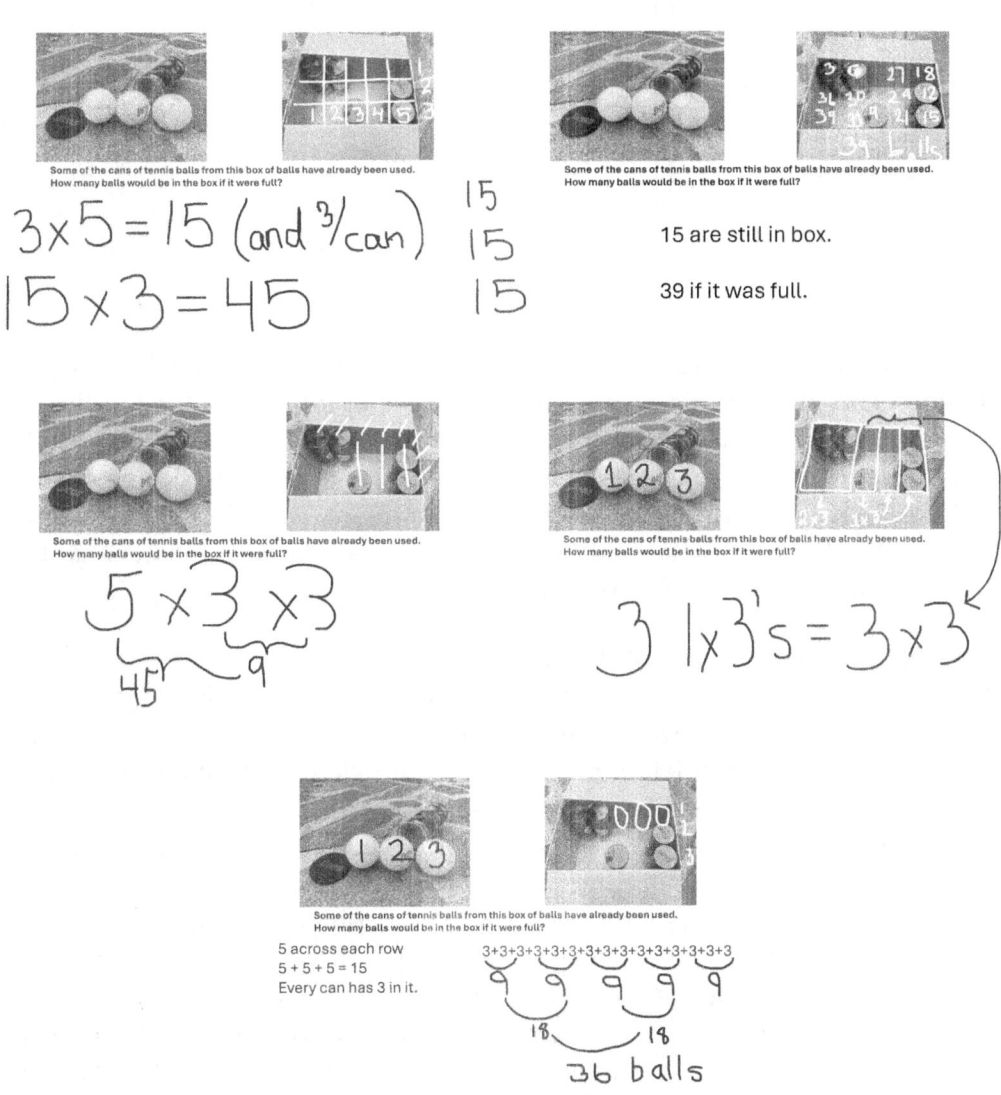

Figure 8.6 A set of sample student solutions for the tennis ball task.

Table 8.1 A Template to Plan Facilitation Moves for Discussing Learner Thinking

| Facilitation Moves for Discussing Learner Thinking |||
Teacher Responsibility	Think	Facilitation Moves
Get the learner's idea out into the open	What could you say or do to introduce this piece of work to the group?	
Help others to engage in this idea	What could you say/do to get the group to engage in the ideas shown in that work? Consider initial moves and also follow-up moves.	
Surface the important mathematics	What is a big idea you anticipate might surface from the conversation?	
	What could you say to help the group see and hold on to that idea?	

solutions and select three that they would use to structure a whole-class discussion. The mathematical goals involve developing an understanding of arrays, multiplication, and multiplicative equations. They then plan specific questions to get each learner's strategy out in the open, help others engage with the idea, and surface the important mathematics behind the strategy (Table 8.1). Working collaboratively, teachers craft targeted questions and then have the chance to rehearse those questions with peers.

Direct Support of Classroom Enactment

Asking teachers to try responsive teaching practices in their classrooms between professional development sessions is a powerful way to ensure that new learning is implemented. Building knowledge about a practice and developing a clear vision of what it looks like in action, followed by repeated cycles of trying it out and receiving feedback, enables teachers to deepen their understanding and more accurately assess their ability to enact it. Teachers can then return to subsequent professional development sessions with greater clarity about the areas where they need more practice or support, and therefore with increased engagement and more focused questions.

As teachers begin to try out responsive teaching practices, having direct support from a partner in the classroom can be extraordinarily beneficial. This partner could be a coach, mentor, or peer who has established a trusting relationship with the teacher and, ideally, has some familiarity with the students in the classroom. Partners are uniquely positioned to support the transition to classroom enactment when they are prepared to provide two critical types of support: (1) just-in-time, non-evaluative help with implementing responsive practices and (2) assistance with background tasks that enable the teacher to focus on instruction. Partners do not just act as passive observers; like the participants in the hivemind simulation, they can be consulted for in-the-moment decisions. They can also directly engage with a student or subset of students, or just be there to help remind the teacher of a relevant strategy. For example, a teacher might confer with their partner to help them formulate a response to a student's question or choose the most appropriate piece of student work to start the classroom discussion. A partner can also support tasks that alleviate some of the burden on teachers, such as monitoring group work or assisting with materials management and timekeeping. When a partner takes on some of these tasks, the teacher can focus more intentionally on the new and sometimes daunting responsive practices they are working on implementing.

Direct support of classroom enactment is most effective when the teacher and experienced partner have established a relationship built on trust and mutual respect, and when the teacher works consistently with the same partner over time. Partners need to set clear expectations and boundaries for engagement from the outset. Setting aside time after the enactment to reflect on the use of responsive teaching practices and the dynamics of the interaction between the teacher and the experienced partner is also critical. This reflection helps surface insights, clarify next steps, and strengthen this collaborative relationship that can support ongoing growth.

Create and Sustain Collaborative Learning Communities

We have also found that providing teachers with regular opportunities to engage in collaborative learning communities—focused on planning, implementation, and reflection—is a highly effective way to support meaningful and sustained instructional change. When these opportunities are offered in tandem with practice-based professional development, they can be particularly effective in bridging the gap between what is learned in professional development and what occurs in the classroom, addressing what Kennedy (1999) calls "the problem of enactment." When the community includes educators with varying levels of responsive teaching experience, they have opportunities to learn from and with one another, helping to break the all-too-common isolation of classroom teaching and fostering a shared sense of growth and support. While there are many ways to structure professional learning communities, engaging

214 ◆ Becoming a Responsive Mathematics Teacher

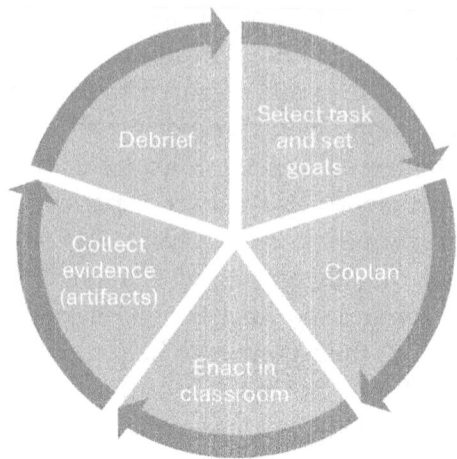

Figure 8.7 Collaborative planning, enactment, and reflection cycle.

teachers in iterative cycles of planning, enactment, and debriefing responsive mathematics lessons provides opportunities for them to apply and refine new practices in the context of their own classroom.

Collaborative Responsive Lesson Design, Enactment, and Debriefing

This section presents a structure for collaborative lesson design in which teachers engage in cycles of five interconnected components—selecting a task, co-planning, enacting, collecting artifacts, and debriefing (Figure 8.7). In the first meeting of a cycle, teachers collaboratively plan a lesson around a mathematical goal, focusing on the four main areas of the model: launching, facilitating productive struggle, discussing learner thinking, and connecting, consolidating, and collecting evidence of student learning (see Chapter 6). After creating a common plan, each teacher enacts the lesson in their own classroom. The teachers bring specific artifacts from the enactment (e.g., student work or a video clip) to debrief their lesson experiences in the next meeting.

Collaborative Planning Sessions

The collaborative planning process allows participants to bring different perspectives and experiences into the design of responsive mathematics problem-solving lessons, as shown in the vignettes in Chapter 6. Embarking on this work as a group provides opportunities for teachers to deepen their mathematical knowledge by sharing potential solving strategies, useful visual models, and potential scaffolds or supports to meet the needs of all learners. Collaboratively working through the planning process enables teachers to generate a variety of solution strategies to explore and unpack, while also leveraging multiple perspectives on how to approach, sequence, and facilitate different parts of the lesson. Over time, teachers become more adept at anticipating how students might respond and can draw upon past experiences with a task to identify potential challenges.

One of the most powerful parts of collaborative planning sessions is the dialogue sparked by teacher-generated questions (e.g., "How should we address the concept of a 'square'?"). Meaningful debates, in which teachers consider the pros and cons of a range of instructional decisions, outside the immediacy of the classroom, present opportunities to deepen understanding of responsive teaching practices. Sometimes these conversations conclude with the group coming to a consensus. Other times, teachers may try different options in their classrooms and revisit the question in a subsequent meeting.

The following excerpt from a collaborative planning session highlights a conversation between a group of fourth-grade teachers and a facilitator as they met to plan the Sharing Crackers task, shown below (and described in vignettes in Chapters 3 and 6). In this excerpt, a teacher poses a question about when to introduce and how much to focus on students' understanding of the term "factor" during the lesson, which leads to a rich conversation.

Sharing Crackers Task

There are 36 crackers in a box. The crackers are to be shared equally among friends. What are all of the different ways that friends can share the 36 crackers? How do you know that you found all of the different ways?

(Boaler et al., 2018, p. 78)

Laura:	I am not sure how worried to be about the language, or whether to focus more on the solving of the problem. So, I was curious how other people are going to approach the language?
Facilitator:	Do you mean the language of factors?
Laura:	Yes. Should I focus on the terms or on representing the thinking?
Facilitator:	That is a really great question. I have thoughts, but I want to throw it back to the group if anybody else is thinking about how they would do that.
Bobbi:	I think you could use it as an opportunity to introduce the factors. So, as they're coming up with a list that's hopefully substantial, you could say these are factors of 36. But I don't think they need the vocabulary to be successful, and I don't think I would necessarily

	give it to them to make sure they are using it in their explanation, if that makes sense.
Serena:	I wouldn't make them use it in their explanation. What I would do is, at the end, that's how I would sum up the lesson, as my takeaway. This is my takeaway: what you just learned how to do is find factors. And factors are the two numbers that you multiply together to get a product. So, I would kind of bubble it up like that, as a takeaway. They don't know the academic language, but they don't need it in the beginning, like Bobbi said, to actually solve the problem.
Laura:	Thank you, I wasn't sure. I was going back and forth.
Facilitator:	That's what I would say, too. While they are solving, it's not important that they talk about factors or think about factors. Some of them might, most of them probably will not. That portion of the lesson where you connect and consolidate is where you help them to put language onto something that they already did. And then you have that. Anytime people don't know what it is, you can say, "Remember with the friends and the crackers. Those are factors." It creates prior knowledge that you can access. They have a connection to what that word means, not just a dry definition.
Serena:	And not only that, they now have a strategy they can use to actually find the factors of a number. So I think that's the more important part. Not knowing that it's a factor, but knowing how to find the factor of a number.

In this rich discussion about introducing the mathematical vocabulary of factors, the group uses Laura's question as a jumping-off point to articulate the importance of developing student understanding before layering the vocabulary on top of that understanding, which is an important responsive teaching practice. They then identify opportunities in the connect and consolidate phase of the lesson to anchor the vocabulary to mathematical practices that the students have already completed. They also contemplate the important knowledge and usable strategy that this lesson will give them in the future when they encounter problems that deal with factors of a number. This brief example highlights the benefits of collaborative planning and illustrates the valuable teacher learning that can emerge from participating in a collaborative learning community focused on planning.

Collaborative Debrief Sessions

After teaching a collaboratively planned lesson, taking time to reflect through a debrief with other teachers is a critical step in formalizing and building on the instructional experience. This process deepens teacher learning and provides an opportunity to revise and annotate the lesson plan—capturing what worked well, what could be improved, and how to make future iterations go more smoothly. This kind of collaborative planning and refinement, a central characteristic of Japanese lesson study, has been shown to contribute to instructional improvement in various contexts where the model has been adopted (Stigler & Hiebert, 1999; Yoshida, 1999). Above all, working alongside colleagues can give teachers both the support and the accountability needed to sustain momentum and continue making progress toward more responsive teaching.

Debriefing common lessons gives teachers a safe space to reflect on their practice, celebrate successes, and troubleshoot challenges. A debrief discussion can be even richer when it centers on lesson artifacts, such as video, audio clips, or pictures of teacher-generated materials (e.g., a launch board). Earlier in this chapter, we introduced *direct support of classroom enactment* to foster the translation of skills learned in professional development to diverse classroom settings. Similarly, collaborative lesson debrief sessions can be a type of *indirect support of classroom enactment*. Although the peers are not physically present in the classroom with the teacher, lesson artifacts offer a tangible and meaningful way to share in the experience. While watching videos of one's teaching can feel risky, it is a powerful tool for reflection and provides insights and perspectives that otherwise

> *It is very humbling to [video] tape yourself, and the fact that teachers are willing to do that and then look at it and make changes, I think that's huge. It's such a valuable practice, so you can really see where changes need to be made. And if you're not able to see the positives, others can point them out for you. Be proud of yourself, see what you're doing, and also have other people look at it.*
> —Teacher Leader

may be difficult to access. Even a short, two-minute video clip, captured on a phone during a moment of pride or uncertainty, can be the foundation for a rich group discussion. Cultivating a space where it is safe to make mistakes and be vulnerable in the process of learning together is a critical component of a productive learning community.

A debrief session should also include time for individual reflections, captured in journals or on a shared group document. Providing time for individual reflections allows each participant to consolidate their thoughts on their experience before conferring with the group. When prompted to reflect on something that went well in the lesson and something that was challenging or did not go as planned, each teacher will come to the discussion with potential advice to offer others and a place to grow from.

After individual reflection, each participant should have time to share their artifact and receive feedback from the group, using a focusing question to guide the discussion. The focusing question should direct the group's attention to a specific aspect of the artifact—such as an instructional move the teacher makes, how a component of responsive teaching is addressed, or a question the teacher poses about their practice—to guide targeted feedback.

Sample Focusing Questions for the Lesson Debrief

Launch
- How does the teacher help the students to make sense of the task?

Facilitating Productive Struggle
- How does the teacher elicit student thinking?
- What does the teacher say to help the student move forward?

Discussing Learner Thinking
- What questions does the teacher ask to facilitate the discussion?
- What did you notice about student discourse?

Connect and Consolidate
- How did the teacher connect student ideas to the mathematical goals of the lesson?
- What is the evidence of student understanding of the key mathematical ideas?

The teacher who is sharing briefly introduces the artifact, offering any pertinent context for others to make sense of what they are seeing, and then poses or restates the focusing question. The presentation of the artifact is kept brief (2–3 minutes). Time is then given for the group to address the question(s) and share advice. Often, teachers discover that they encounter common challenges, and they frequently learn as much, if not more, from discussing a colleague's lesson as they do from reflecting on their own. Making the notes public in a shared document shapes the discussion and facilitates connections across experiences (A template is provided in the online extras: www.routledge.com/9781032882222). In addition, participants can access the document afterward if they need reminders about the conversation or recommendations that were shared.

As with the planning sessions, the exchange between participants in a lesson debrief creates powerful opportunities for differentiated learning. The following excerpt follows the same fourth-grade teachers as they reflect on the implementation of the Sharing Crackers task, with the focusing question, "How does the teacher elicit the student's understanding or point of struggle?" Coral, a novice teacher leader, has just shared a short video of her practice during which she is facilitating productive struggle with a student who was working independently on the problem.

Facilitator:	Before we let Coral talk, I just want to hear from anybody else. What are some things that you saw or heard Coral do while she was facilitating that student's productive struggle?
Laura:	You asked back to see if you were representing his thinking correctly, which was great.
Bobbi:	I just loved your energy around having the conversation and continually going back to that child and checking in I think. And the importance of emphasizing "where are the friends?", and "where are the crackers?"
Serena:	I loved the way you questioned him so he could explain his answers, explain his thinking, and what he was doing in the process, so I really got to know what he was thinking through the questions that you asked.
Facilitator:	I love the "can you tell me more about that" question because the child immediately reflected on their answer and changed it. And you didn't have to do the thing the teachers sometimes do, which is "Are you sure about that?" [shaking head no] You just asked, and they thought to themselves, so that was really nice.
Facilitator:	Anything you want to say about the lesson, Coral?
Coral:	So the lesson was a lot of fun, it was really great. One thing that I noticed was that it was really hard to help a student who was making a mistake without telling them what they did wrong. I wanted to use their own ideas to help them see where they went wrong, but it was hard to think of what questions to ask. I could have done a little bit better responding to some students. But, overall, I thought it was great.
Facilitator:	That would be a great thing for us to focus some time on in the next planning session. I will make a note.

In this excerpt, the participants identify important responsive teaching moves that Coral made in the video clip, focusing on what she did and why her moves were necessary for student sensemaking and maintaining ownership of ideas. Even though teachers are sometimes daunted by the idea of sharing a video of their practice, they often feel validated and more confident when their peers identify things that they did well. At the same time, they gain new ideas from their peers and leave motivated to continue improving their practice.

At the end of the session, it is important to reserve some time to reflect on themes across artifacts and set goals for continued improvement. A helpful practice is to have each participant write down or say out loud one thing they want to try based on the discussions of that session. Stating these goals publicly creates accountability, encouraging teachers to apply what they have learned to their own instruction, and may even inspire them to aim higher in their practice by learning from the aspirations and commitments of their peers. Articulating these ideas as a group also helps to concretize the rich learning of the community.

> It is nice to hear that people have similar struggles and to get fresh perspectives on what is going on in my classroom. Sometimes it's hard when you are in it to sort of step back and see it ... but it is also nice for somebody else to say, well, you know, have you tried this? Or have you explored that?
> —Middle School Teacher

Pairing Practice-Based Professional Development with Collaborative Lesson Design Cycles

As mentioned at the beginning of this section, intentional interweaving of collaborative lesson design, enactment, and reflection cycles with practice-based professional development sessions can be a particularly effective way to support teacher learning (see Figure 8.8). These two forms of professional development are synergistic and mutually supportive. In practice-based professional development, educators expand and deepen their understanding of responsive teaching practices, developing a common language and adaptive expertise. This serves as a scaffold for enacting lessons that teachers plan through collaborative lesson design. In turn, through engagement in lesson design cycles, participants try out, adapt, and contextualize responsive teaching practices to make them work for their situation, grade level, content, and context.

Creating a common focus across these two types of professional learning can provide a cohesive experience for participants. For example, if teachers focus on the launch in professional development sessions by decomposing

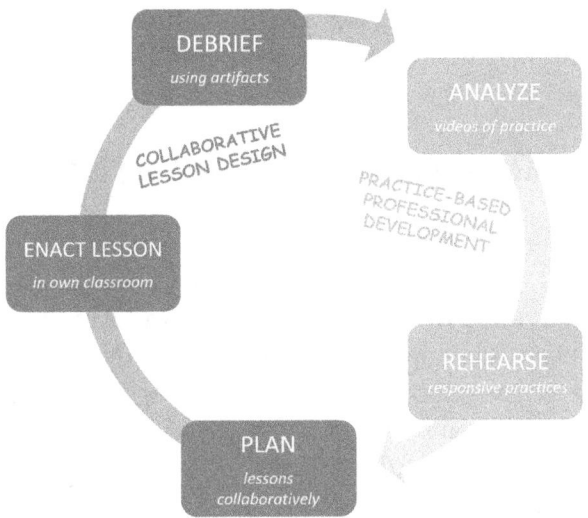

Figure 8.8 Pairing collaborative lesson design cycles and practice-based professional development.

a launch video and engaging in simulations, then a complementary collaborative lesson design cycle could concentrate on planning the launch during the lesson design session and then debriefing video artifacts from the launches. Having a supported opportunity to try out newly developed launching skills will allow teachers to return to practice-based sessions with a more fine tuned understanding of launching in their own context, new questions to pose, and a readiness to learn more sophisticated facilitation.

When groups of teachers have established a shared vision and work together around common goals, they can hold each other accountable while they put that vision into practice (Ebby et al., 2025). For example, in a fourth-grade collaborative planning session, when one participant teacher suggested adapting the task to make it more accessible for her students, the group wrestled with whether the change would lower the cognitive demand and thereby reduce access to important grade-level content. Ultimately, the teacher was convinced to provide targeted support for students when she noticed they were struggling or stuck, rather than changing the task for everyone. This accountability to the guiding principles of responsive mathematics teaching,

> *It is very rare that we get an opportunity to kind of share ideas or share what has worked and what has not and so meeting in a small group and then meeting in a larger group has allowed me, the second grade teacher, to collaborate with people across my grade band—different schools, different settings, different populations—and I feel like when you can collaborate with your peers you are really learning new ways and better ways to instruct in your own classroom.*

as described in Chapter 1, guides and circumscribes in-the-moment decision-making to help create inclusive learning environments.

Facilitating the Learning of Responsive Teaching Practice

Throughout this chapter, we have outlined how facilitators can design meaningful professional learning opportunities for individuals and groups of teachers. We now shift our focus to the skills and practices facilitators and leaders need to effectively support the ongoing development of responsive mathematics teaching within professional learning environments. Intentional structures, shared vision and discourse, strong leadership support, and relational trust are essential for cultivating authentic learning communities (Bryk & Schneider, 2002; Grossman et al., 2001). Fostering this kind of learning community involves establishing and co-constructing a set of norms that support productive collaboration, such as monitoring one's participation, remaining open to others' perspectives, and minimizing distractions to give full attention to the group and learning process.

> *I am not perfect. The beautiful thing I feel about talking with other teachers is that the minute you are vulnerable and show your vulnerability, it is almost like everybody's shoulders are just relaxed. All of a sudden, everybody is just like, "Oh, okay. Yeah, I did that. I made that mistake too."*
> —Teacher Leader

The teacher leaders we worked with reflected that creating a safe and supportive learning community required humility, a willingness to model vulnerability, and a clear message that everyone, regardless of experience, was embarking on a common journey.

The role of a facilitator in a collaborative learning community differs from the traditional view of an instructional leader or coach as the expert, authority figure, or evaluator. The idea of an expert who holds the knowledge and passes it onto the rest of the group runs counter to how a collaborative learning community functions. Instead, facilitators in responsive learning communities position themselves as co-learners and create space for shared inquiry and mutual support. While the facilitator does not need to be an expert or even the most experienced group member, some key practices and stances can help create a productive learning experience for all participants.

First, the group facilitator can take on responsibilities outside of the meeting times to support productive work during the session. This includes logistical tasks such as scheduling meetings, sending reminders, and creating agendas that ensure all participants have time to share, give, and receive feedback. Before a collaborative lesson planning meeting, the facilitator can prompt participants to solve the task and anticipate possible solution paths beforehand. For collaborative debrief sessions, they can remind teachers to bring or submit relevant lesson artifacts.

> *It was important for me to create a space where everybody felt comfortable. I wanted to come across as, "Listen, I'm in this with you guys. I enjoy it as much as you do. I was chosen as the leader, but I'm in no way any more knowledgeable or above anybody."*
> —Teacher Leader

A clear set of learning goals serves as a critical support for facilitation, ensuring that teacher learning remains focused and is continually driven toward a deeper understanding of responsive teaching practices. During professional learning sessions, there are some core responsive facilitation moves, shown in Table 8.2, that support productive discourse around instructional practice (Ebby et al., 2024).

Structuring moves include reminding participants of the learning goal(s), guiding the group through the agenda while managing time and participation, and keeping the conversation focused on the goal(s), ensuring a productive session. In planning and debrief sessions, the facilitator can engage as a group member by sharing ideas, asking questions, and responding to others, while keeping things moving and adhering to the agenda. Sometimes facilitators may need to gently but firmly redirect individuals or the group to ensure that the meeting doesn't get sidetracked by other issues or devolve into a venting session.

Cultivating moves build community, establish trust, and reinforce norms. Facilitators can use these moves to intentionally support participants in sharing their ideas and expertise, ensuring that the group benefits from everyone's input and feels safe sharing and critiquing their practice. In the vignette, the facilitator encouraged and cultivated group expertise by inviting other participants to respond rather than jumping in to answer a question that was posed ("I have thoughts, but I want to throw it back to the group if anybody else is thinking about how they would do that").

An adept facilitator will also pay attention to the learning of individuals and the group as a whole and use eliciting and connecting moves to maximize professional growth. ***Eliciting moves*** involve inviting participants to share their ideas and then following up with clarifying questions or pressing for pedagogical reasoning. For example, in the fourth-grade planning session, the facilitator asked the presenter to clarify the question they were posing ("Do you mean the language of factors?") so that everyone in the group was on the same page when giving feedback.

Table 8.2 Responsive Facilitation of Collaborative Learning Communities Tool

Supporting Collaborative Learning Communities	
Structuring Moves keep the group following the plan/agenda for the meeting, considering timing, participation, and learning goals	
Framing a task	• As we watch the video, remember to focus on the questions the teacher is asking
Transitioning	• This has been a very productive discussion about launching. I'm going to move us to the facilitating productive struggle section, so that we have time to work through the whole lesson plan.
Redirecting the conversation	• We seem to have gone off on a tangent. Let's table that discussion for another time. • I hear Patty naming a challenge. Has anyone successfully addressed a similar issue?
Cultivating Moves help people feel safe to participate or be vulnerable with each other	
Inviting participants to contribute	• Did anybody else have that difficulty? • What do other people think about Meredith's question?
Connecting to one's own or others' teaching experience	• That reminds me of what Harold said about making space for mistakes.
Reinforcing norms	• I appreciate how brave you all are for bringing up things that you don't think you did perfectly.
Affirming a participant	• I love your use of wait time with Khalid. I struggle with that myself. • I'm so proud of you for sticking with that student without telling them how to solve it. I know that's something you've been working on.
Eliciting Moves help an individual or the group to clarify, say more, think deeper, or understand an idea better	
Asking a clarifying question	• Were they working by themselves, or were they working in partners or groups? • Did the possibility of multiple solutions come up in your launch?

(Continued)

Table 8.2 Responsive Facilitation of Collaborative Learning Communities Tool *(Continued)*

Pressing for more information	• *If you showed these two strategies ... what could you ask to help the students who didn't do it this way?*
Pressing for pedagogical reasoning	• *If you shared these two strategies, which one would you show first, or what order would you think would be more effective?*

Connecting Moves help participants deepen their understanding of responsive mathematics teaching or student learning

Analyzing student work or thinking	• *Why do you think he circled 8 dots? I don't see that anywhere in his equation.* • *Let's brainstorm some ways we could help facilitate productive struggle with a student who can't get started.*
Offering potential next steps or alternative steps	• *I think that maybe giving them a non-working example would help them think about it.* • *What questions could you have asked?*
Making explicit the purpose behind an instructional decision	• *In Mary's video, I noticed that she asked the students to try to explain someone else's work. Why do you think she did that?*

Facilitators can use *connecting moves* to help participants link specific instructional decisions with the underlying reasoning behind them, as well as link shared ideas to language and components of responsive mathematics teaching, or other key concepts introduced in professional development. In the fourth-grade planning session, the facilitator responded to a suggestion to use the vocabulary of factors at the end of the lesson by referring to the purpose of the connecting and consolidating phase of responsive mathematics teaching. This terminology held a shared meaning for the group members.

Facilitators in a collaborative learning community are in a unique role because they wear two hats, engaging both as a learner and bearing responsibility for creating a productive learning experience for the group. We have found that over time, groups that meet consistently will often have participants other than the facilitator begin to use cultivating, eliciting, and connecting moves as they work to deepen their understanding and capacity with responsive teaching practices. However, ensuring that the group continues to meet and uses that meeting time productively and intentionally is an important role of the facilitator.

Establishing clear learning goals for each session helps ensure that the time is purposeful and focused, and it also guides the facilitator in deciding how to select and order the activities that align with the goal. At the same time, facilitators need to be flexible and recognize that learning is not always linear. Unexpected questions, challenges, or moments of insight may require a shift in focus. This dynamic interplay between intentional planning and real-time responsiveness is as central to effective professional learning design and facilitation as it is to the facilitation of response lessons for students. Translating these ideas into practice, however, requires careful consideration of the specific context in which the learning will occur.

Bringing It Home: Supporting Responsive Teaching in Your Context

The components of professional learning described in this chapter can take different forms in different contexts. Designing a plan to roll out these opportunities for professional learning requires attention to multiple factors and constraints, including time, participants, format, facilitators, and alignment. Below, we outline some of the important questions and considerations.

Time: How Much Time Do You Have, and Where Can You Find Additional Space?

Do you have an academic year? Multiple years? A semester? A summer? Or some combination? Where can you build in space for additional time?

Collaborative problem-solving sessions can be offered at regular intervals throughout the school year or semester (after school or during professional development days) or in a weeklong summer intensive. Both models can be effective if teachers have repeated opportunities to engage and reflect on the experience. If your school schedule already has space for teachers to plan together during the school day, you might utilize some or all of that time to have teachers engage in collaborative planning and reflection of responsive mathematics lessons. You might also find ways to compensate teachers to meet in collaborative learning communities after school.

Participants: Who Will Participate, and How Will the Groups Be Organized?

Will you start with specific grades or engage the whole school? Will you have teachers volunteer, or will you require everyone to participate?

The composition of groups should be informed by the component of professional learning you are supporting. For example, while problem-solving sessions benefit from having a larger group of participants from a broad range of grades, collaborative planning and reflection sessions tend to be more effective when smaller groups are organized by grades or grade bands. For practice-based professional development sessions, it can be helpful to have the flexibility to meet as a large multi-grade group for discussions of responsive teaching practice and then break up into smaller grade-level groups to engage in simulations and reflections.

Format: How Will Your Participants Engage?

Will sessions be held in person or virtual formats? Are there parts that can be done asynchronously?

Both face-to-face and online formats for each of these types of professional learning can be effective. It can be easier to build community and relationships in face-to-face formats. However, online sessions offer a convenient way to bring busy people together, especially when they are coming from different locations. Problem-solving sessions can also be offered in hybrid, stretched-out formats: participants come together online to launch the task, solve the task independently, and then come back together to discuss strategies and reflect. This format also works well for teachers and preservice teachers taking a course that meets regularly.

Facilitators: Who Will Lead the Sessions?

Do you have a designated mathematics coach or lead teacher? Is there a classroom teacher who has the potential to become an instructional leader? Can you bring in an external partner or consultant?

Consider who in your school or program is best positioned to lead this work. Facilitators should be trusted by their peers and be able to model responsive teaching practices in classroom contexts. If internal capacity is limited, bringing in an external partner or consultant can provide expertise and momentum to get things started. As teachers participate in professional learning, keep an eye out for those who show potential, initiative, and interest in continued growth and mentor them as instructional leaders. Regardless of who leads, facilitators need time, support, and opportunities for professional learning and growth.

Alignment: How Does Responsive Mathematics Teaching Fit with Other Initiatives and Goals of Your School or Program?

What else are teachers being asked to learn or do? Are there potentially competing priorities or messages?

It is important to reflect on what else teachers are being asked to implement—such as curriculum changes, assessment practices, or other instructional strategies—and whether these initiatives support or conflict with the guiding principles of responsive mathematics teaching. Are teachers receiving consistent messages about instructional priorities, and do they have the time and space to try new approaches in their classroom? Are there competing demands that might cause confusion or overload? Exploring this alignment ensures that responsive mathematics teaching is not just perceived as "one more thing to do" but rather as a meaningful approach that complements and deepens existing efforts. It is also important for school leaders to show their commitment and support. Attending professional learning sessions as a participant (not an observer) is one important way to do this. Asking teachers what they are learning, what they are trying out, and how it is going sends the message that their efforts are valued, and that responsive mathematics teaching is a shared priority, not just an individual initiative. This kind of engagement fosters a culture of trust, reflection, and continuous learning, where teachers feel supported in taking risks and refining their practice, as the following reflection from an elementary teacher illustrates.

> I loved that both my colleagues and our principals attended the professional development sessions together; one of my former principals credits them for making him a much better mathematics leader in his school. He had lacked confidence in providing content feedback to the middle school mathematics teacher, but this professional learning enabled him to dig deeper into the standards and better support teachers. My colleagues and I would share how the responsive mathematics lessons utilizing challenging tasks went after we tried them. We refined our practices and challenged each other to engage in productive struggle. I also formed tight intellectual bonds with the other mathematics teachers since we interacted so frequently at professional development and engaged in problem solving and debriefing together.

Change Takes Time

Regardless of the path leaders take to engage educators in developing responsive teaching practices, it is critical to remember that instructional change takes time. The vignettes at the beginning of this chapter illustrate that even a well-designed professional development experience is not enough to support lasting shifts in teachers' practice. Professional development is most effective when sustained and ongoing with opportunities for active and continuous learning, reflection, and feedback (Darling-Hammond et al., 2017; Desimone, 2009; Loucks-Horsley et al., 2010). The professional learning activities introduced in this chapter are grounded in ongoing cycles of learning something new, trying it out in practice, reflecting on the experience, and receiving and responding to feedback.

The first essential component of supporting teacher learning—developing a common vision of responsive mathematics instruction—is supported by opportunities to experience and observe responsive teaching across various settings and tasks so that the vision can become deep and multi-faceted. The second component, prioritizing practice-based approaches to professional learning, breaks down responsive teaching into smaller pieces that can be represented, decomposed, and approximated in a supportive setting. Ideally, multiple sessions are spent exploring just one aspect of responsive teaching in depth. Time and continuity are important in the third component of creating and sustaining collaborative learning communities. These communities become most impactful when teachers are given time to try out new practices repeatedly, return to debrief with peers, and refine their instruction based on shared reflection and feedback.

The time it takes for an individual teacher to take up a new instructional practice will vary depending on prior knowledge and experiences, as well as time dedicated to professional development. There is no one-size-fits-all timeline. Designing ongoing learning experiences and giving teachers multiple opportunities to refine and deepen learning will allow all participants to continue along their responsive development journey at their own pace.

Like most complex learning, learning to teach more responsively is not a linear process. Leaders can expect it to take time and be bumpy, with periods of progress, moments of standstills, and even instances that feel like regression. Normalizing this struggle and providing layered opportunities for reflection, feedback, and support is important. One of the most reassuring insights a facilitator can share with their teachers is acknowledging that teaching responsively is challenging and that the effort, reflection, and persistence involved are all part of the learning process. It is important to honor the hard work teachers invest in developing their practice and to frame their productive struggle as a vital part of progress and learning, just as we do with students.

> *My favorite part about this experience is truly being part of a community of educators who are working together to navigate the current educational landscape. The colleagues in my small group for lesson planning really push me every day to think differently about my mathematics instruction and how to best support the teachers that I coach. I'm just really thankful for the experience.*

Just as student learning is enhanced through collaboration, teacher learning is enhanced when they have opportunities to embark on this journey together with their peers. Working alongside colleagues to improve mathematics instruction allows teachers to feel safe trying new things out, get feedback from others who are facing the same challenges, and hold each other accountable to the guiding principles of responsive teaching.

Guiding Principles for Responsive Mathematics Teaching
1 Prioritize mathematical sensemaking
2 Promote collaborative learning communities
3 Support a positive mathematical identity
4 Ensure all students have access to mathematics

These guiding principles are not a checklist to be completed, but rather a compass to steer our collective efforts to improve mathematics instruction in more equitable and effective directions. The work of centering sensemaking, building inclusive learning communities, supporting every student to see themselves as capable mathematicians, and ensuring that all students have access to mathematics is complex and evolving. As the teachers and leaders we have worked with often remind us, the journey can be challenging, but it is also deeply rewarding. As you move forward, we hope you will find joy in the questions, experimentation, reflection, and the learning—both your students' and your own—that comes from centering student thinking in the mathematics classroom.

References

Aguirre, J., Mayfield-Ingram, K., & Martin, D. B. (2013). *The impact of identity in K-12 mathematics: Rethinking equity-based practices*. National Council of Teachers of Mathematics.

Ashcraft, M. H. (2002). Math anxiety: Personal, educational, and cognitive consequences. *Current Directions in Psychological Science*, 11(5), 181–185. https://doi.org/10.1111/1467-8721.00196

Ball, D. L., & Cohen, D. K. (1999). Developing practice, developing practitioners: Toward a practice-based theory of professional education. In L. Darling-Hammond & G. Sykes (Eds.), *Teaching as the learning profession: Handbook of policy and practice* (pp. 3–32). Jossey-Bass.

Bartell, T. G., Wager, A. A., Edwards, A. R., Battey, D., & Sherman, M. F. (2017). *Equity and mathematics education research: Toward a new era of scholarship*. Springer.

Battey, D., Neal, R. A., Leyva, L. A., & Adams-Wiggins, K. R. (2016). The interconnectedness of relational and content dimensions of quality instruction: Support for equitable mathematics learning. *Journal for Research in Mathematics Education*, 47, 1–48.

Baxter, J. A., Woodward, J., Olson, D., & Robyns, J. (2002). Blueprint for writing in middle school mathematics. *Mathematics Teaching in the Middle School*, 8(1), 52–56.

Baxter, J. A., Woodward, J., & Olson, D. (2005). Writing in mathematics: An alternative form of communication for academically low-achieving students. *Learning Disabilities Research & Practice*, 20(2), 119–135.

Beilock, S. L., & Maloney, E. A. (2015). Math anxiety: A factor in math achievement not to be ignored. *Policy Insights from the Behavioral and Brain Sciences*, 2(1), 4–12. https://doi.org/10.1177/2372732215601438.

Black, P., & Wiliam, D. (1998). Inside the black box: Raising standards through classroom assessment. *Phi Delta Kappan*, 80(2), 139–148.

Boaler, J. (2008). *What's math got to do with it? Helping children learn to love their least favorite subject—and why it's important for America*. Penguin.

Boaler, J. (2015). *Mathematical mindsets: Unleashing students' potential through creative math, inspiring messages, and innovative teaching*. Jossey-Bass.

Boaler, J., Munson, J., & Williams, C. (2018). *Mindset mathematics: Visualizing and investigating big ideas, grade 3*. Jossey Bass.

Borko, H., & Livingston, C. (1989). Cognition and improvisation: Differences in mathematics instruction by expert and novice teachers. *American Educational Research Journal, 26*(4), 473–498.

Boston, M. D., & Wolf, M. B. (2006). *Assessing academic rigor in mathematics instruction: The instructional quality assessment toolkit.* CSE Technical Report 672. National Center for Research on Evaluation, Standards, and Student Testing (CRESST).

Bruner, J. S. (1966). *Toward a theory of instruction.* Harvard University Press.

Bryk, A. S., & Schneider, B. (2002). *Trust in schools: A core resource for improvement.* Russell Sage Foundation.

Carpenter, T. P., & Lehrer, R. (1999). Teaching and learning mathematics with understanding. In E. Fennema & T. A. Romberg (Eds.), *Mathematics classrooms that promote understanding* (pp. 19–32). Lawrence Erlbaum Associates.

Chapin, S. H., & O'Connor, C. (2007). *Classroom discussions in math: A teacher's guide for using talk moves to support the Common Core and more.* Math Solutions.

Cheng, E. (2022). *The joy of abstraction: An exploration of math, category theory, and life.* Cambridge University Press.

Cobb, P., Gresalfi, M., & Hodge, L. L. (2009). An interpretive scheme for analyzing the identities that students develop in mathematics classrooms. *Journal for Research in Mathematics Education, 40*(1), 40–68.

Cobb, P., Jackson, K., Henrick, E., Smith, T. M., & Mapp, K. L. (2018). *Systems for instructional improvement: Creating coherence from the classroom to the district office.* Harvard Education Press.

Cohen, E. G. (1994). *Designing groupwork: Strategies for the heterogeneous classroom* (2nd ed.). Teachers College Press.

Cohen, E. G., & Lotan, R. A. (1997). *Working for equity in heterogeneous classrooms: Sociological theory in action.* Teachers College Press.

Cohen, E. G., Lotan, R. A., Abram, P. L., Scarloss, B. A., & Schultz, S. E. (1998). Talking and working together: Equitable groupwork in the mathematics classroom. *The Journal of the Learning Sciences, 7*(4), 313–350.

Countryman, J. (1992). *Writing to learn mathematics: Strategies that work.* Heinemann.

Danielson, C. (n.d.). *Which One Doesn't Belong?* Retrieved from https://wodb.ca

Darling-Hammond, L., Hyler, M. E., & Gardner, M. (2017). *Effective teacher professional development.* Learning Policy Institute. https://learningpolicyinstitute.org/product/effective-teacher-professional-development-report

Daro, P., Mosher, F. A., & Corcoran, T. B. (2011). *Learning trajectories in mathematics: A foundation for standards, curriculum, assessment, and instruction.* Consortium for Policy Research in Education.

Desimone, L. M. (2009). Improving impact studies of teachers' professional development: Toward better conceptualizations and measures. *Educational Researcher*, *38*(3), 181–199. https://doi.org/10.3102/0013189X08331140

Devlin, K. (2009). *The math instinct: Why you're a mathematical genius (along with lobsters, birds, cats, and dogs)*. Basic Books.

Dewey, J. (1910). *How we think*. D.C. Heath.

Duckworth, E. (1987). *The having of wonderful ideas and other essays on teaching and learning*. Teachers College Press.

Dweck, C. S. (2006). *Mindset: The new psychology of success*. Random House.

Ebby, C. B., Hess, B., Pecora, L., & Valerio, J. (2024). Facilitating collaborative inquiry into practice around artifacts of mathematics teaching. *Journal of Mathematics Teacher Education*, 1–24.

Ebby, C. B., Hulbert, E. T., & Broadhead, R. M. (2021). *A focus on addition and subtraction: Bringing mathematics education research to the classroom*. Routledge. https://doi.org/10.4324/9781003038337

Ebby, C. B., Valerio, J., Hess, B., Goldsmith-Markey, L., Davis, J. A., & Pecora, L. (2025). Developing equitable teaching practices through facilitated teacher learning communities. In C. Koestler & E. Thanheiser (Eds.), *Building community to center equity and justice in mathematics teacher education: AMTE professional book series* (Vol., 6). Association for Mathematics Teacher Educators.

Fetter, A. (2016). *Ever wonder what they'd notice?* [Video]. National Council of Teachers of Mathematics. https://www.youtube.com/watch?v=a-Fth6sOaRA

Flavell, J. H. (1976). Metacognitive aspects of problem solving. In L. B. Resnick (Ed.), *The nature of intelligence* (pp. 231–236). Erlbaum.

Franke, M. L., Kazemi, E., & Battey, D. (2007). Mathematics teaching and classroom practice. In F. Lester (Ed.), *Second handbook of research on mathematics teaching and learning* (pp. 225–256). Information Age Publishing.

Freire, P. (1970). *Pedagogy of the oppressed* (M. B. Ramos, Trans.). Continuum.

Grootenboer, P., & Marshman, M. (2016). *Mathematics, affect and learning: Middle school students' beliefs and attitudes about mathematics education*. Springer.

Grossman, P. (Ed.). (2018). *Teaching core practices in teacher education*. Harvard Education Press.

Grossman, P., Compton, C., Igra, D., Ronfeldt, M., Shahan, E., & Williamson, P. (2009). Teaching practice: A cross-professional perspective. *Teachers College Record*, *111*(9), 2055–2100.

Grossman, P., Wineburg, S., & Woolworth, S. (2001). Toward a theory of teacher community. *Teachers College Record*, *103*(6), 1–10. https://doi.org/10.1111/0161-4681.00140

Gutiérrez, R. (2018). The need to rehumanize mathematics. In I. Goffney & R. Gutiérrez (Eds.), *Rehumanizing mathematics for Black, Indigenous, and Latinx students* (pp. 1–10). National Council of Teachers of Mathematics.

Hardy, G. H. (1992). *A mathematician's apology*. Cambridge University Press.

Hattie, J. (2011). *Visible learning for teachers: Maximizing impact on learning*. Routledge.

Hegarty, M., Mayer, R. E., & Monk, C. A. (1995). Comprehension of arithmetic word problems: A comparison of successful and unsuccessful problem solvers. *Journal of Educational Psychology, 87*(1), 18.

Heritage, M. (2010). *Formative assessment: Making it happen in the classroom*. Corwin Press.

Hiebert, J., Gallimore, R., Garnier, H., Givvin, K. B., Hollingsworth, H., Jacobs, J., Chui, A. M., Wearne, D., Smith, M., Kersting, N., Manaster, A., Tseng, E., Etterbeek, W., Manaster, C., Gonzales, P., & Stigler, J. (1997). *Making sense: Teaching and learning mathematics with understanding*. Heinemann.

Hiebert, J., & Grouws, D. A. (2007). The effects of classroom mathematics teaching on students' learning. In F. K. Lester (Ed.), *Second handbook of research on mathematics teaching and learning* (Vol. 1, pp. 371–404). Information Age Publishing.

Hulbert, E. T., Petit, M. M., Ebby, C. B., Cunningham, E. P., & Laird, R. E. (2024). *A focus on multiplication and division: Bringing research to the classroom* (2nd ed.). Routledge. https://doi.org/10.4324/9781315163611

Humphreys, C. & Parker, R. (2015). *Making number talks matter: Developing mathematical practices and deepening understanding, grades 3-10*. Routledge.

Hyde, A. A. (2006). *Comprehending math: Adapting reading strategies to teach mathematics, K–6*. Heinemann.

Illustrative Mathematics. (n.d.). *Grade 8, Unit 3, Lesson 5: Linear relationships*. https://im.kendallhunt.com

Jackson, K. J., Garrison, A., Wilson, J., Gibbons, L. K., & Shahan, E. C. (2013). Exploring relationships between setting up complex tasks and opportunities to learn in concluding whole-class discussions in middle-grades mathematics instruction. *Journal for Research in Mathematics Education, 44*(4), 646–682.

Jackson, K. J., Shahan, E. C., Gibbons, L. K., & Cobb, P. A. (2012). Launching complex tasks. *Mathematics Teaching in the Middle School, 18*(1), 24–29.

Jansen, A. (2020). *Rough-draft math: Revising to learn*. Stenhouse Publishers.

Karp, K. S., Bush, S. B., & Dougherty, B. J. (2019). Avoiding the ineffective keyword strategy. *Teaching Children Mathematics, 25*(7), 428–435.

Kazemi, E., & Hintz, A. (2014). *Intentional talk: How to structure and lead productive mathematical discussions*. Stenhouse.

Kennedy, M. M. (1999). The role of preservice teacher education. *Teaching as the Learning Profession: Handbook of Policy and Practice, 54*, 85.

Ladson-Billings, G. (1995). Toward a theory of culturally relevant pedagogy. *American Educational Research Journal, 32*(3), 465–491.

Ladson-Billings, G. (1997). It doesn't add up: African American students' mathematics achievement. *Journal for Research in Mathematics Education, 28*(6), 697–708. https://doi.org/10.2307/749638

Lampert, M. (2010). Learning teaching in, from, and for practice: What do we mean? *Journal of Teacher Education, 61*(1–2), 21–34. https://doi.org/10.1177/0022487109347321

Liljedahl, P. (2020). *Building thinking classrooms in mathematics, grades K-12: 14 teaching practices for enhancing learning.* Corwin Press.

Lockhart, P. (2009). *A mathematician's lament: How school cheats us out of our most fascinating and imaginative art form.* Bellevue Literary Press.

Loucks-Horsley, S., Stiles, K. E., Mundry, S., Love, N., & Hewson, P. W. (2010). *Designing professional development for teachers of science and mathematics* (3rd ed.). Corwin Press.

Louie, N. L. (2017). The culture of exclusion in mathematics education and its persistence in equity-oriented teaching. *Journal for Research in Mathematics Education, 48*(5), 488–519.

Martin, D. B. (2000). *Mathematics success and failure among African-American youth: The roles of sociohistorical context, community forces, school influence, and individual agency.* Routledge.

Martin, D. B. (2009). Researching race in mathematics education. *Teachers College Record, 111*(2), 295–338.

Middleton, J. A., & Jansen, A. (2011). *Motivation matters and interest counts: Fostering engagement in mathematics.* National Council of Teachers of Mathematics.

Muhammad, G. E. (2020). *Cultivating genius: An equity framework for culturally and historically responsive literacy.* Scholastic Inc.

Munson, J. (2018). *In the moment: Conferring in the elementary math classroom.* Heinemann.

Munter, C., & Correnti, R. (2017). Examining relations between mathematics teachers' instructional vision and knowledge and change in practice. *American Journal of Education, 123*(2), 171–202.

Nasir, N. S., Hand, V., & Taylor, E. V. (2008). Culture and mathematics in school: Boundaries between "cultural" and "domain" knowledge in the mathematics classroom. *Review of Research in Education, 32*(1), 187–240. https://doi.org/10.3102/0091732X07308962

National Council of Teachers of Mathematics. (2000). *Principles and standards for school mathematics.* Author.

National Council of Teachers of Mathematics (NCTM). (2014). *Principles to actions: Ensuring mathematical success for all.* NCTM.

National Governors Association Center for Best Practices & Council of Chief State School Officers. (2010). *Common Core State Standards for Mathematics.* Authors.

National Research Council (NRC). (2001). *Adding it up: Helping children learn mathematics*. National Academy Press.

Paivio, A. (1986). *Mental representations: A dual-coding approach*. Oxford University Press.

Petit, M. M., Laird, R. E., Ebby, C. B., & Marsden, E. L.. (2023). *A focus on fractions: Bringing mathematics education research to the classroom* (3rd ed.). Routledge. https://doi.org/10.4324/9781003185475

Petit, M. M., Laird, R. E., Wyneken, M. F., Huntoon, F. R., Abele-Austin, M. D., & Sequeira, J. D. (2020). *A focus on ratios and proportions: Bringing mathematics education research to the classroom*. Routledge.

Piaget, J. (1960). *The psychology of intelligence*. Littlefield, Adams.

Polya, G. (1957). *How to solve it: A new aspect of mathematical method* (2nd ed.). Princeton University Press.

Pugalee, D. K. (2001). Writing, mathematics and metacognition: Looking for connections through students' work in mathematical problem solving. *School Science and Mathematics, 101*(5), 236–245.

Pugalee, D. K. (2005). Writing to develop mathematical understanding. *Mathematics Teacher, 98*(6), 1–6.

Remillard, J. T., Ebby, C. B., Lim, V., Reinke, L., Hoe, N., & Magee, E. (2014). Increasing access to mathematics through locally relevant curriculum. In K. Karp (Ed.), *Annual perspectives on mathematics education* (pp. 89–96). NCTM.

Resnick, L. B. (2017). *Toward a culture of productive teaching and learning*. Learning Research and Development Center, University of Pittsburgh.

Robertson, A. D., Scherr, R. E., & Hammer, D. (Eds.). (2016). *Responsive teaching in science and mathematics* (pp. 1–35). Routledge.

Secada, W. G., & Berman, P. W. (1999). Equity as a value-added dimension in teaching for understanding in school mathematics. In E. Fennema and T. Romberg (Eds.) *Mathematics classrooms that promote understanding* (pp. 33–42). Routledge.

Seda, P., & Brown, K. (2021). *Choosing to see: A framework for equity in the math classroom*. Dave Burgess Consulting, Incorporated.

Shaughnessy, M., DeFino, R., Pfaff, E., & Blunk, M. (2021). I think I made a mistake: How do prospective teachers elicit the thinking of a student who has made a mistake? *Journal of Mathematics Teacher Education, 24*, 335–359.

Skemp, R. R. (1976). Relational understanding and instrumental understanding. *Mathematics Teaching, 77*(1), 20–26.

Skultety, L., Saclarides, E. S., Bajwa, N. P., Brown, K., Poetzel, A., & Gerardo, J. M. (2023). Making sense of elementary pre-service teachers' mathematical wounds: A proposed framework for practice. *International Electronic Journal of Mathematics Education, 18*(2), em0738. https://doi.org/10.29333/iejme/13170

Smith, M. S., & Stein, M. K. (2018). *Five practices for orchestrating productive mathematics discussions* (2nd ed.). NCTM/Corwin Press.

Sousa, D. A. (2022). *How the brain learns* (6th ed.). Corwin.

Stein, M. K., Grover, B. W., & Henningsen, M. (1996). Building student capacity for mathematical thinking and reasoning: An analysis of mathematical tasks used in reform classrooms. *American Educational Research Journal, 33*(2), 455–488.

Stigler, J. W. (1999). *The TIMSS videotape classroom study: Methods and findings from an exploratory research project on eighth-grade mathematics instruction in Germany, Japan, and the United States*. US Department of Education, Office of Educational Research and Improvement, National Center for Education Statistics.

Stigler, J. W., & Hiebert, J. (1999). *The teaching gap: Best ideas from the world's teachers for improving education in the classroom*. Free Press.

Su, F. (2020). *Mathematics for human flourishing*. Yale University Press.

Tate, W. F., Ladson-Billings, G., & Grant, C. A. (2014). The brown decision and mathematics education: Lessons learned and future directions. *Review of Research in Education, 38*(1), 106–136.

Vygotsky, L. S. (1978). *Mind in society: Development of higher psychological processes* (M. Cole, Ed.). Harvard University Press.

Warshauer, H. K. (2014). Productive struggle in middle school mathematics classrooms. *Journal of Mathematics Teacher Education, 18*(4), 375–400.

Warshauer, H. K. (2015). Strategies to support productive struggle. *Mathematics Teaching in the Middle School, 20*(7), 390–393.

Watanabe, T. (2021, March 5). Teaching through problem solving: Japanese model. *Tad Watanabe Blog*. https://tadwatanabe.wordpress.com/2021/03/05/teaching-through-problem-solving-japanese-model-%e5%95%8f%e9%a1%8c%e8%a7%a3%e6%b1%ba%e5%ad%a6%e7%bf%92/

Wilhelm, A. G. (2014). Mathematics teachers' enactment of cognitively demanding tasks: Investigating links to teachers' knowledge and conceptions. *Journal for Research in Mathematics Education, 45*(5), 636–674.

Wiliam, D. (2021). Why there is no such thing as a formative assessment. *Assess for Learning*. https://www.assessforlearning.eu/news/article?id=54310

Yackel, E., & Cobb, P. (1996). Sociomathematical norms, argumentation, and autonomy in mathematics. *Journal for Research in Mathematics Education, 27*(4), 458–477.

Yoshida, M. (1999). *Lesson study: A case study of a Japanese approach to improving instruction through school-based teacher development* (Doctoral dissertation, University of Chicago). ProQuest Dissertations Publishing.

For Product Safety Concerns and Information please contact our EU
representative GPSR@taylorandfrancis.com
Taylor & Francis Verlag GmbH, Kaufingerstraße 24, 80331 München, Germany

www.ingramcontent.com/pod-product-compliance
Lightning Source LLC
Chambersburg PA
CBHW060312240426
43661CB00059B/2739